Hancock COUNTY GEORGIA

Superior Court Minutes

- 1794-1805 -

(Volume #1)

Compiled by:
Michael A. Ports

Southern Historical Press, Inc.
Greenville, South Carolina

Copyright 2019
By: Michael A. Ports

All rights reserved. No part of this publication may be reproduced, stored in a retrieval system, transmitted in any form, posted on to the web in any form or by any means without the prior written permission of the publisher.

Please direct all correspondence and orders to:

www.southernhistoricalpress.com
or
SOUTHERN HISTORICAL PRESS, Inc.
PO BOX 1267
375 West Broad Street
Greenville, SC   29601
southernhistoricalpress@gmail.com

ISBN #0-89308-757-2

Printed in the United States of America

Introduction

The Georgia General Assembly created Hancock County on December 17, 1793, from parts of Greene and Washington counties, and established Sparta as the seat of its government. Part of Baldwin County, east of the Oconee River, was part of Hancock County prior to 1807. A portion of Hancock County was taken to form Taliaferro County in 1825. The Legislature divided the state into judicial districts, assigning Hancock to the Western Circuit, comprised of Elbert, Franklin, Greene, Jackson, Lincoln, Oglethorpe, and Wilkes counties. The judges, elected to serve three year terms, held court in each county at least twice per year, as they traveled from county to county within their circuit. The Superior Court had Jurisdiction over all criminal matters, most civil cases, appeals from the Inferior Courts and Justice's Courts, divorces, grand juries, naturalizations, admissions to the bar, and registration of land deeds.

The first volume of Superior Court minutes begins February 1, 1794 and continues through February 21, 1805. The following transcription includes the first 383 pages through August 26, 1800 and comes from the microfilm photographed at the courthouse in Sparta December 2, 1960 by the Genealogical Society of Salt Lake City, Utah and avaialable at the Georgia Archives in Morrow, Georgia and the Family History Library. The heading on the microfilm reads

State of Georgia
Hancock County

Superior Court
Minutes

Book 1794 – 1805

Index No

On the outer spine of the volume is printed

Minutes

1794 – 1805

On the inside cover, the clerk wrote

Forgery 427

Judge Mitchell's Charge to Grand Jury 287

Murder Page 14 -16

Grand Jury Presentments 56

Ints Courthouse 57

Cattle Stealing

The original record volume is not indexed; however, a complete full-name index follows the transcription. The reader should note that a surname appearing in the index without a first name indicates that no first name was entered in the minutes, for example Mr. Smith, Smith and Company, Captain Smith, or said Smith. An index entry in the form ___, Jesse indicates that a first name was entered in the minutes, but without any surname, as in Jesse, a free person of color, or the surname is obliterated by a torn page, ink blot, or other imperfection. The clerk entered consecutive numbers at the top of the original pages. The numbers in the transcription appearing between brackets, for example [72], signifying the original page numbers, entered in the upper right-hand corner of each original page.

Thomas P. Carnes, David B. Mitchell, William Stephens, William Stith, Jr., Benjamin Taliaferro, and George Walton presided as judge during the period covered by the following transcription. Henry Graybill and Martin Martin served as clerks during the same period; although, based solely upon the handwriting, at least four or five others served as deputy clerks. For the most part, their handwriting is legible, making the transcription straightforward and not too difficult. The occassional ink smear or other imperfection is noted within brackets, for example [smear], [torn], or [illegible].

Sometimes the clerks formed the letters "a" and "o" in a very similar manner, making abbreviations such as Jas. and Jos. and sunames Harman and Harmon or Low and Law impossible to distinguish. At other times, the letters "a" and "u" are too similar to differentiate between such names as Burnett and Barnett or Barton and Burton. The formation of the letters "i" and "e" sometimes makes it difficult to distinguish between such names as Melton and Milton, for example.

Also, the clerk formed the capital letters "I" and "J" identically. Determining which letter usually is not a problem when the first letter of a surname, but entirely a guess when a middle initial. Sometimes the clerk crossed the letter "t" by extending the horizontal line across most or all of a word, making it difficult to distinguish between the such surnames as Cutter, Cutler, and Culter or Cotton and Colton. Occasionally, the clerk failed to cross the letter "t" at all, leaving the reader wondering if the name was Jewett or Jewell, for example. The transcription follows Sperry's recommended guidelines for reading early American script.[1]

The transcription does not correct any grammar or spelling, no matter how obvious the errors, but does add a few commas, semicolons, apostrophes, and periods for clarity. Finally, the clerk entered a vertical squiggly line to delineate case citations and other headings, duplicated by the symbol } in the transcription. Careful researchers will consult either the original record or the microfilm copy either to confirm the transcription or formulate alternative interpretations of the clerks' handwriting.

Generally, the transcription maintains the overall format of the minutes, but presents the case citations, jury panels, lists of witnesses, and other court proceedings in a standard and consistent format. The minutes contain numerous original signatures, beyond merely those of the judge and the clerk, including those of many attorneys, individuals filing bonds for appeals and stays of execution, and their securities, as well as those subscribing to various oaths.

When abbreviating words, the clerk often entered a symbol resembling a tilda over the end of the abbreviation. For example, the abbreviation for the word Execution frequently appears as

That symbol is not repeated in the transcription.

The book is dedicated to the memory of the author's numerous Georgia ancestors, although none ever were residents of Hancock County. Many thanks are offered to the kind, patient, and generous staff of the Georgia Archives, for their assistance

---

[1] Sperry, Kip. *Reading Early American Handwriting.* Genealogical Publishing Company, Inc., Baltimore, Maryland, Sixth Printing, 2008.

and suggestions, not only in locating the original records, but in understanding their historical context. Thanks also are offered Labruce Lucas of the Southern Historical Press for his sage professional advice and counsel. Special thanks are offered to my mother, Ouida J. Ports, who helped instill in me a deep appreciation of American history and genealogy.

Superior Court Minutes

1794 to 1805

Office of the Superior Court Clerk of Hancock County 1st February 1794 [1]

The Jury list for the said County being corrected, a Sufficient number being selected to serve as Grand Jurors and the remaining Number to serve as Pettit Jurors, being separated the following persons were drawn to serve as Grand Jurors and Petit Jurors at the next Term in said County.

Grand Jurors

1. James Horton
2. Seth Tatum
3. Jarratt Burch
4. Alexander Reed
5. John Bailey
6. John Studivant
7. Jesse Veazey
8. Henry McCoy
9. James Wood
10. Thaddeus Beale
11. Roberds Thomas
12. Thomas Rains
13. William Clark
14. James Adams
15. John Veazey
16. Stephen Bishop
17. William Owsley
18. George Bagby
19. Britain Rogers
20. Robert Sims
21. Theodosius Turk
22. James Alford
23. John Herbert

Petit Jurors [2]

1. Elijah George
2. Jesse Thompson
3. Frier Robison
4. Richard W. Oates
5. Azariah Butts
6. Joseph Carson
7. Lewis Bandy
8. James Rutledge
9. Thomas Hill
10. John Wooten
11. William Welsh
12. James Murphy
19. John Parker
20. Richard Pope
21. Drury Cook
22. Robert Hill
23. George Earnest
24. Joshua Bishop
25. Mial Monk
26. Thomas Grace
27. Jeremiah Spillers
28. Charles Polk
29. James Thomas
30. John Harvey

13. Thomas Heath
14. George Strother
15. James Cathell
16. William Brown
17. John Kelley
18. William Low

31. Jeremiah Morgan
32. John White
33. Thomas Dickinson
34. Henry Pope
35. Aaron Wood
36. Thomas Fail

Attest. Hen. Graybill, C. S. C.   Ex^d W. Stith, jun^r

At a Superior Court began and held in and for the County of Hancock [3] on the third day of June in the year 1794, in pursuance of an act of the General Assembly entitled an act to lay out a County, out of part of the Counties of Washington & Green, passed on the Seventeenth day of December 1793, and in Conformity to an appointment made and duly Published by the Honorable William Stith, Junior, one of the Judges of the said State, and George Walker, Esquire, Attorney General, under a Concurred resolution of both branches of the legislature.

Present, his Honor Judge Stith, Esquire.

The following Grand Jurors appeared and were sworn.

James Adams, foreman
Seth Tatum
Alex^r Reed
John Bailey
John Studivant
Jesse Veazy
Henry McCoy
James Wood
Roberts Thomas
Thomas Rains

John Veazey
Stephen Bishop
Wm Ousley
Britton Rodgers
Robert Sims
Thadeus Beall
John Haverd

The following Petit Jurors appeared.   [4]

Thomas Hill
William Welsh
George Strother
James Cathell
Wm Brown
John Kelly

Thomas Grace
James Thomas
Aaron Wood
Elijah George
Richard W. Oats
Hazariah Butts

Wm Lowe   Jn° Harvey
John Parker   Jeremiah Morgan
Richard Wood
Drury Cook
George Earnest
Joshua Bishop
Mial Monk

State   }
  vs   } an Indictment
Joseph Hutchinson } assault

A True bill.   James Adams, foreman

William Stark }
  vs   } Case
William Weeks }

William Weeks, Senr came into Court and entered himself Special bail for the defendant in the above Case.

The Court then adjourned till tomorrow morning 10 O'Clock.   [5]

Ex^d   W. Stith, jun^r

Wednesday 4 June 1794 the Court met according to adjournment.

Present, Judge Stith.

John White and Thomas Grace returned of the Petit Jury were excused on account of sickness, and Wm Brown had leave of absence till tomorrow.

James Harvey   }
  vs   } Debt
Ja^s Christopher, Adn^r }
of Henry Greer   }

The defendant came into Court by Peter Carnes, his Attorney, and proclamation being made according to an Act of the General Assembly in such cases made and provided, and nothing being said to the contrary, the following Judgement by confession was ordered.

7

By virtue of a Warrant of Attorney incorporated in the bond Within enclosed. I do appear for the defendant and confess Judgment for the sum of Eighty pounds & Cost, with Interest from the first of April until paid.

Peter Carnes, for Def^t

Blanford Davis }
    vs   } Debt
Vachel Davis }   [6]

The defendant came into Court by John E. Anderson, his Attorney, and proclamation being made according to an Act of the General Assembly in such cases made and provided, and nothing being said to the contrary, the following Judgement by confession was ordered.

I do hereby Confess a Judgement by Virtue of a Power of Attorney against Vachel Davis for One hundred pounds Sterling 4th June 1794.

John E. Anderson
Attn^y pro Defend^t

Michael & Lawrence }
    vs   } Case
Edward Moore }
Drury Cook }
Etheldred Wood }
& Richard Wood }

Edward Moore and Zachariah Glass came into Court and acknowledged themselves Special bail for the defendants in the above Case.

The State }
    vs   } assault
Joseph Hutcherson }

The defendant being arraigned, pleads guilty and ordered that he be fined in ten shillings & to pay the cost of prosecution & be discharged.

James Harper }
    vs   }   [7]
William Glass }

Writs of fi fa levied on a negro man named Frank, as the property of the defendant, and claimed by Richd Wood, on which the Sheriff made report that the right of property may be tried, and now the following Jury was Sworn, to wit.

Thomas Hill	Jno Kelly	Jo^s Thomas
Wm Welch	Jno Parker	Aaron Wood
Ge^o Strother	Joshua Bishop	Elijah George
Ja^s Cathell	Mial Monk	Richd W. Oates

The Jury come into court and declared they could not agree, whereupon the parties consented to withdraw a Juror & postpone the trial.

The State   }
   vs   } Murder
Garrett Sutton, al^s}
Gary Sutton   }

A true Bill.   Ja^s Adams, foreman

The prisoner was brought into Court and on his arraignment pleaded Not Guilty.

Wm Reily   }
   vs   } Case
Wm Thomas }

Settled at the defendant's Cost, the Attorney's fee paid.

John Hamill   }
   vs   } Case
Joseph Minton &   }
Samuel Townshend }

Settled at Defendant's Cost.

John Hamill   }
   vs   } Case
Abram Reddick }

Settled at Defendant's Cost.

Michael & Lawrence }
    vs   } Case
James Holton &   }
Henry Graybill   }

The defendant, James Holton, being dead, the Other defendant, Henry Graybill, confesses Judgm^t as Security for the said James Holton for the sum of twelve pounds eight shillings and one penny & Costs of the Suit, with stay of Execution until the first day of January next.

                                              Hen. Graybill

Michael & Lawrence }
    vs   }
Thomas Johnston   }

Settled & Cost paid.

The State   }
    vs   } Indictment Forgery
Michael Whatley }

A true Bill.   Ja^s Adams, foreman

The prisoner was brought into Court, on being arraigned, pleaded Not Guilty.

The State   }   [9]
    vs   } Ind^t Adultery
Benjn Averett & }
Elizabeth Salyers }

A true Bill.   Ja^s Adams, foreman

The defendant, Benjamin Averett, came into Court and was arraigned & plead not Guilty.

Charles Moore }
    vs   } Case
Isham Hogan   }

The parties to submit all differences and matter of Controversy relative to this case to the arbitration and award of Needham Jernigan, Jonas Shivers, & Robert Flornoy, and their award to be returned the next Superior Court, or a Majority of them.

State }
    vs } Indmn^t for Adultery
Benjamin Averett & }
Elizabeth Salyers }

The said Benjamin Averet, with Daniel McDowell his Security, came into Court and acknowledged themselves indebted to his Excellency the Governor and his successors in office for the Sum of fifty pounds each, to be levied on their Several and respective goods and chattels, lands and tenements to be void upon Condition that the said Benjamin Averett shall appear at the next Superior Court to be held for this

County to answer the said Indictment and not depart without leave of the [10] Court.

The said Elizabeth Salyers not appearing, ordered that a Bench warrant issue against her returnable to the next term.

Michael & Lawrence }
    vs } Case
Levi Lancaster }

Thadeus Holt came into Court & Entered himself Special bail in the above Case for the defendant.

William Reiley }
    vs } Case
James Thomas }

Settled at the Defendant's Cost.

Michael & Lawrence }
    vs } Case
Benjamin Jones }

I do confess a Judgement for the Sum of Nine pounds Eight shillings and four pence three farthings and Cost of suit, with stay of levy Untill the first day of January next. 4th June 1794

                                        Benjamin Jones

The State   }
    vs   } Tippling
Daniel Waller }

No bill.   Ja^s Adams, foreman

The State   }   [11]
    vs   } In^t for selling spirits
Edmond Bazor } without license

A true Bill.   Ja^s Adams, foreman

The Defendant came into Court and being arraigned pleaded Guilty. Whereass, it is ordered that the Defendant pay the sum of ten pounds, one half to and for the use of the County & the other half to the use of Allen Whatley, the informer, according to an Act of Assembly in such cases made & provided.

State   }
    vs   } Perjury
Michael Whatley }

And thereupon came the said Michael Whatley, with Daniel Whatley and George Strother, his Securities, who acknowledged themselves indebted to his Excellency the Governor and his successors in Office, the said Michael Whatley in the sum of two hundred pound, the said Daniel and George in the sum of One hundred pounds each, to be levied on their goods and chattels, lands and tenements, to be void upon Condition that the said Michael Whatley shall appear at the next Superior Court to answer the above indictment and not depart without leave of the Court. ~~The Court adjourned~~

John Barron   }   [12]
    vs   }
Michael Gilbert }

Settled at defendant's Cost.

The Court then adjourned till 10 O'Clock to morrow morning.

ex^d W. Stith, jun^r

Thursday 5 June 1794 the Court met according to adjournment. Present, Judge Stith.

Michael & Lawrence }
      vs   } Case
Robert Lethro   }

William Ousley came into Court and entered himself Special bail for the defendant in the above Case.

The Special bail came into Court and Surrendered his Principal in discharge of his Recognisance.

Michael & Lawrence }
      vs   }
William Yarborough }

Jesse Thompson & Benjamin Brantley came into Court and entered themselves Special bail for the defendant in the above case.

Michael & Lawrence   }
      vs   }
Abner Bankston & others }

We do confess a Judgement for the Sum of fourteen Pounds sixteen Shillings and seven pence, with costs of Suit, with a stay of Levy untill the first day January next. June 5th 1794

                                     Abner Bankston
                                     Daniel Bankston

Michael & Lawrence   }   [13]
      vs   } debt
John Holsom & Richd Ship }

We do confess a Judgement for the sum of Seven pounds seventeen Shillings & Eight pence one farthing and Cost of Suit, with a Stay of levy untill the first day of January next. June 5th 1794

         Moses Lucas
         Richard Ship

Michael & Lawrence }
   vs   }
Edward Moore   }
Drury Cook   }
Etheldred Wood   }
& Richard Wood   }

We do confess Judgment for the sum of fifteen pounds eight Shillings, with interest from the first day of November last, and for the further sum of forty five Shillings, making in the Whole Seventeen pounds thirteen Shillings, and cost of Suit, with Stay of execution nine Months.

June 5th 1794   P. J. Carnes, for Defend[ts]

The Court then adjourned till 10 O'Clock to Morrow Morning.

         W. Stith, jun[r]

     Friday 6th June 1794

The Court met according to adjournment. Present, Judge Stith.

The State   }
  vs   } Murder
Garrett Sutton, al[s]}
Garry Sutton }

[14]

The prisoner being brought to the bar for his trial, the follow Jury was drawn & sworn, to wit.

Elijah George	George Earnest	Andrew Borland
William Welsh	John Harvey	Thomas Harrison
James Cathell	Edmond Crowder	Henry Bankston
John Parker	Ward Daniell	James Britain

who returned the following verdict. We, the Jury, find the prisoner, Garry Sutton, Guilty of the most agravated Murder and recommend him to the Mercy of God only.

Edm^d Crowder, foreman

William Starks }
    vs   } Trover
Jeremiah Bonner }
& Robert Bonner }

John McKenzie came into Court and entered himself special bail for Jeremiah Bonner, and Richard Bonner came into Court and entered himself special Bail for Robert Bonner.

Ex^d W. Stith, jun

Court adjourned till tomorrow 9 O'Clock AM.

Saturday 7 June 1794

The Court met according to adjournment. Present, Judge Stith.

Ordered, that a petition from Martin Armstrong relative to a bridge over Ogechee and a petition from David Smith to be exempt from paying poll tax, with the recommendations of the Grand Jury thereon, be refered to the inferior Court.

Ordered, that the presentments of the Grand Jury be published in the State Gazettee agreeably to their request.

The State }
    vs   }
Moses Harris}

The Defendant being three times Solemnly called and failing to appear and his Securities, James Wood and Edward Moore, being also called and required to produce the body of the said Moses Harris and failing so to do. Ordered, that their Recognizance be estreated and that a Scire Facias issue against the said Moses Harris and his securities requiring them to appear at the next Superior Court requiring them to shew cause, if any they have, why their said recognizance should be absolutely forfeited.

The State   }   [16]
    vs   } murder
Garrett Sutton, otherwise }
called Garey Sutton }

The prisoner, being found guilty, was brought to the bar and demanded if he had ought to say why Judgment of death should not be pronounced against him. Mr Dickinson, on his behalf, Moved in arrest of Judgment alledging the want of a proper caption to the Indictment, and that one of the Jury was one ~~of~~ in the affray at the time the deceased received his death Wounds. the Court said ~~it~~ the Indictment was Well and perfectly conformable to the constant course of practice & precedent in the Superior Courts of this State. And that the objection to the Juror was insufficient.

Whereupon, it is ordered and adjudged by the Court that the said Garrett Sutton, otherwise called Gary Sutton, be remanded from the bar into the custody and safe keeping of the Sheriff until friday, the seventeenth day of this present month, and that on the said friday, the seventeenth instant, between the hours of eleven o'Clock in the forenoon and one of the Clock in the afternoon, that he Garrett Sutton, otherwise called Garey Sutton, be carried

to the place of execution and hanged by the neck until he be dead.   [17]

The Court adjourned till Court in Course.

ex^d   W. Stith, jun
                                      7 June 1794

~~Tuesday March the 24th 1795 the Court met according to adjournment. Present, Judge Stith.~~

~~The following Petit Jurors appeared.~~

~~Lewis Barnes~~   ~~Zephaniah John~~
~~Joseph Chapel~~   ~~Jno Orear~~
~~Willis Spears~~   ~~Littleton Rees~~
~~Saml Gann~~ ~~James Turner~~
~~Jno Gan~~   ~~Thaddeus Holt~~
~~Henry Miller~~   ~~Wm Ousley~~

~~John Barren~~   }
     vs   } ~~Case~~
~~William Sallard~~ }
~~& Eppes Brown~~   }

~~I Confess Judgm^t for the sum of Twenty Six pounds Eleven Shillings & Eight pence, with In^t from the Second day of Jany 1793 & Cost of suit, with a stay of Execution four Months.~~

$$\text{William Sallard}$$

Ex^d c n

$$\text{Office of the Clerk of the Superior Court} \quad [18]$$
$$\text{of Hancock County 8 September 1794}$$

The following persons were drawn to serve as Grand Jurors at the next Term of the Superior Court to be held ~~be held~~ in the County aforesaid.

1. John Lamar
2. John Weekes
3. Joseph Cooper
4. John Mapp
5. Robert Harper
6. Edm^d Butler, Senr
7. Aaron McKinzie
8. Alexander Reed
9. Harman Reynolds
10. William McLung
11. Jonathan Adams
12. John Mitchell
13. Edm^d Crowder
14. William Alford, Senr
15. Joseph Turner
16. Thomas Dent
17. Charles Moore
18. James Lucas
19. William Cain
20. George Ross
21. Charles Abercrombie
22. Tully Choice
23. Mark Sanders

And the following persons were drawn to Serve as Petit Jurors the same Term.

1. John Gann
2. Benjamin Boice
3. Saml Gann
4. Joseph Rogers
5. James Christopher
6. Thos Chappell
7. John Shakleford
8. William Lancaster
9. Micajah Harris
10. Saml Goode
11. Thos Lofton
12. Nicholas Hughes
13. Thadd^s Holt
14. Nathan Smith

15. Tho[s] Moore	26. Henry Miller [19]
16. Edward Parrist	27. Francis Moreland
17. Drury Mitchell	28. Eppes Brown
18. Thomas Bradford	29. William Spears
19. Benjamin Grant	30. Hugh Beatty
20. William Wright	31. William McInvail
21. Joel Hurt	32. John White
22. William McGaughey	33. Josiah Coleman
23. James Loyd	34. Abner Abercrombie
24. Samuel Reed	35. Daniel Murphy
25. Joseph Chapple	36. Nicholas Smith

Attest. Hen. Graybill   Ex[d] W. Stith, jun[r]

At a Superior Court begun and held in and for the County of Hancock on the second day of December 1794. Present, the honorable Judge Stith, Esq[r].

The Attorney General being ordered to attend the Legislature, the persons summoned to appear on the Grand Jury who appeared were discharged.

William Reiley }   [20]
    vs   } Case
Zachariah Glass }

Edward Moore, Sen[r] came into Court and entered himself Special Bail for the defendant.

Samuel Williamson }
    vs   } Case
John Bivins   }

Settled at the defendant's Cost.

The Adm[r] of Hamilton }
    vs   } Case
Rob[t] Montgomery   }

Harris Nicholson came into Court and entered himself Special bail for the defendant.

Noel Mitchell }
    vs   } Trespass
William Grantham }

James Thomas came into Court and entered himself Special bail for the defendant.

James Rutledge }
    vs   } Case
Bolling Hall   }
Joseph Turner }

Settled at the Plaintiff's Cost.

Robert Flournoy }   [21]
    vs   } Case
Ullysses Rogers }

Settled at the ~~defendant's~~ Plaintiff's Cost.

Thomas Flournoy }
    vs   } Case
Ullysses Rogers }

Settled at the Plaintiff's Cost.

Thomas Cooper }
    vs   } Debt
Thaddeus Holt }

I do appear in this Case and acknowledge the Service of the within Declaration and by virtue of a Warrant of Attorney incorporated in the body of the bond within declared upon, do confess Judgment for the Sum of twelve pounds Sterling.

                                        Matthews, Att[y]

Execution to be Stayed three Months on good Security therefore. Stith

Edward Butler, Sen[r] Entered himself Security for the Defend[t].

Ordered, that the present term be and it is hereby adjourned & continued till the fourth tuesday in March next, at which time all Jurors, parties, witness, & others are ordered and directed to take notice & to appear

and that the Clerk advertise this order in at least four public places in the County, for at least two weeks before the time of the said adjournment. [22]

Ex[d]   W. Stith, jun[r]

Tuesday March 24th 1795 the Court met according to Adjournment. Present, Judge Stith.

The following Petit Jurors appear'd.

John Barron   }
       vs   } Case   28th March 1797 paid
W[m] Sallard   }   Sam[l] Barron this Judg[t]
& Eppes Brown }   over to Plff

I confess Judgm[t] for the sum of Seventy Six pounds Eleven Shillings & Eight pence, with Interest from the Second Day of Jan[y] 1793 and Cost of Suit, with a stay of Execution four months.

                              William Sallard

{24[th] March 1797 rec[d] £33.9.8¾   }
{in full for Principal & In[t]. M. Martin }

John Barron   }
       vs   } Case
W[m] Sallard   }
& Epps Brown }

I confess Judgm[t] for the Sum of Nine Pounds Sixteen Shill & Nine Pence, with Interest from this thirteenth day of December 1792, with Cost, Stay of Execution four months.

                              W[m] Sallard

Exec[n] Issued for both these 22nd March 96.

John Barron }   Exec^n Issued 22nd March 1796   [23]
     vs   } Case
William Sallard & }
William Mitchell }

I Confess Judgment for the Sum of Twelve pounds Six Shillings and five pence, with Interest from the Twenty Eighth day of December 1793 and Cost. Stay of Execution four Months.

                 William Sallard

Michael & Laurence }
     vs   }
Zachariah Maddox }
& Jesse Cormell   }

Settled at the defendant's Cost.

Ex^d W. Stith, jun^r

The Court Adjourn'd tomorrow 10 o'Clock.

Wednesday 25 March 1795 The Court met according to adjournment. Present, Judge Stith.

The following Petit Jurors Appeared & qualified.

     1. Saml Gann   7. Bouldin Hall
     2. Henry Miller   8. Francis Ross
     3. William Rees   9. Richd Bonner
     4. James Turner   10. Ja^s Waller
     5. Thaddeus Holt   11. Richd Whatley
     6. Wm Ousley   12. Wm Maddox

John Millar   }   [24]
     vs   } Case
Martin Gilbert & }
Michael Gilbert   }

the above Jury sworn.

We find for the Plaintiff the sum of Twenty two Pounds.

                              Thaddeus Holt, foreman

The 30th day of March 1795 Martin and Michael Gilbert appeared, paid the Cost, and Joseph Smith entered him self as Security for them for the Stay of Execution. Witness, Hen. Graybill, Clk

Mich^l & Laurence }
      vs   } Case
William Gilbert   }

Judgment confest for Seventeen Pounds fourteen Shillings & one penny half penny, with Interest from this date, with cost of Suit, with Six Months Stay of levy.

                              William Gilbert

I do acknowledge myself equally bound with William Gilbert for the Above Judgment.

Witness, Hen. Graybill, Clk   Edm^d Butler

Mich^l & Laurence }
      vs   } Case
Robert Lithgo   }

Judgm^t confessed for the sum of Twelve Pounds Nineteen Shillings & three pence & Cost.

Test. Jn° Griffen   Robert Lithgo

~~The following Grand Jurors app~~   [25]

John Jones   }
      vs   } Slander
Benjamin Averett}

The following Jury sworn, to wit.

      1. Richd W. Oats   7. William Lawson
      2. Henry Townsen   8. Robert Simms

3. Josʰ Chapel
4. Thoˢ Gorden
5. Ben Anderson
6. James Briton
9. James Wood
10. George Thompson
11. Wiley Abercrombie
12. William Spear

We find for the Plaintiff Twenty Shillings, with Cost of Suit.

James Wood, foreman

John Chandler }
    vs   } Case
Wᵐ McInvaile }

The following Jury Sworn.

1. ~~Richard W. Oats~~
2. ~~Henry Townsen~~
3. ~~Joseph Chapel~~
4. ~~Thoˢ Gorden~~
5. ~~Ben Anderson~~
6. ~~James Britain~~

1. Samˡ Gann
2. Henry Miller
3. Littleton Rees
4. James Turner
5. Thaddeus Holt
6. Wᵐ Ousley

7. Francis Ross
8. Richᵈ Bonner
9. James Waller
10. Richᵈ Watley
11. Wᵐ Maddox
Edmᵈ Abercrombie

We, the Jury, find for the Plaintiff Thirty One Pounds Thirteen Shillings.

Thaddeus Holt, foreman

Jnᵒ Brown }   [26]
    vs   } Case
Merideth Price & }
Joel McClendal }

I do hereby confess Judgmᵗ to John Brown for the sum of Twenty four Pounds Sterling, with Inᵗ from the first of Decemʳ 1793 and Cost, this 25ᵗʰ March 1795. Stay of Execution Two months.

Merideth Price

Isham Hogen }
    vs   }
Zachariah Glass }

Ordered, that all matters respecting the said suit be refered to Etheldred Wood, Esqr and Mr Benjamin Welsh, with power of umpirage, their Award to be made in writing on or before the next term and to be made the judgment thereof.

Mich^l & Laurence }
      vs   } Case
Jno H. Walker   }

Judgm^t confess'd for the sum of Nine Pounds and cost, with stay of Execution four months.

Walker, Att^y for Defen^t
25th March 1795

I acknowledge myself jointly & severally bound with the Defendant for the payment of the above judgment.

Test. Seaborn Jones   (Signed)   Wm Walker

Mich^l & Laurence }   [27]
      vs   } Case
Etheldred Wood &}
Richd Wood   }

Judgm^t confess'd for the sum of Twenty Pounds Seven Shillings & Six pence & Cost. Stay of Execution [faint]

Walker, Att^y for Defend^t
25th March 1795

Michael & Laurence }
      vs   } Case (Page 180 Carried to)
James Wood   }

The same Jury as in the case of Jno Jones vs Benjamin Everet, Only Saml Pope sworn in the place of James Wood.

We find for the Plaintiff the Sum of Nineteen Pounds Ten Shillings, with lawfull In^t from the 25 Decem^r 1793 Until Paid,

Robt Simms, forem

The 28 March James Wood Entered an app^l in the above Case, Daniel Whatley, Security.

Test. Hen. Graybill

Michael & Laurence }
      vs   } Case
William Walker   }

Judgm^t confessed for the sum of Twenty three Pounds Two Shillings & penny. Stay of levy till the 1st day of December 1795.

                              Wm Walker

I acknowledge myself Jointly & severally bound with the defendant for the payment of the above Judgm^t.

                              Jno H. Walker

Michael & Laurence }   [28]
      vs   } Case
Richd Wood &   }
Etheldred Wood   }

Judgm^t confessed for the Sum of Twenty three Pounds Eight Shillings & Ten Pence & Cost. Stay of Execution four months.

                              Walker, Att^y for the Def^t
                              25th March 1795

Michael & Laurence }
      vs   } Case
William Yarborough }

Judgm^t confes'd for the sum of Nine Pounds nineteen Shillings & Nine Pence & Cost, & if Security given within Ten days there is to be a Stay of Levy four months.

                              Walker, Att^y for the Def^t
                              25th March 1795

Whereupon, William Reddock came into Court & Acknowledged himself Security in terms of the Confession.

Michael & Laurence }
    vs   } Case
John Hamlin   }

Settled at the Defendant's cost. Att^y fee paid.

Michael & Laurence }   [29]
    vs   } Case
Barnaby Pope   }

Judgment confessed for the sum of Twenty three Pounds thirteen Shillings & three Pence. and on Security being entered in Ten days, there is to be a Stay of ~~Execution~~ levy four Months.

                                     W. Stith, Senr, Def^t Att^y
                                     25th March 1795

I acknowledge myself to be Jointly & severally bound with the Defendant for the Paym^t of the above Judgm^t.

                                     W^m McGeehee

Michael & Laurence }
    vs   } Case
Danl Richardson   }

Settled at mutual Cost.

Ben Maddox   }
    vs   } Case
James Wood &   }
Ben Thompson   }

I confess Judgm^t for the sum of Twenty One Pounds nine Shillings, with Interest from the first of January 1794 untill paid. Stay of Execution four Months.

                                     Walker, Att^y for the Def^t
                                     25th March 1795

Needham Jernagan }
    vs   } Case
Wm Gilliland }

Judgm^t confessed for the sum of thirteen pounds Six Shillings & four pence & Cost. Stay of Execution for thirty five Dollars untill the first of May & till the first December for the balance.

                              Walker, Att^y for D^t

Felix Gilbert }   [30]
    vs   } Case
Barnaby Pope }

Judgm^t confest for the sum of Nine Pounds four Shillings & One Penny, with Interest from the first of February 1791 untill paid of Cost of Suit and Stay of Execution Six Months on giving Security.

                              P. J. Carnes, Deft^s Att^y

Michael & Laurence }
    vs   } Case
Joseph Cooper   }

The Jury as in the case of Jno Candler ag^t McInvaile, only Bouldin Hall, Senr in the place of Abercrombie.

We find for the Plaintiff forty three Pounds Eleven Shillings & Nine pence, with Interest for the same from the time it became due till paid.

                              Thaddeus Holt, foremⁿ

The Court Adjourned untill tomorrow Nine O'Clock.

Ex^d   W. Stith, jun^r

Thursday 26th March 1795 the Court met according to adjournment.   [31]
Present, Judge Stith.

Van Allen

Peter L. Van Alen having made application for admission to practice in the Several Courts of Law & Equity within this State, and being found duly qualified, he was admitted [blot] after taking the Usual Oaths and his name ordered to be enrolled amongst the list of Attornies, Solicitors, & proctors.

Philip Spitters }
    vs }
W^m McInvail & }
Robt Mgintee }

The following Jury Sworn, to wit.

    1. Richd Oats   7. Wiley Abercrombie
    2. James Britain   8. Willis Spear
    3. Jos^h Chappel   9. Saml Gann
    4. Wm Lawson   10. Littleton Rees
    5. Robert Simms   11. James Turner
    6. James Wood   12. Wm Ousley

We, the Jury, find for the Plaintiff the sum of Twenty Six pounds against William McInvail, with lawfull Interest from the first of Jany 1793 till paid, with Cost of Suit.

                                      Robert Simms, form

John Barron }   [32]
    vs } Case
Wm Huddleston }

I confess Judgment for the sum of fifteen pounds Sterling, with In^t from the first day of April 1794, with stay of Execution 'till the first of Decem^r next upon giving Security for the debt.

                                      P. J. Carnes, Att^y for Def^t

Whereupon, James Huddleston came into Court and became Security.

Daniel Watley }
    vs } Case
Andrew Bouldin }

The following Jury Sworn, to wit.

    1. Henry Miller   7. John Barron
    2. Edm^d Abercrombie   8. Jesse Clemonds
    3. James Walker   9. Ben Thompson
    4. Wm Maddox   10. Richd Hamlin
    5. Ben^j Anderson   11. Saml Barron
    6. George Thompson   12. Mich^l Gilbert

We, the Jury, find no cause of action, the Plaintiff pay Cost.

                        Edwd Abercrombie, form^n

The 28th Day of March 1794 Daniel Whatley came & Entered an appeal in the above Cause and paid the Cost, James Wood, his Security.

Witness, Hen. Graybill

William Starks   }   [33]
    vs   } Case
William Weekes }

Continued by consent.

Walter Dent   }
    vs   } Case
Thos Mullings & }
Jno H. Walker   }

We confess Judgment for the sum of Sixteen pounds five Shillings, with Int^t from the 25th day of December 1793 until paid & Cost of suit, with stay of Execution four Months.

                        G. Walker, Att^y for Def^t

~~Michael & Laurence~~ }
    vs   } Case
~~Jno H. Walker~~   }

[blank]

Michael & Laurence }
    vs   } Case
Richard Hamlin }

Settled at the Defendant's Cost.

Hutcheson }
   vs   } Case
M. Price }

Dismissed.

Jnº T. Spencer }
    vs   } Case   [34]
James Rutledge }
& Wᵐ Wiley }

Continued on the plaintiff's affidavit.

Joshᵃ Williams }
   vs   } Case
Jnº Whatly & }
Jnº Pounds }

Continued on the plaintiff's affidavit.

Willᵐ Stark }
   vs   } Case
Jeremiah Bonner }
& Robᵗ Bonner }

Discontinued.

Jnº Linsey }
   vs   } Case
Moses Harriss }

Continued by consent and any Sett off of Defᵗ to be admitted.

Michael & Laurence }
    vs   } Case
Levi Lancaster   }

Continued On Defendant's Affidavit.

~~Harden & Hamlin~~ [35]

Michael & Laurence }
    vs   } Case
John H. Walker   }

Judgment Confessed for the Sum of eighteen pounds Seven Shillings and Six pence & costs, to be discharged by the payment of the full quantity of twenty-six hundred and thirty-five weight of Nett Inspected Crop tobacco delivered at Augusta clear of charges within eight months, till which time there Shall be a Stay of Levy.

                                        Walker, Att[y] for Def[t]

I acknowledge myself jointly and Severally bound with the Defendant for payment of the above judgment.

Test. Seaborn Jones   W[m] Walker

W[m] Low   }
    vs   } Attachment
Ge[o] Dooly }

Dismissed for divers errors.

Joseph Woodward } [36]
    vs   } ffi ffa
James Wood &   }
Joseph Carson   }

By Report of the Sheriff for illegality, withdrawn.

Michael & Lawrence}
    vs   } Debt
George Vest   }

I confess judgment for the Sum of thirteen pounds four Shillings and ten pence & Costs. Stay of levy till 25th day of December next.

Test. Seaborn Jones   George Vest
                                       26 March 1795

The following persons were drawn to serve as Grand Jurors at the next term, to wit.

1. Theophilus Turk 2. George Bagby 3. Wm Clark 4. Thomas Reins 5. Britain Rogers 6. Jn° Sturdivant 7. Edm^d Crowder 8. Robert Simms 9. Jn° Mitchell 10. William McClung 11. Jn° Baily 12. Jn° Harbirt 13. Henry McCoy 14. Harmon Runnels 15. Alex^r Reed

16. John Weeks 17. Jn° McKenzie 18. David Adams 19. George Ross   [37]
20. Tully Choice 21. Jn° Lamar 22. Charles Abercrombie 23. James Horton 24.

The following were drawn to serve as Petit Jurors, to wit.

1. Saml Wilson 2. James W[smear] 3. Demsy Stanley 4. David Hurley 5. [smear] 6. William Ryan 7. Jesse Permento 8. Wm Smith 9. Seth Tatum 10. Jesse Ellis 11. Jos^h Robt Clark 12. Jn° Carter 13. William Maddox, Senr 14. John Whatley 15. James Cain 16. Jonathan Black 17. Wm Gilbert 18. Sheldrick Brown 19. Ben Leonard 20. Joseph Howell 21. Henry Rogers 22. Elisha Whatley 23. William Edwards 24. Allen Pope 25. John Orear 26. James Turner 27. Jn° Low 28. Jn° P. Isaac Hern 29. Wm Turner 30. Jn° Barnes 31. John Pattison 32. Edm^d Noles 33. Zachariah Noles 34. Jn° Castleberry, Senr 35. Walter Ellis 36. Saml Williamson

Ordered, that certain suits removed from the County of Greene be placed by the Clerk at the head of the trial Dockett for the

term & that they stand there peremtorily for trial.   [38]

The Court adjourned till Court in Course.

Ex^d   W. Stith, jun^r

Tuesday the 2nd June 1795 The Court met according to Adjournment. Present, the honorable Judges Walton and Stith, Esq^rs.

The following persons attended and were Sworn as Grand Jurors.

   1. Chas Abercrombie, foreman   12. Harman Runnels
   2. Theodosius Turk   13. Alex^r Reed
   3. Wm Clark   14. Jno Weekes
   4. Thos Rains   15. Jno McKinney
   5. Britain Rogers   16. Jno Lamar
   6. Edm^d Crowder   ~~Thomas~~
   7. Robt Sims   17. James Horton
   8. John Mitchell   18. Tulley Choice
   9. Jno Bailey
   10. Jno Harbirt
   11. Henry McCoy

~~The State~~ }   [39]
   vs   }
[blank] ~~Coulter~~ }

The Court being Opened and the Grand Jury Sworn and the room for doing business Appearing to be too Small and Confined for the Season of the Year, the Commissioners were called upon to Report the State of the Court house created by Law, Who accordingly made the following Report, to wit.

We, the Commissioners appointed by the Legislature of the State of Georgia for tolling the Court house of the County of Hancock do hereby Report to the Honorable the Judges of the Superior Court, that the said Court house is now in Order for temporary use. Given under our hands this 2nd day of June 1795.

       Signed   Matt Rabun, Com^{rs}
             Ja^s Adams, Com^{rs}
             John Mitchell

Whereupon, it is Ordered that when this Court adjourns on this day it be to meet at ten O'Clock tomorrow at the Court house established by Law and that the Charging the Grand Jury with the duties & business &c the Term be Refered to that meeting.

The State   }
   vs   } Murder
William Coulter }

The Defendant being Confined in the Jail of Washington County. Ordered, that the Sherif do Cause him to be Removed thence to the Court house of this County to be proceeded

Against and that the Sherif or Keeper of the Common Jail of the [40] County of Washington is hereby directed to deliver the body of the said William Coulter to the Sherif on his order.

Ex^d W. Stith, jun^r
                               Ge^o Walton

The Court adjourned.

Wednesday 3rd June 1795 the Court met according to Adjournment. Present, the Honb^l Judge Walton.

The State   }
     vs   } Purjury
Mich^l Watley }

The following Petit Jurors Sworn, vis.

      1. James Waller   7. William Maddox
      2. William Thomas   8. Jonathan Black
      3. William Ryan   9. Ben Leonard
      4. Jesse Permetar   10. Allen Pope
      5. Jesse Ellis   11. James Turner
      6. Jno Carter   12. Wm Turner

Witnesses Sworn, Thaddeus Holt, Martha W. Holt, Hilry Phillips, Thomas Gray, Edwd Hunter, Esqr, Chares Abercrombie, Esqr, in behalf of the State

Daniel Whatley, Mary Anderson, Elisha Whatley, James Page, George Strother, in behalf of the Defendant

We, the Jury, do find the Defendant not Guilty of the Charge ag^t him.

                                                   James Waller, foreman

William Starks   }   [41]
    vs   } Case
William Weekes }

The same Jury as in the case of the State vs Mich^l Whatly.

We find for the Plaintiff the sum of Seventeen Pounds Sixteen Shillings & Nine pence.

                                                   Jonathan Black, form^n

John Barren   }
    vs   } Case
Isham Hogen & }
Etheld^d Wood } Exon iss^d 29th April 1799

We Jointly & Severally Confess a Judgment for the amount of the within described bond, with In^t & Cost. acknowledge Service of process. Rec^d Declaration, the amount being Twenty two pounds Sixteen Shillings & Eight pence Sterling, with a Stay of Execution to the 5th of January next. To Jno Barren, Adm^r of Alexander Miller, this 3rd Day of June 1795.

                                                   Isham Hogins
                                                 Eth^d Wood

Joshua Williams }
    vs   } Debt ~~Case~~
John Whatley & }
John Pounds   }

The same Jury as in the case of William Starks ag^t Wm Weeks.

We, the Jury, do find for the Plaintiff the sum of Twenty Seven Pounds Eighteen Shillings & three pence.

                                                   Jesse Ellis, foreman

The State   }   [42]
    vs   } Indictm^t Murder
Ben Breadlove }

A True Bill.   Charles Abercrombie

The State   }
    vs   } assault
Hezekiah Linsacomb }
& James Miller   }

A True Bill.   Charles Abercrombie, formⁿ

The State   }
    vs   } Indictm^t Larceny
Henry Clark   }

Not a true Bill.   Charles Abercrombie, form

The State   }
    vs   } Indictm^t Libel
Abner Bankston }

A true Bill.   Charles Abercrombie, form

The State   }   [43]
    vs   } Adultery
Jason Parmeton }

A true Bill.   Charles Abercrombie, form

The State   }
    vs   } assault
Hezekiah Lincicomb }
& James Miller   }

A true Bill.   Charles Abercrombie, formⁿ

The State   }
    vs   } Indictm^t Riot & Assault
Jesse Clements   }
Philip Clements   }
Frederick Ross   }
Jacob Rust &   }
Wm Brown }

Not a true Bill.   Charles Abercrombie, form^n

                                    Ge^o Walton

The Court adjourned till to morrrow 10 O'Clock.

Thursday 10 O'Clock the Court met according to Adjournment, present the honb^e Ge^o Walton.

Michael & Laurence }
  vs   } Case
Levi Lancaster }

Edm^d Crowder, Witness for the Plaintiff The

The following Petit Jurors Sworn, vis.   [44]

  1. William Thomas 7. Benjamin Leonard
  2. William Ryan   8. Allen Pope
  3. Jesse Permeter   9. James Turner
  4. Jesse Ellis   10. William Turner
  5. John Carter   11. John Barron
  6. William Maddox 12. Jno Castleberry

We find for the Plaintiff the Sum of Twenty Pounds Nine Shillings & Nine Pence, with Inter^t & Cost.

                                    William Thomas, forem

Charles Moore }
  vs } Case
Isham Hogin }

Award for the sum of Eight Pounds Eleven Shillings, with the accruing Cost, with stay of Execution till June Term.

Jno T. Spencer }
  vs   } Case
J. Rutledge & }
Wm Wylie }

Moses Wiley came into Court & entered himself Security on which the Plff's Att[y] consented to Stay of levy until the next term.

Hen. Graybill & Jn[o] Bailey, Esq[rs] Witn[d]

We find for the Plaintiff the sum of fifteen pounds, with In[t] thereon from the 25th Decem[r] 1793 till paid, with cost of suit. Execution Issued 2 May 1796.

W[m] Thomas, foreman

Jane Burne } [45]
    vs } Case
William Andrew }

Edm[d] Crowder, James Wood, Witn[s] Plaintiff

The same Jury as in the case of Michael & Laurence vs S. Sannard.

We, the Jury, find for the Plaintiff the Sum of Six pounds Nineteen Shillings & two pence, with cost of suit.

William Thomas, foreman

Jane Burne }
    vs } Case
William Andrew }
& Edm[d] Moore }

Jury as in the above Case.

Jn[o] Grear, Jn[o] Hamil, Witn[s] for Plainff

We, the Jury, find for the Plaintiff the sum of Two hundred and Eighty Six pounds Thirteen Shillings, with Cost of Suit.

William Thomas, form[n]

John Hamlin } [46]
    vs } Case
Hez[h] Jn[o]Son & }
Jesse Clemons }

Ansel Hudgin, Absalom Frazier, & Ge^o Scurlock, Witnesses for Plff

The following Jurors Sworn, vis.

1. Richd Bonner	7. Richd Risby
2. Mich^l Gilbert	8. Matthew Hawkins
3. Jno Coulter	9. Caleb Bayzer
4. Levi Lancaster	10. [illegible] Lawson
5. Lewis Barnes	11. Wm Ousley
6. Anderson Comer	12. James Wood

Ordered, the Plaintiff have leave to amend his Declaration so as to make an averment that Hezekiah Johnson was not good, according to the Defendant's engagement.

We, the Jury, find for the Plaintiff the Sum of fourteen Pounds, with In^t thereon from the 25th Decem^{er} 1793, with Cost of Suit.

           Wm Ousley, forem^n

The State   }
 vs   } Indictm^t Riot
Thos Johnson }
Job Jackson   }
Hez^h Johnson & }
Stephen Jackson }

A true Bill.   Charles Abercrombie, forem

The State }
 vs   } Ind^t Murder
William Colier }

A true Bill.   Charles Abercrombie, forem

The State   }   [47]
 vs   } Indictm^t Forgery & Anti dating a Plat & Survey
Micajah Williamson }

A true Bill.   Charles Abercrombie, forem

William Pound }
    vs   }
John Whatley }

In this Case, the parties have agreed to refer all matters in dispute to the final Arbitration and determination of Harmand Runnels & Peter Boyle.

With power of Umpirage, provided their award be returned under their hands & Seals on or before the first day of the next Term of the Honble Superior Court to be held in and for the County of Hancock on the first Tuesday in Decemb^r next, then and there to be made the Judgm^t of the Court.

                                { William Pound
                                { John X Whatley, his mark

The State   }
    vs   } Ind^t Adultery
Silas Downs & }
Nany Maddox }

Not a true bill.   Charles Abercrombie, forem^n

The State   }
    vs   } Assault
James Miller }

A true Bill.   Charles Abercrombie, forem

~~Henry Bonner~~ }   [48]
    vs   } Case
~~Jeremiah Bonner~~ }

Jones Bonner, Richd Bonner, Wyat Bonner, Plf Witness's

James Thweatt, Hilry Phillips, Wyat Bonner, Def^{ts} Witness

The same Jury as in the case of Jane Burne vs Wm Andrew & Edm^d M

not tried.

The State   }
    vs   } Ind^t Libel
Abner Bankston   }

Continued.

And thereupon came in said ~~Jacob~~ Abner Bankston with Isham Hogin & Jacob William, his Securitys, who acknowledge themselves Indebted to his Excellency the Governor & his Successors in Office. The said [blot] Abner Bankston in the sum of Two hundred Pounds, the s^d Isham and Jacob in One hundred Pounds each, to be levied on their Goods & Chattels, lands and Tenaments, to be void on Condition that the said J[blot] Abner Bankston do Appear the next Superior Court to Answer the above Indictment and not depart without leave of the Court.

The State   }   [49]
    vs   } Indictm^t Forgery & Ante Dating a Plat & Survey
Micajah Williamson }

Continued.

On said Micajah Williamson's coming in with Thaddeus Holt and Edmund Crowder, his Securities, who acknowledge themselves Indebted to his Excellency the Governor or his Successors in Office, the Said Micajah Williamson in the sum of Fifty Pounds Sterling. The said Thaddeus Holt and Edmund Crowder in Twenty five Pounds each, to be levied on their Goods and Chattels, lands and Tenaments, but to be void on Condition if said Micajah Williamson do Appear the next Superior Court to be held in and and for the County of Hancock the first Tuesday in Decem^r next to answer the above Indictm^t & not depart without leave of the Court.

The State   }
    vs   } Ind^t Libel
Abner Bankston   }

Continued.

And therefore [blot] came into Court with James Wood, Robert Abercrombie, Ezekel Smith, and Richd Castleberry and acknowledged themselves Indebted to his Excellency the Governor or his Successors in Office in the sum of Twenty Pounds Each, to be levied on their Goods & Chattels, lands & Tenem^{ts}, But to be void on Condition of the above Cowden to be & a[tt] at the next Superior Court in & for the County of

County of Hancock, then and there to give in Testimony in behalf of the State and not dep[t] without leave of Court. [50]

The State }
    vs   } Ind[t] Forgery &c
Mic[h] Williamson }

James Adams, Es[r], Godfry Martin, Sam[l] Alexander, and Rob[t] Harper and acknowledged themselves Indebted to his Excellency the Governor or his Successors in Office in the sum of Twenty Pounds each, to be levied on their Goods & Chattels, lands and Tenements, but to be void on Consideration of the s[d] James, Godfrey, Samuel, & Robert appearing on 4th Decem[r] next at Superior Court to be held in and for the County of Hancock, then and there to give in Testimony in behalf of the State & not depart without leave of the Court {blot}

Henry Bonner }
    vs   } Case
Jeremiah Bonner }

Jones Bonner, Rich[d] Bonner, Wyat Bonner, Plf's Witnesses

James Thweat, Hilry Phillips, Wyat Bonner, Def[ts] Witnesses

By consent, it is Ordered that all matters in dispute between the parties be refered to the final award of Peter Boyle and John Hamilton, Esq[rs], with power of Umpirage, and to investigate all disputes between the parties from the beginning of the world to this day without regard to any Arbitrations or Judgments heretofore had. The said Jeremiah Bonner on his part acknowledging a payment of four Thousand and fifty Weight of Tobacco paid in part of the negro named Esther to Humphrey Richards & James Hall. And the award made by the said Arbitrators or by them or either of them and the Umpire under their hands to be received and made the Judgment of the Court, if returned on or before the next term. John McKinzey came into Court and acknowledged himself Jointly and Severally bound with Jeremiah Bonner to pay the award if made against said Jeremiah, and Richard Bonner in like manner acknowledged him Self bound for the said Henry Bonner. [51]

                                    Ge[o] Walton

The Court adjourned till to morrow 10 O'Clock.

Friday 5th June The Court met according to Adjournment. Present, the Hon. Judge Walton.

The State }
    vs } Indictm^t Riot
Thomas Johnson }
& Others }

Therefore came Job & Stephen Jackson and acknowledged themselves [52] Indebted to his Excellency the Governor & his Successors in Office in the sum of Twenty pounds Each, to be levied on their Goods and Chattels, lands and Tenaments, to be void in Consideration of s^d Johnston appearing during the present term to ans^r the above Indictm^t &c and not depart hence without leave of the Court.

The State }
    vs } Ind^t Murder
Wm Coulter }

Jos^h Howard, Turner Harwood, Thos Dent, Mary Colter, Jno Colter, Witn^s State

Peter Colter, Ge^o Thompson, Def^s Witn^s

The following Jury Sworn, vis.

    1. William Ryan   7. Levi Lancaster
    2. Ben Leonard   8. Lewis Barnes
    3. Jesse Parmeter   9. Caleb Bayzer
    4. Allen Pope   10. Jesse Thompson
    5. Wm Turner   11. Jno Carter
    6. Jno Barren   12. Ben Maddox

We, the Jurors, find the Prisoner at the Bar Guilty of Murder.

                      Lewis Barnes, forem^n

The State }   [53]
    vs } Ass^t
James Miller }

Jacob Williams, Gabriel Hubbard, James Bonner, Paul Williams, Witn^s for State

The following Petit Jury Sworn, Vis.

1. Richd Bonner
2. James Wood
3. Edwd Hunter
4. Mich^l Gilbert
5. Edwd Woodham
6. James Thomas
7. William Thomas
8. Francis Lawson, Es^r
9. Matthew Hawkins
10. Zephaniah Harvey
11. James Christopher
12. Jachaniah Moore

On Motion, the Defendant was permited to withdraw his plea of not guilty and to plead guilty, whereupon a Juror was withdrawn by consent and the Jury discharged.

The prisoner Plead Guilty and fined five Shillings.

The State }
   vs   } Indct^t [illegible] Stealing
Abraham Borland }

Not a true Bill.   Charles Abercrombie, form

The State   }   [54]
   vs   } Ass^t
James Miller, Junr }

The defendant being arraigned & Plead guilty and was by the Court fined five Shillings.

The State   }
   vs   } Ass^t
Hezekiah Linsacomb }
& James Miller, Junr }

fined five Shillings.

The State   }
   vs   } Ass^t
Hezekiah Linsacomb }
& James Miller, Senr }

fined Twenty Shillings.

Buckner Harriss }
     vs   } Debt
Joseph Dickison }

We find for the Plf the Sum of Twenty five pounds One Shilling & Nine pence, with In^t from the Twenty first of Decem^r 1793.

                                 Francis Lawson, form

William Ryly }   [55]
     vs   } Case
Zachariah Glass }

Continued.

Noel Mitchell }
     vs   }
William Grantham }

Richd Bonner, Jno Burge, Abel Johnson, Ben Thompson, Bat Wyche, Witn^s for Plff [blot]

James Pinkston, Jno Pinkston, Bamalea Pope, Jn^a Parham, Alex^r Walker, Witn^s Def^t

The same Jury as in the case of Buckner Harris vs Jos^h Dickison, only Eps Brown sworn in the place of Richd Bonner.

Abraham Bouldin Sworn in the place of James Thomas. It appearing that James Thomas, being sworn one of the Jury in the case, was special bail for the defendant, he was removed and another sworn in his place.

We find for the Plaintiff Twenty five Pounds and Cost for Plaintiff.

                                   Edwd Hunter, foreman

The Grand Jury brought in their presentments which were Ordered to be   [56] published with the Charge.

His honour the Judge's Charge to the Grand Jury

Gentlemen of the Grand Jury,

Among the advantages attending the Exercise of a free Constitution and form of Government, the Opportunity afforded to every Citizen freely to attend the Tribunals of Justice and see for him Self the course of legal proceedings is not the least. And when it is seen that the laws are Admr^d Equally and fairly to all, Individuals will feel a full confidence in their Security, both in person and property and will be initiated in the Support of the Government, without which neither the Community can prosper, or the part thereof be happy. I Say this because this part of the Country has been newly Settled and by persons from divers other Countries; because also that busy and restless men are often spreading forth false reports and disturbing the general confidence, it should be our business, therefore, to unite and fix our attention to the Objects for which the Constitution and the laws have call'd us together, and they are to render Justice between man and beast and to enquire into and punish those who have broken the publick law. For myself, Gentlemen, you may rely on my intention to do right and in you I have the utmost confidence.

With respect to yourselves, Collectively,

Collectively, it is your first Business to attend to the Business which shall [57] be lain before you by the Att^y Genl. Some it is said will be cases of Capital Crimes. These will command and Obtain your Serious attention.

From his usual conduct in Office, I am persuaded he will lay before you no light or trifling business, but prosecutors are Often urgent, so as sometimes to force cases of this Kind into publick decree. Should any such business come before you, let it not have your sanction. The Justice of the Court is the glory of the law, while the litigation in them is a reproach. When these publick duties are discharged, the law has required it of you to decide in Civil Cases between your fellow Citizens, on appeal, And these are important trials, being the last resort of the parties. At present, there are few such on the Docquet.

The power of directing and superintending the public roads, ferries, and Bridges in the County is invested in the Inferior Jurisdiction, but if there should be any insufficiency of either, or any abuse of them already established, it will be within the immediate line of your duty to present it to the Court. And due notice shall be taken of it.

Any other matter or thing existing as a Grievance in your County and Capable of legal redress, being presented, shall be attended to.

George Walton

The presentments of the Grand Jury [58]

1st We, the Grand Jury of Hancock County, upon Oath present as a Grievance of the most serious & interesting nature to Georgia The breach of confidence by her Legislature in assuming the unexampled authority to sell contrary to the general voice of their Constituents, save a special [blot] our western lands, the birth right of the present and Succeeding ages, and that for an incompetent sum, Shall the Principals of Republicanism and the flower of Liberty that over Shone so bright in American Breasts, become extinguished, to the eternal disgrace of those who lit the Lamp of freedom for Europe, in the light of which millions are crowding to the Standard of liberty? Is it not a crime of the first magnitude to Wrest with a Sacrilegious hand the Trophies God and nature have hung upon the Standard of Liberty for us and our Children? Shall national firmness and fidelity, under the patronage of uniting Council of the benificent parent of nature, be unhinged and insulted by practical enemies of Republican Interest? Shall the Shades of Anarchy and the gauling Yoke of Despotism, from which we have extricated ourselves, be again fabricated upon the American Shoar for us and our Offsprings? Oh Georgia! cannot you mutually view the throbbing

ing breast and falling tear of thousands in the bosom of nature, [59] lamenting the irreparable loss they have sustained by one nefarious act? Is not our freedom visionary? Are not all the advantages of republicanism connected with freedom visionary? If no redress can be Obtained in this hour of political darkness, into which we are now festering.

In as much as the Incquitors Act passed the Second of January last, respecting the sale of the Western lands, is subversive of the Rights of the Citizens of this State, and the most daring piece of prostitution that we disgraced the annels of a free people. Therefore, we recommend to our Representatives in the next Legislature to take such measures as in their Judgment may seem proper towards repealing the above said Act. And having the same erased from the Records, so that no such piece of infamy be handed down to posterity.

2) We present as a grievance that the major part of State Officers, whom the publick have placed confidence in & promoted not only to hon[ble] but profitable Offices, have united with a corrupt Legislature in Order to share the public

property amongst themselves. Therefore, we recommend to our next legislature to remove from Office every person anyways concerned in the sale of the Western Territory, either as buyers or Sellers. And that the names, together with their crimes, be published throughout the Union, on Order that those concerned may be Stigmatized in such a manner as will more effectually prevent them from imposing upon some other part of the union.

3rd We present as a Grievance that the Majistrary is not properly regulated [60] in this County and that the multiplicity of Justices of the peace has rendered the Office Contemptible, and unless the number be reduced to a reasonable standard, we do not conceive that any person of respectability can think it his duty to serve in that Office.

4 We present as an alarming grievance that there is no law to prevent hawking and Pedling in this State, as by the Tolerance of such practices we are drained of much circulating Specie and a Spirit of Extravagance is introduced amongst the people.

5th) We present as a Grievance the bad State of the Roads in General in this County.

We return his hon^{or} Judge Walton our thanks for his Judicious Charge to the Grand Jury and his faithful attendance to the business of the County and request that these presentments with his honour's Charge be printed in the Public Papers.

                              Charles Abercrombie, for

John Lamar	Jno McKinzie	[61]
John Weeks	James Horton	
Thomas Reins	Tully Choice	
Henry McCoy	Alex^r Read	
John Bailey	Robt Sims	
William Clark	Harmon Runnels	
Britain Rogers	Edm^d Crowder	
John Mitchell		
Theodosius Turk		

The State   }
   vs   } Ind^t [62]
Isham Hogin }

Carried over from Green C^y.

The Defendant discharged by proclamation.

Charles Finch }
    vs   } Debt
Thomas Brown }

I do acknowledge the service of this Declaration and by virtue of a power of Att^y to me directed and contained in the body of the bond within declared upon, do confess Judgm^t for the sum of three hundred ~~pounds~~ Seventy five pounds.

Jno Mathews, Att^y Def^t

Saml

State }
    vs   } Indm^t for Adultery
Jesse Permeter }

The Defendant recognised in thirty pounds, John Booth his Security in the like sum, for the appearance of the Defendant at the next term and not to depart without leave.

Samuel Gordon }   [63]
    vs   } debt
Edm^d Tayler }

By virtue of a warrant of Att^y to me directed and Incorporated in the body of the bond declared upon, I do acknowledge the service of this declaration, appear for the Def^t and confess Judgm^t for the sum of Three hundred pounds, with cost.

Jno Mathews, Att^y

The State }
    vs   } Indim^t Riot
Job Jackson }
Stephen Jackson }
and others }

Job Jackson, Stephen Jackson, & Thos Johnson Recognised in the sum of 25 £ each, John Lamar, Sect^y for Thos Johnson, Harris Nicholson for the two Jacksons in the like sum of 25 £, for their appearance at the next Superior Court, there to answer the Said Indictment and not to depart without leave.

John Heath & Thomas Heath came into Court and acknowledged themselves indebted to his Excell^y the Governor & his Successors in Office in the sum of fifty pounds each, to be levied on their goods & Chattels, lands & Tenements, on condition of their Appearing the next Superior Court to give Evidence in behalf in ye above case.

Patrick Hayes } [64]
    vs }
Abner Bankston }

I confess Judgm^t against the defendant for the sum of five pounds Eleven Shillings & Eight pence, Cost of suit, & Stay of Execution two months.

June 5th 1795   Peter Williamson, Def^t Att^y

                                           Ge^o Walton

The Court Adjourn'd till tomorrow 10 O'Clock.

Saturday, 6th June the Court met according to Adjournment. Present, his honor Judge Walton.

Ordered, that the Clerk of this Court make out in Columns on one side of Clean Sheets of Paper a list of Persons liable to serve on Jury's, to be laid before the Judge of the next Sup^r Court, then to be regulated and corrected agreeably to the Act.

Isaac Barberae }
    vs } ffi fa
Edward Hunter, Esqr }

[blank]

The following persons were drawn to serve as Grand Jurors at the next term. [65]

1. William McClelland
2. James Scarlett
3. Wm Battle
4. Ja^s Alford
5. Wm Rabun
6. Hart Champion
7. James Thweat
8. David Adams
9. James Harvey
10. Robt Reins
11. Peter Coffee
12. Jonadale Read
13. Saml McGehee
14. Wm Bivins
15. Loyd Kelly
16. Josiah Beal
17. Judkins Hunt
18. Dixon Hall
19. Thos Mitchell
20. ~~Philip Clemonds~~
20. Charles Moore

21. Obadiah Richardson
22. Francis Ross
23. Richd Lockhart

Petit Jury
1. Jno McCullock
2. Wm Holt
3. Wm Bishop
4. Thos Shipp
5. Jno Gay
6. Thos Middlebrook
7. Jonathan Horn
8. Arthur Crocker
9. James Turner
10. Mathew Durham
11. Reubin Slaughter
12. Robt Wilson
13. Jno Miles
14. Alex^r Hooring
15. Jno Carnelo
16. James Lewis
17. Zorababel Williams
18. Blundel Curtis
19. Wm Horn
20. Reubin Slaughter
21. Jno Strother, Junr

22. Martin Gilbert
23. Thomas Peckard
24. Aaron Pryor
25. Philip Barnhart
26. Isaac Dennis
27. Jno C. Holcomb
28. Joseph Burgess

29. Hezekiah Carter [66]
30. Thos Jackson
31. Lumpton Turner
32. Robt Miller
33. Saml Read, Junr
34. Wm Sallard
35. Edwd Woodham
36. James Orr

Saml Giles }
   vs   }
Harriss Nichols}

In this case, the parties have [illegible] agreed to refer all matters in dispute to the final Arbitrament & determination of Robert McGinty, Jn° McKinzey, and Joel McClendon, Esq^{rs} and their award to be final and conclusive, provided it be returned under their hands and seals on or before the first day of the next term of the Sup^r Court, to be held in and for the County of Hancock on the first Tuesday in Decem^r next, then and there to be made the Judgm^t of the Court. The S^d Arbitrators to meet the first Saturday in July next at Jesse Thompson's or any day afterward.

Wm Stith, Plf^s Att^y
P. Wallin, Def^{rs} Att^y

William Marden & }
Thos Hambleton, Exo^{rs} }
    vs } Case
John McKenzie }

Dismiss'd.

Patric Hayes }
    vs } pro
Jn° Price & } Case
Wm Hutchison }

[67]

The following Jury sworn, vis.

Eps Brown	Wm Thomas
James Wood	Francis Saunders
Edwd Hunter	Matt^w Hawkins
Mich^l Gilbert	Zephaniah Harvey
Edwd Woodham	Ja^s Christopher
Abr^m Borland	Jachariah Moore

We find for the Plaintiff the sum of Twenty Seven pounds fifteen Shillings & Six pence Sterling, with In^t from the 5th June 1790 till paid & Cost of suit.

Edwd Hunter, fore^m

Noel Mitchell }
    vs }
Wm Grantham }

James Thomas, who was Special bail in ye above case, came into Court and delivered up the principal, Wm Grantham, into open Court, whereupon the s^d James Thomas was Exonerated.

The State } [68]
   vs   } Murder
Wm Colter }

The prisoner, being brought into Court, The Judge passed the following Sentence, Vis.

That you, William Colter, be remanded to the place of confinement and be there kept until the Second Tuesday in July next, from whence you shall be taken on that day by the proper Officer and conducted to the place of Execution in the Town Sparta, & that then & there between the hours of Ten in the forenoon & two in the afternoon of the same day you be hanged by the neck untill you are dead.

It appearing that the Clerk had made several writs returnable to last March, thru Neglect. Upon motion of the Attorney General, it is ordered that this Term be considered as the first and the writs amended.

Upon the Petition of Jesse Thompson. It is Ordered that a rule be issued to shew cause upon the administration of John Wooten why the letters to him should not be revoked next term.

Exam^d   Ge° Walton

The Court adjourned until Court in Course. [69]

Tuesday December 1st 1795 The Court met according to Adjournment. Present, his honor Judge Stith.

The following persons attended and were sworn as Grand Jurors, Viz.

       1. Francis Ross, foreman   9. Dixon Hall
       2. William Battle   10. Thos Mitchell
       3. William Rabun   11. Obadiah Richardson
       4. David Adams   12. Hart Champion
       5. James Harvey   13. Josiah Beall
       6. Peter Coffee   14. Robert Rains

    7. William Bivins   15. James Scarlett
    8. Judkins Hunt

On Affidavit of Charles Moore that he was over age, the Court dismissed him of Service as a Grand Juror.

Henry Bonner }
      vs   } Case
Jeremiah Bonner }

The Arbitrators made the following return, which was ordered to be entered of Record & made the Judgment of the Court, viz. Hancock County. In Conformity with an order of the Honorable Superior Court of said County, bearing date June Term 1795. Wherein the final decision of all debts, Judgments, Arbitrations, disputes &c between Henry Bonner, Plaintiff, & Jeremiah Bonner, Defendant, bring to us Peter Boyle, John Hamilton, & our Umpire

Submitted, we making choice at the same time of Henry Mitchell, Esqr [70] as Umpire, entered on the investigation of said business, & after hearing the Evidence on both sides & duly & maturely considering the same, we adjudge & award that Jeremiah pay to Henry Bonner the full Sum of thirty two Dollars & eighty four cents, together with the legal costs of suit, in full satisfaction of all debts, dues, & demands. In witness whereof, we have hereunto set our hands this 27th day of July 1795.

                                            P. Boyle
                                            John Hamilton
                                            Henry Mitchell

Francis Willis }
      vs   } fi fa
Jere^h Bonner }

Staid on affidavit of Def^t that the negro levied was free, the affidavit dismissed on the arbitrations of the case of Armstrong & Clarr in Wilkes.

The Grand Jury being empannelled represented to the Court that a general belief had prevailed in the County that a Court would not be holden the present term, of course the suitors were generally unprepared. And the petit Jury not being Summoned, & on the recommendation of the Grand Jury, the Court will adjourn till Court in Course. [71]

Ordered, that all recognizances returnable to the present term be continued over to the next term.

Elisha Pruit }
    vs }
Benjamin Oliver }

Judgment Confessed for the sum of two hundred and Eighty pounds eleven shillings and two pence & Cost of suit, to be paid in Dollars at four shillings and Eight pence each.

                Signed   Benjn B Oliver, his mark
                                        1st Decr 1795

Exon iss^d 3rd Jany 1798.

4 June 1799 Satisfied as p^r a Rec^t from Elisha Pruitt 17th Octr 1797 filed in Office brot by Def^t. Mar Martin, Clk

The Court adjourned till Court in course.

Ex^d W. Stith, jun^r

Hancock County } Clerk's Office of the Superior Court 1st of March 1796 {72}

In pursuance of an Act of the General Assembly, entitled "an Act to regulate the Judiciary System of this State," passed at Louisville on the twenty third day of february in the year of our Lord 1796, the times for holding Courts being altered; no Jury being drawn at the last term and the Judge not having attended; a majority of the Judges of the Inferior Court, being present, corrected the Jury list, and a sufficient number being selected for the Grand Jury, agreeably to the forecited Act, the following persons were drawn to Serve as Grand and Petit Jurors at the next Term.

                                Grand Jurors

        1. Daniel Low   10. Eppes Brown
        2. Peyton Tucker   11. Charles Statham
        3. Anderson Comer   12. Francis Lawson

4. John Harbirt
5. Levin Ellis
6. Daniel Muse
7. Stephen Kirk
8. John Strother
9. Robert Bailey

13. Richard Shippe
14. Solomon Jordan
15. Thomas Mathews
16. Barnaby Pope
17. Jesse Battle
18. Needham Jernigan

19. William Lawson, Jun[r]
20. Jesse Pope
21. Andrew Borland
22. Robert Hill
23. James Lamar
24. Thomas Johnston

25. Benjamin Shippe [73]
26. Robert Montgomery
27. James Bishop
28. John Brown
29. John Brewer, Jun[r]
30. Henry Burnley

Petit Jurors

1. George Gray
2. Henry Peak
3. John S. Williams
4. John Owsley
5. Jesse Herod
6. John Brown
7. Edward Beard
8. Thomas Fields
9. Reuben Mobley
10. Robert Montgomery
11. Isaac Stroud
12. Dennis Trammel
13. Stephen Ellis
14. Thomas Pebbles
15. Thomas Bailey
16. Abraham Peavy
17. George Brewer
18. William Mapp
19. Joseph Braswell
20. William Lawson, Sen[r]
21. Alexander Johnston
22. John Griggs

23. Caleb Kennedy
24. Samuel Harris
25. Zachariah Williamson
26. Aaron Feagan
27. Benjamin Chappell
28. John Parker
29. William Scurlock
30. Curtis Hay
31. Greene Lee
32. Austin Morris
33. Samuel Turner
34. Daniel Muse
35. Charles Johnston
36. John Fulsom
37. John Peace
38. Lewis Bailey
39. James French
40. John Grier
41. Richard Ryon
42. Elisha Hearn
43. Richard Barfield
44. John Dickinson

45. Thomas Callaway
46. Benjamin Gilbert
47. John Spear
48. Lewis Barnes
49. Richard Moon

50. George Miller [74]
51. William Bivins, Junr
52. William Thornton
53. Lewis Bandy

Attest. Mar Martin, Clk   Ex^d David Dixon
Pr Boyle
John Hamilton

Hancock County [75]

At a Superior Court began and held in & for the County of Hancock on the first day of September 1796. Present His Honor Benjamin Taliaferro, Esquire, Judge.

The following persons appeared and were sworn as the Grand Jury. (Viz.)

1. ~~Daniel Low~~
    John Harbirt, Esqr, foreman
2. Levin Ellis
3. Robert Bailey
4. Epps Browne
5. Francis Lawson
6. Thomas Matthews
7. Jesse Battle
8. Needham Jarnigan
9. William Lawson, Junr
10. Jesse Pope
11. Andrew Borland
12. Robt Hill
13. Thos Johnson
14. Robt Montgomery
15. James Bishop
16. John Brewer, Junr
17. Michael Gilbert
18. Thaddeus Holt
19. Stephen Horton
20. John Weeks
21. William Cureton, Jn^r
22. Peyton Tucker
23. Solomon Jordan

The following persons appeared ~~and were~~ of ~~Sworn~~ the Petit Jury. (to wit.) [76]

1. Jesse Harwood
2. John Browne
3. Abraham Peavy
4. John Griggs
5. Saml Harris
6. John Parker
7. William Scurlock
8. Astin Morris
9. Saml Turner
13. Richard Moone
14. William Thornton
15. Dennis Trammil
16. John Spier
17. Lewis Bandy

57

10. John Greer
11. Benjamin Gilbert
12. Lewis Barnes

John Gibson }
    vs   } Case
George Thompson }

[77]

Dismissed.

Micajah Williamson }
    vs   } Case
James Adams }

The death of the Defendant Sugested in the usual way.

21)

William Pound }
    vs   } Case Hancock County
John Whatley }

Agreable to an order of the Superior Court of said County, appointing as the Subscribers Arbitrators, in a certain case depending in said Court, wherein William Pound, as plaintiff, & John Whatley, defendant. Therefore we, the said arbitrators did meet at the House of James Thomas on the 25th day of August 1795 and, after hearing the said parties, and in examining into the Merits of the case. We do award that John Whatley pay unto William Pound the Just Sum of twenty six dollars and Seventy one Cents, as a full compensation for Said debt. in Witness whereof, we have hereunto set our hands and seals this day & year first written. 20 March 1797 we the principal, Wm Pound Plff

                        P. Boyle
                        H. Runnels

Exon for Cost iss^d 23rd July 1796.

The State }
    vs   } Indict^{mt} for Adultery
Lena Shaw & }
Jason Parmeter }

[78]

~~Fined two Dollars.~~

In this Case, the defendants came into Court and plead guilty, & the prosecutor interceding for the defendants. Whereupon, it is ordered that they be fined in the sum of two dollars.

Mich^l & Laurence }
     vs   } Debt
Aaron Wood   }

We do hereby confess a Judgment to the Plaintiffs for the sum of fifty three Dollars & fifty four Cents, with Stay of Execution till 25th December next.

1st Septr 1796   Aaron Wood
Test. John Griffin   Will Penticost

Richd Smith, ex dem }   [79]
of John Lamar   }
     vs   } Ejectment
William Stiles &   }
Richard Bonner   }

The following Jurors Sworn.

      1. Jesse Harwood   7. William Scurlock
      2. John Brown   8. Austin Morris
      3. Abraham Peavey   9. Saml Turner
      4. John Griggs   10. John Greer
      5. Saml Harris   11. Benjamin Gilbert
      6. John Parker   12. Lewis Barnes

We, of the Jury, do find verdict for the plaintiff, John Lamar.

                                           Benjamin Gilbert, Foreman

The Court then adjourned till 10 O'Clock tomorrow.

                                           Ben Taliaferro

Immediately after the Grand Jury were empanneled, the following   [80]
Rules were read in open Court and ordered, to be entered of record.

Rules for regulating the proceedings & practice of the Superior Courts to be held in the Counties of this State.

The style of address shall be that which has been heretofore Customary.

The principles of admission of Attorneys having a knowledge of the Laws and the Practice of Courts, a liberal examination shall be had in these respects.

For the sake of a decent conformity to ancient Custom in the profession, the Attornies ought to be heard in a black Robe, especially in Criminal Cases, but this is not to be insisted on with those who shall not have provided themselves with Such habits until the Second Term.

The order of pleading shall correspond with that laid down by Judge Blackstone and in no Case shall more than one of the Council be head in Conclusion.

In cases where Bail is required, the Sheriff shall take Bond in usual form with a condition to the following effect, "that if the above bound (the Defendant) do appear at the next Superior Court to be held in and for the County of [blank] on the [blank] day of [blank] next, to answer the Plaintiff in an Action of [blank] for [blank] dollars (the Sum for which Bail is ordered) then this Obligation to be void and of None effect, otherwise to remain in full force and virtue." Sealed &c. In Cases of Special Bail, the Same shall be offered as the Law directs, and shall be entered in the Court books in the following words, or to the like effect, "I (the Defendan) & we (the Securities) with their Additions) acknowledge ourselves jointly and Severally bound to (the plaintiff) in the sum of (the sum mentioned in the Sheriff's bond) on this Condition, that if (the Defendant shall be cast in this Suit, he (the Defendant) will pay the condemnation money or surrender himself as the Law directs, or we will do it for him. Taken and acknowledged before &c. A. B. &c.

And exceptions to Special Bail shall be taken When the same is offered, [82] Motion of the Plaintiff, or his Attorney, & the same shall be perfected on or before the rising of the Court, [blot] in default whereof the Plaintiff shall be at liberty to proceed on the Bail bond by Assignment, which Shall be made under the hand and Seal of the Sheriff in the presence of two Witnesses, in words to the following effect, "I [blank] the Sheriff of the County of [blank] do hereby Assign, transfer, and set over the within Bond to the plaintiff in the within mentioned Action. In witness &c &c."

No Attorney or other officer of the Court shall be bail in any Suit or Action depending or determined in Court, and no Attorney shall be permitted to appear either for plaintiff of Defendant until he produces a Warrant for that purpose.

Doquets of Original Writs &

& Processes shall be made out by the Clerk, who Shall furnish a fair [83] & correct Copy for the use of the Court and deliver the same at the first opening thereof. The Clerk shall also keep a Remembrance Book, in which shall be alphabetically entered all Judgments obtained in Court and shall Keep a Docket of all Executions, which Shall be called the Execution Doquet.

When the Plaintiff, or his Attorney, shall receive satisfaction for debt or damages upon a Judgment & the Costs, Satisfaction shall be forth with entered up by the plaintiff or his Attorney, on pain of being proceeded against for a contempt.

The Sheriff shall make Returns at the opening of the Court of the names of the Justices, Coroners, & Constables for their respective Counties to the Clerk of the Court, who shall not depart therefrom without leave.

The Justices of the Peace shall deposit or transmit to the Clerk of the Court, Attorney or Solicitors General all informations, examinations,

Examinations, and Recognizances by them taken, at least one day [84] before the sitting of the Court. And that they direct all persons who shall be bound to prosecute, that they attend the Attorney or Solicitor General on the first day of the Court.

In any Case of trial by Appeal before a Special Jury, it shall not be in the power of the plaintiff to claim the right of suffering a Nonsuit, but the Verdict thereon shall be final and Conclusive, to which end there shall be no necessity to call the plaintiff, when the Special Jury have returned with their Verdict, the Appellant's Attorney being answerable for the fees.

The Judiciary Law having taken away the right of the Inferior Courts having Cognizance in the trial of Real Estates, and as there are suits of this nature depending in said Inferior Courts and it not being directed by said Act in what manner the said Suits shall be removed to the Superior Court, it is Ordered that the following mode be observed. that is to Say. The

The party desiring to move the Cause shall take out a Writ of Certiorari [85] from the Clerk of the Superior Court, which writ shall be made out of course without any delay, and the same being carried to the Clerk of the Inferior Court, all the proceedings had shall be sent up to the Clerk's Office of the Superior Court, with a Return on the Certiorari, & thereupon the cause shall be entered on the Doquet of the Superior Court, and other proceedings take place as if the Suit had Originated there, but no suit so removed shall be allowed to come to trial without a written notice of the removal being given to the opposite party or his Attorney, if in the County, at least twenty days before the meeting of the Court and Service of such notice proved by Affidavit, or admitted, or in case the said opposite party or his Attorney shall not reside in the County where the said cases shall be depending, then the said notice shall be published in one of the Public Gazettes of this State at least twenty days before the Meeting of the Court.

Court, and the said publication proved as aforesaid or admitted. [86]

In cases of proceedings for foreclosing Mortgages of personal property, the party in possession shall be liable to be held to Bail to the amount of the debt, upon the Oath of the party claiming, or his Attorney.

When cases in the first instance require the powers of a Court of Equity the mode of proceeding shall be by Bill or Petition. & the usual Process of Subpoena shall issue, and Copies of Bill and Subpoena Served on the Defendant, if in the State as in common cases; if out of the State, the Subpoena shall be published six months in one of the public ~~Public~~ Gazettes to bring in the Defendant to answer, the Defendant on appearance shall have Such reasonable time to answer as the Court shall find to be Equitable. When the Defendant remains in default or contempt, the Plaintiff shall be entitled to have his Petition or Bill taken so far confessed as to justify an interlocutory order being passed thereon, and which shall intitle the Complainant to have his Case

Case exparte submitted to the Jury, who may decree on the merits of the [87] Case laid before them.

As all cases at common Law are directed to ~~proceed by~~ originate by petition and process, and some of those cases may require equitable interposition, when a common Law remedy is not adequate, either party, plaintiff or defendant, may State the facts supported by Affidavit of which the Court will Judge, & if the application is sustained, either party shall be compelled to answer on Oath at Such reasonable time on notice as may be deemed proper, so as no unnecessary delay be occasioned. Subsequent proceedings shall be the same as in other equity cases.

In regard to the establishment of Copies of Papers under the Act of the 22nd February 1785, all applications for the purpose shall be made in open Court only, and accompanied with proof on Oath to the Satisfaction of the Court. The following is prescribed as the form of the Rule Nisi

Nisi, the affidavit and the Rule absolute in Such cases, that is to say.　　　[88]
The Rule Nisi on the petition of A B stating that being possessed of a Note of hand signed C D bearing date [blank] for the sum of [blank] Dollars, a Copy whereof as nearly as your petitioner could recollect was annexed to the said petition, is now lodged in the Clerk's Office, together with an Affidavit pursuant to the Act of 22nd february 1785, that the said Note was lost or destroyed during the late War, and praying the benefit intended by said Act, and other circumstantial proof being all laid before the Court. it is Ordered that the said Note be established as directed by the said Act, on the said A B his publishing a Notice as therein required, & for the space of six Months in one of the public Gazettes of this State, unless cause shall be shewn to the contrary within the said six Months, or other matter shall appear to the Court against the same.

The form of the Affidavit

State of Georgia }　　　　　　　　　　　　　　　　　　　　　　　　　　[89]
[blank] County　} I, A B & C, being duly Sworn, maketh Oath that, pursuant to a Rule of Court of the [blank] last, he the deponent did cause to be published for the space of six months in the public Gazette of [blank] a Motion of his intention of establishing a Note of hand Signed C. D. bearing date [blank] for the sum of [blank] Dollars, a Copy whereof is filed ~~of Record~~ in the Clerk's Office of this County, which publication will appear by the Gazette hereunto annexed, & that no person hath to the Deponent's knowledge appeared to gainsay the same.

Sworn to the [blank] day of

before ~~me~~

The Rule Absolute

On Motion of Mr W., Counsel for A. B., (referring to the Rule of the [blank] last) acompanied by an Affidavit of the said A. B. that the several matters required of him had been duly perfected,

Perfected, which affidavit remains of Record in this Court. It is Ordered, [90] That the said Rule Nisi be now made absolute, no person having appeared to gainsay the same. And in case any person ~~should~~ Shall appear within the term to gainsay the establishment of such Paper, he shall file his objections in writing in the nature of a plea in the Clerk's Office, and the said Petition and Plea shall make a Record on which may be found an issue of either Law or fact according to circumstances.

The Mode of foreclosing Mortgages shall be as heretofore, in Such Cases when the State is a party and the Rule absolute in other cases varied so far as to direct Executions to issue in terms of the Judiciary Act.

Such Rules of Practice as have been heretofore adopted, not repugnant to the Judiciary Law, and the foregoing Rules are declared to be in force.

Done at Louisville this

this Nineteenth day of July in the year of our Lord One thousand Seven [91] hundred and Ninety Six.

                                 W. Stephens
                                 Ben Taliaferro
                                 W. Few
                                 D. B. Mitchell
                                 H^y Caldwell

A true Copy from the Original.

Attest. Mar Martin, Clk

Friday 2nd September 1796 the Court met According to adjournment. [92] Present, Judge Taliaferro.

State of Georgia }
Hancock County } To the Honorable the Superior Court for the County aforesaid

The petition of Hart Champion humbly sheweth that Violet Horn, a free Mulatto woman, is now held in Slavery in the County aforesaid. Your petitioner on behalf

& at the request of the said violet Horn prays that the Honorable Court will appoint him Guardian to the said Violet Horn and your petitioner will ever pray.

2nd Sept' 1796   Hart Champion

Petition Granted And ordered that Hart Champion be appointed Guardian to said Violet Horn.

John Loyed   }   [93]
    vs   } case
Philip Allen }

dismissed at Mutual Cost.

William Walker, ass^e }
    vs   } case
Benjamin Maddox   }

Dismissed at Defendant's Cost.

The following Jurors attended and were Sworn, Viz.

    1. Jesse Harwood   8. John Greer
    2. John Brown   9. Benjamin Gilbert
    3. Abraham Peavy   10. Lewis Barnes
    4. John Griggs   11. William Thornton
    5. Samual Harris   12. Dennis Trammel
    6. William Scurlock
    7. Samuel Turner

William Street   }
    vs   } Slander
Joshua L. Acee   }

The above Jurors Sworn.

We, of the Jury, do find Verdict for the plaintiff to the Amount of one hundred Dollars, with cost of Suit.

                        Ben^j Gilbert, foreman

William Turner } [94]
    vs   } Case
Levin Smith   }

The parties agree to submit all matters of dispute in the above Case to the award & determination of Charles Abercrombie, David Dickson, Peter Boyle, and John Bailey, Esquires, with power in case of disagreement to appoint an Umpire, whose award or Umpirage to be made in writing and returned to the Clerk's Office of the Superior Court on or before the first day of the next term, which Award or Umpirage shall be final and conclusive.

                                             W. Stith, Pff Att^y
                                              Levin Smith

N° (1)

The State   }
    vs   } Indctm^t Horse Stealing
Abner Pierce }

True Bill.   John Harbirt, foreman

N° 2   [95]

The State   }
    vs   } Cattle Stealing Indctm^t
Thomas Pickard }

True Bill.   John Harbirt, foreman

N° 3

The State   }
    vs   } Indctm^t Misdemeanor Bastardy
Larkin Turner }

Nole proseque.

True Bill.   John Harbirt, foreman

Nº (4)

The State }
   vs   } Cattle Stealing
Thomas Pickard }

True Bill.   John Harbirt, foreman

Nº 5

The State }
   vs   } Larceny
William Fitzgeareld }

Not a true Bill.   John Harbirt, foreman

Nº 6   [96]

The State }
   vs   } Misdemeanor Bastardy
John Coventon }

Not a true Bill.   John Harbirt, foreman

Nº (7)

The State }
   vs   } Indctm^t for Trespass
William Lawson, Senr }

A True Bill.   John Harbirt, foreman

Nº (8)

The State }
   vs   } Indctm^t for Trespass
Francis Lawson }

A True Bill.   John Harbirt, foreman

Nº (9)

The State   }
    vs   } Indctm^t for Trespass
James Lawrence }

A True Bill.   John Harbirt, foreman

Nº (10)   [97]

The State   }
    vs   } Indctm^t for Riot
William Lawson, Senr }
Francis Lawson   }
Thomas Lawson &   }
James Laurence &   }
Jane Lawson   }

A True Bill.   John Harbirt, foreman

Nº (11)

The State   }
    vs   } Indctm^t for Trespass
Thomas Lawson }

A True Bill.   John Harbirt, foreman

Nº (12)

The State   }
    vs   } Ind^t Ass^t
Isham Hogan }

A True Bill.   John Harbirt, foreman

John Torrence   }   [98]
    vs   } Case
John De Yambert }

68

In this Case, Robert Owsley, the Security, came into Court and delivered up the Defendant, whereupon James Wood came into Court and entered himself Special bail in the following manner, to wit. We, John De Yambert and James Wood, do acknowledge ourselves jointly and Severally bound to John Torrence in the sum of three hundred and eighty four Dollars, on this Condition, that if the said defendant shall be cast in this suit, he pay the condemnation money, or will Surrender himself into Court as the Law directs, or I (the said Wood) will do it for him. Taken and acknowledged in open Court this 2nd of Septr 1796.

Before
Mar Martin, Clk

John de Yampert
James Wood

The State }
 vs } Libill
Abner Bankston }

[99]

Continued till to morrow.

The following Jurors Sworn, Viz.

  1. Richard Moone   7. Micajah Harris
  2. John Spiers   8. Randolph Rutlin
  3. Lewis Bandy   9. James Ross
  4. Jecamiah Moore   10. Astin Morris
  5. John Parker   11. Zepheniah John
  6. Richard Rispas   12. ~~James~~ Jones Bonner

Joseph Cooper }
 vs   } Case
John Jack }

~~The same Jury as in the Case the T~~

The same Jury as in the Case the State vs Abner Bankston.

We the Jury find for the plaintiff ninety Dollars eighty seven and an half Cents.

             Randolph Rutland, foreman

Appealed to page 184.

Exon iss^d 16th May 1797

John Lindsy }
   vs   } Case   [100]
Moses Harris }

The same Jury as in the Case Street vs L. Acee.

We, of the Jury, do find a Verdict for the Plaintiff for two hundred & forty Dollars & Seventeen Cents, with Interest included.

                                 Ben^j Gilbert, foreman

Execution iss^d 14 March 1797.

Richard Hamlin }
   vs   } Case
Hezekiah Johnston }
& Evan Harvey }

The Same Jury as in the Case of Cooper vs Jno Jack.

We find for the Defendant.

                                 Jones Bonner, foreman

Appealed.

The Court then adjourned till 10 O'C Tom morrow.

                                 Ben Taliaferro

               Saturday 3rd ~~June~~ Septr 1796   [101]

The Court met according to Adjournment. Present, the Honorable Judge Taliaferro.

The State   }
   vs   } Ind^t Libel
Abner Bankston }

At September Term 1796, the defendant, with leave of the Court, withdraws the plea of "not Guilty," pleads guilty, and Submits to the Mercy of the Court, with leave to file exculpatory Affidavit.

Walker, for def^t

Solomon Wood }
     vs   } debt
Alexander Herring }

Settled at the defendant's Cost.

	D Ct^s
Att^y	2.00
Clk	1.50
Shff Lamar	1.50
	5.00

Exon iss^d 16th May 1797.

John Robertson }   [102]
     vs   } case
William Hinson }

The following Jury sworn in this case.

1. Richard Moon   7. Astin Morris
2. John Spier   8. Zepheniah John
3. Lewis Bandy   9. Jones Bonner
4. John Parker   10. Saml Harris
5. Randolph Rutlind   11. Saml Turner
6. James Ross   12. Benjamin Gilbert

We, of the Jury, find for the plaintiff One hundred & Seven Dollars & forty three Cents.

Jones Bonner, foreman

Mich^l & Laurence }
    vs   } Debt
Barnaby Pope   }
Isaac R. Pope & }
William Jenkins }

Continued.

Robert Montgomery }
    vs   } case
Isaac Daniel   }

The Same Jury as in the Case of Robertson vs Hinson.

We, of the Jury, find for the plaintiff one hundred twenty nine dollars 51 Cents.

                                Jones Bonner, Foreman

N^o (6) Septr 1796   [103]

John Pound   }
    vs   } Debt
William Morgan }

In this case, the defendant came into Court with John Booth, Senr, his security, who entered himself Special bail, in terms of the Act, to wit. We, William Morgan and John Booth, do acknowledge ourselves jointly and Severally bound unto John Pound, the Plaintiff, in the sum of four thousand eight hundred dollars, on this Condition, that if said Defendant is cast in this Suit, he will pay the Condemnation Money, or Surrender himself into Court as the Law directs, or I (John Booth) will do it for him. Taken & acknowledged in open Court this 3rd of September 1796.

Before Mar Martin, Clk

Arther Long   }
    vs   } assault
Thomas Johnson }

Settled.

                                                 Attorney   2$00
                                                 Clk   1.50
                                                 Shff   1.50
                                                                    5.00

Exon iss^d 16th May 1797.

Lewis Barnes }   [104]
     vs   } Case
Joseph Turner }

The following Jurors Sworn.

      Jesse Harwood   Dennis Trammell
      John Brown   Stephen Kirk
      Abraham Peavey   Alexander Reid
      John Griggs   Thos Cooper
      William Scurlock   John Kelly
      Wm Thornton   James Wood

We, the Jurors, find for the plaintiff one hundred dollars, With the lawfull Interest.

                                          James Wood, foreman

appealed.

Whereupon, the defendant paid Cost, entered an appeal, ~~Security~~ for ~~the payment of the above sum~~ with Andrew Borland, his Security, as follows. We acknowledge ourselves bound in the above Verdict & all Cost that may accrue thereon, & if said Turner fails to pay as aforesaid, or Surrender himself in Court, or Andrew Borland will do it for him.

Taken in open Court   Ja^s Turner
Attest. Mar Martin, Clk   And^w Borland

Thomas Eliot   }
     vs   } Case
Joshua Scurlock }

The death of the defendant Suggested in due form of Law.

Exon iss^d 16th May.

Iss^d 16th May 1797.

Walter Dent }
    vs   } Case
Thomas Mullins & }
John Hunter Walker }

The same Jury as in the Case of Montgomery vs Daniel.

We, of the Jury, find for the plaintiff one hundred dollars.

                                    Jones Bonner, foreman

Ex^n Is^d 14th March 1797.

Whereupon William Silman came into Court, Acknowledged himself jointly & Severally bound with def^t for the Stay of Execution Sixty days.

John Kilgore }   [105]
    vs   } case
Saml Townsend }
& Joseph Milton }

The same Jury as in the case of Barnes vs Turner.

We, the Jurors, find for the plaintiff thirty seven dollars & ninety three cents, With all lawfull interest that has accrued from that note.

                                      James Wood, foreman

Thaddeus Holt }
    vs   } case
Rubin Blankinship }

The Same Jury as in the Case of Barnes vs Turner.

We, the Jurors, find for the plaintiff One hundred & twenty dollars, with lawfull interest.

                                      James Wood, foreman

Ex^n issued 27th March 1797.

N^o (13)

The State   }
    vs   } Inditement for arson
William Fitzgerreld }

A True Bill.   John Harbirt, foreman

(7)   [106]

The State   }
    vs   } Ind^t Trespass
William Lawson, Senr }

Arraigned and plead not guilty. Traversed until Next Term.

(8)

The State   }
    vs   } Ind^t Trespass
Francis Lawson }

Arraigned & plead not guilty. Traversed until next Term.

The State   }
    vs   } Ind^t Trespass
James Lawrence }

Arraigned & plead not guilty. Traversed until next Term.

The State   }
    vs   } Ind^t Riot
William Lawson, Senr }
Francis Lawson   }
Thomas Lawson &   }
James Laurence &   }
Jane Lawson   }

Arraigned & plead not guilty. Traversed until next Term.

75

The State }   [107]
  vs } Ind^t Trespass
Thomas Lawson }

Arraigned and plead not guilty. Traversed until next Term.

In the five foregoing Indictments, Ezekiel Smith Acknowledged himself bound to his Excellency the Governor & his successors in Office in the sum of five hundred Dollars, to be void in Case the said Defendants do appear at the Next Term and do not depart without leave of the Court. the 3rd of Septr 1796

Before Mar Martin, Clk   Ezekiel Smith

Henry Parrish }
  vs } Case
Moses Harris }

Dismissed.

Exon iss^d 16th May 1797.

Andrew King }   [108]
  vs } Case
James Works }

In this Case, the Defendant came into Court with John Bond, his Security, who entered himself Special bail as follows, to wit. We, James Works and John Bond, do jointly and Severally acknowledge ourselves bound to Andrew King in the Sum of one hundred and twenty two dollars, on Condition that, if the Defendant is cast in this suit, he will pay the condemnation money, or Surrender himself into Court As the Law directs, or I (John Bond) will do it for him. Taken and acknowledged in Open Court this 3rd of Septr 1796.

Before Mar Martin, Clk

The Court then adjourned till 10 O'C Monday.

                     Ben Taliaferro

Monday 5th September 1796 [109]

~~Lewis Barnes~~ }
    vs   } ~~Case~~
~~Joseph Turner~~ }

~~In this Case~~

Monday 5th Septr 1796

The Court met according to adjournment. Present, Judge Taliaferro.

Daniel Whatley }
    vs   } Trespass
Andrew Borland }

This day the parties Came into Court by their Attorneys, and thereupon Came a Jury, to Wit.

John Brown	Astin Morris
Abram Peavy	Saml Turner
John Griggs	Lewis Barnes
Samuel Harris	Richd Moone
John Parker	William Thornton
William Scurlock	Stephen Kirk

Witness for plff, Joseph Hearndon, William Ewing

~~And after hearing the Evidence, returned the following Verdict, Viz.~~

The parties being called & the plaintiff failing to Appear, Ordered that he be nonsuited.

Absalom Jackson }   [110]
    vs   } ffi ffa Sheriff's Reports
William Low }

Dismissed on account of the illegality of the Execution.

James Wood } Distress for Rent
    vs   } ~~ffi ffa~~ Sheriff Report
John Cobbs }

Dismissed.

Joseph White }
    vs   } ffi ffa Sheriff Report
Isham Hogan }

The same Jury as in the case of Whatley vs A. Borland.

We, the Jurors, do find for the plaintiff forty five Dollars & Seventy two cents, with lawfull interest.

                            Lewis Barnes, foreman

Laurence Smith }
    vs   } ffi ffa Sheriff's Reports
Isham Hogan }

Dismissed.

William Walton }
    vs   } ffi ffa Sheriff's Reports
Isham Hogan }

Dismissed.

George Bagby}   [111]
    vs   } ffi ffa Sheriff's Reports
Isham Hogan }

Dismissed.

William Johnson }
    vs   } ffi ffa Sheriff's Reports
Isham Hogan }

Dismissed.

Michael & Laurence }
    vs   } ffi ffa Sheriff's Reports
Barnaby Pope &   }
William McGehee }

Continued.

Michael & Laurence }
    vs   } ffi ffa Sheriff's Reports
Waller, et al   }

Dismissed.

Jane Burne   }
    vs   } ffi ffa Sheriff's Reports
William Andrews}

Satisfied.

Simon Day   }   [112]
    vs   } ffi ffa Sheriff's Reports
Charles McDonald}

Dismissed.

Hammil }
   vs   } ffi ffa Sheriff's Reports
Johnson }

Adjudged illegal.

John Barron   }
    vs   } Case
Michael Gilbert }

Settled.

Exon Iss^d 17th May 1797.

Josiah Beal }
    vs   } Case
Zachariah Lamar }
& Thomas Lamar }

We confess Judgement for Seventy Nine dollars & Costs, With Stay of Execution till the 15th day of January next.

                              Z. Lamar
                              Thos Lamar

Samuel Giles }   [113]
    vs   } Case
Harris Nichols }

The arbitrators brought in their award, which was ordered to be entered of record and made the Judgement of the Court, as follows, Viz.

At Jesse Thomson's the 7th day of November 1795, We, the arbitrators being appointed by the Honorable Superior Court in the County of Hancock to decide on all matters in dispute betwixt Samuel Giles, plaintiff, Harris Nicholson, defendant, and on investigation of the business, We agree that Harris Nicholson do pay Samuel Giles forty two dollars & Seventy Cents, or return to the said Samuel Giles a discharge as aforesaid.

As witness our hands and seals the day & date above written.

                              Robt McGinty
                              John McKinzie
                              Joel McClendon

Ex^n issued 27th March 1797.

The Court then adjourned till 10 O'Clock Tomorrow.

                              Ben Taliaferro

            Tuesday 6th September 1796   [114]

Court met according to adjournment. Present, the Honorable Judge Taliaferro.

The State }
   vs   } Ind^t Libel
Abner Bankston }

On examining the affidavits for and against the Defendant, it is therefore ordered by the Court that he be fined five dollars. Which fine being paid, Ordered that the prisoner be discharged.

The Grand Jury returned the following Bills.   [115]

The State }
   vs   } Comp [illegible]
Richard Hamlin }

Not a true Bill.   John Harbirt, Foreman

The State }
   vs   } Ind^t assault
Abner Abercrombie }

A true Bill.   John Harbirt, Foreman

The State }
   vs   } Ind^t Escape
John Hamlin }

A true Bill.   John Harbirt, Foreman

The State }
   vs   } Ind^t Com^d felony
Ansel Hudgens }

Not a true Bill.   John Harbirt, foreman

William Stark }   [116]
   vs   } Trover
Jeremiah Bonner }
& Robert Bonner }

In this Case, Robt Bonner, one of the defendants, came into Court with Gabriel Hubert, his Security, who became Special Bail in the following manner for both

Defendants, that is to Say. We, Robert Bonner & Gabriel Hubert do acknowledge ourselves jointly & Severally bound unto William Stark in the Sum of two thousand one hundred dollars, on this Condition, that if the said defendants shall be cast in this Suit, they will pay the condemnation Money, or Surrender themselves into Court as the Law directs, or I (Gabriel Hubert) will do it for them.

Taken and acknowledged in Open Court the 6th of Septr 1796.

Before Mar Martin, Clk   Robt Bonner
                                           Gab^l Hubert

John Barnett   }
        vs   } Case for words
Bartley McCreary }

Settled.

Eliza Vaughan, Guardian }
         vs   } Case
John Harrison   }

Abated by the death of the plaintiff.

Richard Shipp, ass^e & Att^y }   [117]
         vs   } Case
Job Allen &   }
James Cowden   }

In this case, the defendants being called and failing to appear. Etheldred Wood, the former Sheriff, came into Court and acknowledged himself bound in the Sum of Eight hundred Dollars unto the plaintiff, Richard Shipp, & James Cowden, as follows, to wit, that if said defendants shall be cast in this Suit, they shall pay the Condemnation Money, or Surrender, or said James Cowden will Surrender himself into Court as the Law directs, or I will do it for him. Taken & acknowledged in Open Court the 6th of Septr 1796.

Before Mar Martin, Clk   Eth^d Wood

Richard Shipp, Att^y & ass^e }
    vs   } Case
Job Allen &   }
James Cowden   }

In this case, Etheldred Wood, Came into Court and acknowledged himself bound unto the plaintiff, Richard Shipp, in the sum of one hundred and twenty eight dollars and fifty seven Cents for James Cowden, as follows, to wit, that if said defendant Shall be cast in this Suit, they shall pay the condemnation Money, or said James Cowden will Surrender himself into Court as the Law directs, or I will do it for him. Taken & acknowledged in Open Court the 6th of Septr 1796.

Before Mar Martin, Clk   Eth^d Wood

The State   }   [118]
    vs   } Indictm^t Arson
William Fitzgerald}

State Witnesses, Ezekiel Smith, Senr, Peggy Moffatt, Ezekiel Smith, jun^r, Dudley Milum, William Lawson, jun^r

Witnesses, Dudley Milum, Robt Day, Danl Craft, Danl Bankston, Sarah Lucas, Jno T. Hansel

The following Jurors Sworn, viz.

        John Brown   John Spear
        Abraham Peavey   Dennis Trammell
        John Griggs   Richd Lockhart
        John Parker   Robt Day
        Austin Morris   Chas Moore
        Lewis Barnes   William Alford

who rendered the following Verdict. We, the Jurors, find the defendant not guilty of the charge.

                                            Lewis Barnes, forman

The Grand Jury Returned the following Bills (Viz). [119]

The State }
    vs } Indictm^t Murder
William Wigans }
Thomas Laurence }
Cornelius Clark }
Robt Clark }
Abner Wheloss & }
Nathaniel Sledge }

Not a true Bill.   John Harbirt, foreman

The State }
    vs } Indictm^t Larceny
Moses Harris }

A true Bill.   John Harbirt, foreman

The State }
    vs } Indictm^t for Selling a free Negro
William Braswell }

A true Bill.   Jno Harbirt, foreman

Joseph Palmer } [120]
    vs } Case
Thomas Pickard }

Setled.

The State }
    vs } Indict^{mt} Selling a free Negro
William Braswell }

Arraigned & plead not guilty. Traversed until next Term.

The Court adjourned untill tomorrow 10 O'Clock.

                                              Ben Taliaferro

Wednesday 7th Sept\` 1796 [121]

The Court met according to adjournment. Present, Judge Taliaferro.

William Barksdale }
    vs   } case
Elisha Whatley   }

In this case, the bail was discharged on a common appearance.

Suit continued.

The State   }
    vs   } Ind^t Assault
Abner Abercrombie }

Arraigned & plead guilty & Submits to the Mercy of the Court, with leave to file exculpatory Affidavits.

On examining the Affidavits for and against, it is therefore Ordered that the defendant be fined five dollars. Which fine being paid, Ordered that the defendant be discharged.

Wednesday 7th Sept\` 1796 [122]

The State   }
    vs   } Ind^t Escape
John Hamlin }

Arraigned & plead not guilty.

Witnesses, Nathaniel Waller, Aurther Danielly, Francis Danielly, Frederick Ross, Elijah Simmons, George Vest, William Brown, Michael Madox, Weldon Ousley, Archibald Taylor, William Spencer, for State

Richard Hamlin

The following Jury Sworn.

        Jesse Harwood   Austin Morris
        John Brown   Lewis Barnes
        Abraham Peavy   William Thornton

        John Griggs   Ben^j Gilbert
        John Parker   Jecamiah Moore
        William Scurlock   Edmund Walsh

And returned their verdict as follows, to Wit. We, the Jurors, find for the defendant not guilty of the charge.

                                            Lewis Barnes, foreman

The State   }
    vs   } Ind^t Horse Stealing
Abner Pierce }

Recognisance discharged upon affidavit of the death of said Pierce.

                                      P. L. Van Alen, Att^y [faint]

Andrew Borland }   [123]
    vs   } debt
William Minor   }

In this Case, the defendant came into Court with Gabriel Hubert, his Special Security, who acknowledged themselves jointly and Severally bound to the plaintiff in the Sum of four hundred & twenty eight Dollars, on this Condition, that if said def^t shall be cast in this Suit, he will pay the condemnation Money, or Surrender himself into Court as the Law directs, or I (Gabriel Hubert) will do it for him. Taken & acknowledge in Open Court this 7th of September 1796.

Before Mar Martin, Clk   Will Minor
                                                Gab^l Hubert

Adm^{rs} of John Wooten }
      vs   } Trover
Hardy Wooten   }

Continued.

~~The State~~ }
    vs   } Ind^t Burglary
~~David Lidd~~ }

~~The Grand Jury Returned the following Bills.~~

The Grand Jury Returned the following Bills. [124]

The State }
    vs   } Indit^{mt} Burglary
David Lidd }

Not a true Bill.   John Harbirt, foreman

The State   }
    vs   } Ind^t Perjury
William Fitzgerald }

A true Bill.   John Harbirt, foreman

The Court then adjourned till 10 O'Clock Tomorrow.

                                Ben Taliaferro

              Thursday 8th Septr 1796   [125]

~~Court met according to adjournment. Present, Judge Taliaferro.~~

~~William Lawson }~~
    ~~vs~~   } Case
~~Thomas Cooper, et al }~~
~~Exo^{rs} of Thos Cooper }~~

~~Dismissed & cost paid~~.

The State }
    vs   }
Samuel Gan }

Recognizance for appearance at Court & to keep the peace generally & particularly towards Betsey Greer, the elder.

On Motion of W. Carnes, Att^y for defendant, Ordered that the said Saml Gan be discharged from his recognizance, no proceeding having been had thereon.

Thursday 8th Septr 1796

~~The Court having taken up the petition of Nancy Temple stating the insanity of her husband, Peter Temple, And the consequent injury resulting to his property and person therefrom. And on Motion of Mr Walton, Attorney for the said Nancy Temple. It is Ordered, that a Jury be immediately impannelled to enquire into the Circumstances of Lunacy stated in the petition aforesaid.~~

Upon calling the Grand Jury, it appeared that four of the Original pannel were absent.

Whereupon, Davis Long, Lewis Barnes, John Hamilton, & Littleton Reese were Summoned and Sworn in their steads.

William Street }
    vs   } Slander
Joshua L. Acee }

In this Case, ~~Verdict~~ Judgmt having been obtained against the ~~plaintiff~~ defendant, he paid the costs & craved an Appeal. Whereupon, Harmon Runnels, Esqr came into Court & entered himself Security, On this Condition, that if said defendant shall be cast in this Appeal, he will pay the condemnation Money, or Surrender himself into Court as the Law directs, or I (Harmon Runnels) will do it for him. Taken and acknowledged in Open Court this 8th of Septr 1796.

Before Mar Martin, Clk   J. L. Acee
                                     H. Runnels

John Robison }
    vs   } Case
William Hinson }

In this Case, Judgment having gone against the defendant, he paid cost & craved an Appeal. Whereupon David Lidd and Benjamin Gilbert came into Court and [blot] entered themselves ~~unto~~ Security, on this Condition, that if said defendant shall be cast in this Action, he will pay the condemnation Money, or Surrender himself into Court as the Law directs, or we will do it for him. Taken and acknowledged in Open Court the 8th of Sept' 1796.

Before Mar Martin, Clk   William X Hinson, his mark
                               David Lidd
                               Benjn Gilbert

The Court having taken up the Petition of Mrs Nancy Temple, Stating [128] the insanity of her husband, Peter Temple, and the consequent injury resulting to his person and property therefrom. And on proper Affidavits being exhibited to convince the Court of the insanity of the said Peter Temple, on Motion of Mr Walton, Attorney for the said Nancy Temple, it is Ordered, that Duke Hamilton & Willie Burge be appointed Guardians to the said Peter Temple, with power to take care of his person and property until the meeting of the next Superior Court to be held in this County, on their entering into bond (with approved Security) in the sum of Twelve hundred dollars for the faithful discharge of their duty.

Stephen Horton }
        vs   } Trespass
Allen Burton   }

Settled at def^{ts} Cost. Cost paid.

Joseph Whitehead, for }
the use of James Thweatt }
        vs   } Debt
Etheldred Wood }

Dismissed.

The State   }   [129]
        vs   } Ind^t Breaking Prison
William Grantham }
& Joseph Patterson }

A true Bill, as far as William Grantham is accused, not a true Bill as to Patterson.

                                        Jesse Battle, foreman

Witnesses, Bolling Hall, Saml Hall

Arraigned & plead not guilty & the following Jurors Sworn, viz.

Edm^d Walsh	Austin Morris
Duke Hamilton	Nathaniel Waller
John Lewis, Junr	Benjamin Gilbert
Harmon Runnels	William Thornton
Richard Bonner	Samuel Turner
	John Griggs
	Richard Moon

Who returned the following Verdict, viz. We, the Jurors, find no misdemeanor in the prisoner.

            Nathl Waller, foreman

The State }
  vs   } Ind^t Malpractice
George Bagby }

A true Bill.   Jesse Battle, foreman

The State }
  vs } Ind^t Extortion
Hines Holt }

Not a true Bill.   Jesse Battle, foreman

The State }
  vs   } Ind^t Ass^t
Ezekiel Smith }

A true Bill.   Jesse Battle, foreman

Nathaniel Waller }   [130]
  vs   } Trespass
William Bezar, Senr }
John Bezar &   }
Edward Bezar   }

By consent of the parties, it is agreed that all matters in dispute between them as far as respects the above case be submitted to the award and determination of

James Thweatt, John Hamilton, Esqʳ, Thomas Mitchell, John Bailey, Richard Bonner, Peter Boyle, Andrew Baxter, John Harbirt, John Cook, Senʳ, Mark Sanders, Stephen Kirk, Francis Ross, & Thomas Mathews, Esqʳˢ, whose award, returned on or before the first day of the next Term to the Clerk's Office in writing, to be made the Judgment of the Court.

          N. Waller
          William Bazar
          Edward Bazar
          John Bazar

The State   }   [131]
 vs   } Indᵗ Assault
Ezekiel Smith }

Arraigned, Plead guilty, & Submits to the mercy of the Court.

Whereupon, it is ordered that he be fined five Dollars, which fine being paid, he is discharged.

The Grand Jury brought in their presentments, as follow.

We present as a grievance that there are no boxes provided for Jurys in our Court House. Whereby, from the necessary encumbrance and the intrusion of Speculators, the Sheriff & Clerks are unable to perform the duties of the office with the facility and perspicuity which is necessary. We therefore recommend that the Judges of the Inferior Court enjoin it on the commissions of this court House to have Such repairs as are necessary. We recommend that the Judges of the Inferior Court to appoint commissioners to lay out a Road leading from Littleton Map's, Senʳ to this place the nearest and best way, and recommend that there be Commissioners to lay of & appoint Commissioners to keep open the Road leading from Chambers' Mill to Powelton, thence to Mitchell's Bridge. We further recommend that the Judges of the Inferior Court to appoint Commissioners to Act in Conjunction

With those of Warren County in erecting a Bridge at Lucas's Mill near [132] Powelton on Ogechee River, in case it cost this county not more than fifty dollars.

We present as a grievance that the Law is not put in force against the disturbances of public Worship.

We recommend that the Court examine into the affairs of the Academy Lands. We further desire to Return our Sincere thanks to his honor Judge Taliaferro for his Charge to the Grand Jury and his great attention in discharge of his office. And also recommend that the said Charge with our presentments be made public.

Jesse Battle, foreman

The State }
    vs   } Ind^t Larceny
Moses Harris}

In this Case, the Defendant being arraigned, plead not guilty, it is therefore traversed untill the next Term. Where upon, Austin Morris Came into Court and acknowledged himself bound to his Excellency the Governor for the time being & his successors in office in the full and Just Sum of Five hundred dollars, on condition that he, the said Austin Morris, will render the body of the said Moses Harris into Court on the first day of March next and then stand to and abide the Judgement of said Court, then this recognizance to be void.

Moses Harris
Austin Morris

Ordered, that the foregoing presentments be transmitted to Mr Smith,   [133] Printer to the State, in order for publication.

Michael Rogers, having produced an Affidavit, proving to the Satisfaction of the Court his right & Property to two heifers tolled by Doct^r Jeremiah Nelson before Alexander Reid, Esqr & sold some time last Spring as estrays. Ordered, that the amount of the Sale of said Estrays be paid Said Rogers, deducting the lawful fees therefrom.

The Court then adjourned till Court in Course.

Ben Taliaferro

The following persons were drawn to serve as Grand Jurors next Term.   [134]

George Evans	James Bynum
Jecamiah Moore	Thomas Cooper
George Lee	William Ousely
David Felps	Richd Parker

William Gilliland
Thomas Mitchell
William Lawson
Richd W. Oats
John Adams, Jn^r
Randolph Rutland
John Heath
Philip Levar
Richd B. Ship
Joshua Ellis
John Currie
Henry Mitchell
Thaddeus Holt
Moses Powell

Martin Armstrong
Nathan Jones
James Cooper
Wyatt Collier
Daniel Lewis
David McAlister
Daniel Mitchell
Abraham Womack
Jesse Grigg
William Truman
Jerald Burch
John Holcomb
Martin Johnson
Absalom Harris

Petit Jurors

William Bivins
William Landcaster
William Beardin
Samuel Dent
Edward Bazor

Thomas Kelley
William Bazor
Henry Castlebury
William Barnet
Robert Day

Isham Philips
Edmund Lishman
William Brown
William Hamilton
James Rogers
John Blair
Benjamin Hall
Jerrard Trammil
John Booth, Jn^r
John Butler
Partha Fuquay
John Simmons
Samuel Ewin
George Roan
Joshua Mitchell
Burwell Brown
William Hunt

Allen Cook [135]
Miles Rachels
Thos Trammil
John McKessack
James Baxter
Azariah Butts
Thomas Gillaland
Joshua Gray
James Riley
John H. Walker
John Justice
Wimburn Dickinson
Walter Brown
Francis Mouland, jn^r
William Reives
Littleton Beauchamp
John Frazier

James Braswell	Joseph Paterson
Robert McDaniel	William Griggs
Salathel Culver	Jesse Kelley
Thomas Bradford	Robert Willson
William Hudleston	Asa Morgan
Benjamin Frazier	Allen Brown
Henry Hall	
William Foxwell	
Turner Harwood	
John Leigh	

Examined   Ben Taliaferro

Judge Taliaferro's Charge to the Grand Jury [136]

Gentlemen of the Grand Jury

The event of the late Treaty with the Creek Indians, not having been agreeable to the expectations or wishes of the people of this Country, it is much to be feared that the discontent occasioned thereby will hurry some among us into acts that may involve the State in difficulties, not only with the neighboring Indians, but with the General Government. I feel it a duty therefore to lay before the several Grand Juries (and particularly those of frontier Counties, who are more immediately exposed to Indian depredations) a few observations on that Subject.

Whether the true interest of Georgia has been attended to in the progress of the Treaty, or whether the Commissioners who represented the State have faithfully acquitted themselves, are Questions that we ought to leave to the investigation of our Legislature, they are the proper body to enquire into the Conduct of those Gentlemen, and either approve or censure their Conduct. it is sufficient for us in the present Situation of things to endeavor by every means in our power to prevent any attempt that may tend to frustrate the measures of Government.

Experience has taught us that there are some among us, who regardless of Treaty, Laws, or the more Sacred ties of Humanity, would involve

involve their Country in Scenes of bloodshed, for the ill timed [137] gratification of Killing a Single Indian. If no possible ill could result from the perpetration of Acts like this, there is something so Shocking to every humane and benelovent mind in a wanton effusion of human blood, that I cannot suspect a good man or well disposed Citizen of a wish to commit a crime so horrid, but when we reflect that retalliation is to be the inevitable consequence, without knowing when or where the fatal blow will fall, whether on the person ~~whose~~ whose temerity has led him to the commission of the Act, or on whole families of innocent & defenceless women & children. how can we forbear to censure the man who has been the Author of such Mischief.

It is probable that war with the Creek Indians ought to be preferred to peace, but of this no man is or ought to be a Judge. Neither have the Legislature of your Country the power of determining. That Power is by the Constitution of the United States lodged with the General Government, of course we ought not to exercise it.

Let us examine the consequences of indulging any man or Set of men, unauthorized by Government, with the privilege of drawing a whole Country into war, when war is the voice of a nation, and the several movements & operations are concerted and carried on under the Auspices of Government, every possible contingency is provided for, & when men are called into the field, the money and credit of the Nation is pledged for their pay and Support, there is a perfect

perfect cooperation in all departments, both for defence and annoyance, [138] and victory is the reward of their exertions. but when hurried into war by the Act of a Single man, and perhaps at a time when one half the people are anxious for peace. The Government perplexed, not knowing whether to attempt effective operations or remain inactive, without arms ammunition, provision, or Money to procure them, with the enemy at our door prepared to do us every ~~injury~~ mischief in their power. in this Situation, what have we to expect but defeat, disgrace, and a total desertion of our frontiers, with the loss of many of our most valuable Citizens, before we can make the necessary preparations for defence.

Let us endeavor then to pursue peace with those people, so long as we are under Treaty with them, or if we are forced into hostilities, let it be fairly in our power to evince to mankind that we are not the aggressors, then may we with propriety expect the Aid & cooperation of the Nation to afford us the necessary protection.

That in future no person may justify improper trespasses on the Indians or their Territory by pleading ignorance of the Laws. I will briefly State the Several Acts by which Such offences are forbidden and made punishable. Even the Laws of England

England, which are of force in this Country, where they are not repugnant [139] to our own, declares it a felony to Kill an Alien Enemy within the Kingdom, unless it be in the heat of war, and in the Actual exercise thereof. By the Laws of our own State, it is declared, that to murder any free Indian in Amity with this Provence, is as penal to all intents and purposes, as to Murder a white person. And the Treaty of New York, entered into with the Creek Indians, and two Acts of the General Government founded thereon, for regulating Trade and intercourse with Indian Tribes, declares such Offences highly Criminal.

As to matters that more immediately relate to your County, the Situation of your public Roads ought to be particularly attended to, and all Overseers or Commissioners that have not made the necessary repairs presented. Keepers of unlicensed disorderly tippling houses, common movers, exciters, or maintainers of Vexatious Law Suits, or Quarrels, and in short everything transacted or done within your County that tends to disturb the public peace, or that are of notorious ill example, are Indictable offences and ought to be presented. I shall direct the Clerk to Lay before you the digest of the Tax Returns for your County. The tax Law for the present year makes it your duty to examine it and present all persons that you find to be in default.

           Ben Taliaferro

[blank page]   [140]

        Wednesday 1st March 1797   [141]

At a Superior Court begun and held in and for the County of Hancock. Present, his Honor Judge Taliaferro.

The following persons appeared and were Sworn of the Grand Jury, Viz.

    1. J. Grigg   11. Daniel Mitchell
    2. Jecamiah Moore   12. Abraham Womack Excused
    3. George Lee   13. William Turner
    4. David Felps   14. Jerard Burch
    5. Randolph Rutland   15. John Halcom
    6. Thaddeus Holt   16. Absolem Harris
    7. Moses Powell   17. Jacob Gore
    8. Thomas Cooper   18. Littleton Ross
    9. William Ousley   19. John Lewis, Jn^r
    10. Wyatt Collier

Who retired, returned, and made report that they had Made choice of Jesse Grigg, Esquire as foreman.

Court adjourned till tomorrow ten O'Clock.

Ben Taliaferro

Thursday 2nd March 1797 [142]

The Court met according to adjournment. Present, his Honor Judge Taliaferro.

The following persons attended and were Sworn of the Petit Jury, viz.

1. Saml Dent
2. Edward Bazor
3. Wm Hamilton
4. Ben^j Hall
5. John Butler
6. William Hunt
7. Turner Harwood
8. Thomas Trammill
9. John Justices
10. Wimburn Dickinson
11. Joseph Patterson
12. William Scurlock

William Riely }
    vs   } Case
Zachariah Glass }

The above Jurors on this Case, Who returned the following Verd^t, viz. We, the Jurors, find for the plaintiff forty two dollars eighty seven & an half Cents and costs of suit.

Saml Dent, foreman

Exo^n issued 27th March 1797.

Sparta 2nd March 1797 Received forty four dols prin & In^t for the above Jud^{mt} in full, also four dol for tax fee [faint]

P. J. Carnes, T. P. Carnes, Att^{ys} for Def^t

Upon motion founded on Affidavit Mʳ Abraham Wormack, one of the [143] Grand Jury, was excused from further attendance during this term from indisposition & Martin Armstrong, one of the original pannel having attended, was sworn of the Grand Jury in his Stead.

John Gibson }
    vs   } Case
James Huckaby }

Abated by death of the plaintiff.

Exoⁿ Issᵈ 17ᵗʰ May 1797.

George Taft }
    vs   } Cont
Joseph Smith}

Witness for Dfᵗ, Job McClendon

This day the parties came forward by their Attornies and thereupon came a Jury, to wit.

Abner Atkinson	Hart Champion
Robert Day	Benʲ Gilbert
Jonathan Day	Jaˢ Lawrence
Isham Hagan	Isaac Vaughan
Jacob Williams	William Martin
Nathan Gann	Jnº McKinzie

Who returned the following Verdict (Viz.) We, the Jurors. do agree that the defendant Smith have two months from this day to make the plaintiff good and lawfull Titles to the said Tract of Land, and on failure of making such titles, the said Smith is to pay the penalty of the Bond.

2ⁿᵈ March 1797   John McKinzie, foreman

                Thursday 2ⁿᵈ March 1797 [144]

The State }
    vs   } Indictᵐᵗ for Cattle Stealing
Thoˢ Pickard }

Witnesses pro S, William Morgan, Jn° Reid, Jn° Price, Jn° Booth, Sen', Joel McClendon, Jason Parmington, Henry Beard, Polly Mahan

For Df', Jesse Thompson, Frances Pickard, George Strother, Merryman Pound, Ab^m Myles

The following Jurors Sworn.

<table>
<tr><td>Saml Dent</td><td>Turner Harwood</td></tr>
<tr><td>Edward Bazor</td><td>Thomas Trammell</td></tr>
<tr><td>William Hamilton</td><td>John Justice</td></tr>
<tr><td>Benjamin Hall</td><td>Wimburn Dickinson</td></tr>
<tr><td>Jn° Butler</td><td>Joseph Patterson</td></tr>
<tr><td>William Hunt</td><td>William Scurlock</td></tr>
</table>

Who returned the following Verdict, viz. We, the Jury, find the defendant guilty.

Saml Dent, foreman

Saml Dent, forman

The State }
    vs   } Indictment for Larceny
John Milirons }

The Grand Jury returned the following verdict Report. The Within a true bill.

Jesse Grigg, foreman

Thursday 2nd March 1797   [145]

The State }
    vs   } Indictment for assault
Andrew Maddox }

The Grand Jury returned the following, a True Bill.

Jesse Grigg, foreman

The State }
    vs   } Indictment for Larceny
Francis Beard }

The Grand Jury made the following return, not a True Bill.

                                                          Jesse Grigg, foreman

The State   }
    vs   } Indictment for Larceny
William Stewart }

A True Bill.   Jesse Grigg, foreman

The State   }
    vs   } Indictment for Larceny
William Stewart }

A True Bill.   Jesse Grigg, foreman

                      Thursday 2nd March 1797   [146]

The State   }
    vs   } Indictment for Larceny
William Stewart }

A True Bill.   Jesse Grigg, foreman

The State   }
    vs   } Indictment for Larceny
Michael Ryan }

Not a True Bill.   Jesse Grigg, foreman

The State   }
    vs   } Indictment for Larceny
Lewis Duboise }

Not a True Bill.   Jesse Grigg, foreman

The State   }
    vs   } Indictment for Mal practice
George Bagby }

Witnesses for Def^t, Jesse Kelly

The following Jurors Sworn, viz.

    Rob{{t}} Day   Benjamin Gilbert
    Jonathan Day   Isaac Vaughan
    Isham Hogan   Jn{{o}} McKenzie
    Jacob Williams   Miles Rachels
    Nathan Gann   Jesse Kelly
    Hart Champion   John Lamar

Who returned the following Verdict, viz. We, the Jury, find the defendant not guilty.

2{{nd}} March 1797   John McKenzie, foreman

Court adjourned till to morrow Morning 10 o'Clock.   [147]

                        Ben Taliaferro

              Friday 3{{rd}} March 1797

Court met according to adjournment. Present his Honor Judge Taliaferro.

~~John Myles, one of the original pannel of the Grand Jury and was sworn~~

The State   }
    vs   } Verdict of guilty yesterday
Thomas Pickard }

On Motion of M{{r}} Walker, et al, Councils for Defendant & consent of the Solicitor General, a Rule is granted to shew cause why a new trial should not be granted. On Argument, it is considered by the Court, That a new trial can not be granted.

              Friday 3{{rd}} March 1797   [148]

The adm{{rs}} of Hamilton }
      vs   } Debt
Robert Montgomery   }

This day the parties came forward by their attornies and thereupon came a Jury, to wit.

William Bivins	William Hamilton
William Lancaster	Ben^j Hall
Saml Dent	Jured Trammil
Edwd Bazor	Jn° Butler
Robert Day	Wm Hunt
William Browne	Salathiel Culver

Who returned the following Verdict. We, the Jury, find for the plaintiff two hundred & eleven Dollars and sixty Cents, with Interest from the time it became due & Costs.

Saml Dent, foreman

The State   }
    vs   } Ind^t for Riot
William Lawson, Senr }
Francis Lawson   }
Thomas Lawson   }
James Laurence &   }
Jane Lawson   }

Josiah Thomas
Sarah Thomas proved
Davis McGee [faint] attendant

Mrs Sarah Thomas

The same Jury as in the above case, who returned the following Verdict, viz. We, the Jurors, find the persons contained within to be guilty of a Riot.

Saml Dent, foreman

Whereupon, it is Ordered that each of them be fined five dollars, except Jane Lawson, who is fined twenty five Cents.

Friday 3rd March 1797   [149]

The State   }
    vs   } Indictment for Cattle Stealing
Thomas Pickard]

State Witnesses sworn, Abraham Myles S, John Booth, Senr S, James Graham, William Morgan, Polly Mahan proved 5 days att^d, Sworn in open Court

Def^{ts} Witnesses, Jonathan Day, George Strother, Merryman Pound, Frances Pickard, Jesse Thompson

The following Jurors Sworn.

Henry Hall	William Gilbert
Turner Harwood	Jonathan Day
Allen Cook	Isaac Vaughan
Miles Rachels	John McKenzie
Jeremiah Bonner	Isham Hogan
Abner Atkinson	William Rees

Who returned the following Verdict, viz.

We, the Jurors, find the prisoner [blot] not guilty of Cattle Stealing.

                        John McKenzie, foreman

The Grand returned the following Bills, viz.

The State }
    vs   } Indictment for Larceny
William Smith }

Not a true Bill.   Jesse Grigg, foreman

The State }
    vs   } Indictment for Larceny
James Shirly }

Not a true Bill.   Jesse Grigg, foreman

The State }
    vs   } Indictment for selling liquor without license
Jesse Ellis }

Not a true Bill.   Jesse Grigg, foreman

Friday 3rd March 1797 [150]

Hardy Wooten }
    vs } case
Lewis & Mary Bailey }
Adm^{rs} of Jno Wooten, dec^d }

By consent of parties, ordered that all matters in dispute between them in the Case be referred to the final arbitrament and award of Francis Trawick, Wm Yarborough, Miel Monk, Jesse Thompson, Robt McGinty, Aaron McKenzie, Ja^s Bishop, Absolem Eiland, Jonathan McCrary, Stephen Bishop, Jonathan Anderson, & John Mitchell, Esq^{rs}, Whose award shall be final and conclusive between the parties, provided the same be returned under their hands and seals on or before the first day of the next term.

                      Hardy Wooten
                      Ben^j Skrine, Att^y for Df^t

The Court then adjourned till 10 O'Clock tomorrow.

                      Ben Taliaferro

Saturday 4th March 1797 [151]

Court met according to adjournment. Present, his Honor Judge Taliaferro.

Samuel Dent, one of the Petit Jurors, having made affidavit that he had a suit depending in a Justices Court, obtained leave of absence until Monday next.

The State }
    vs } Indictment for Grand Larceny
John Millirons }

Arraigned & plead not guilty.

State Witnesses Sworn, Jno Whitney, Samuel Parker, William Stewart, James Shirly, ~~William Mosely~~

Deft^s Witnesses, Joseph Cars, William Mosely, William Beard

The following Jury Sworn.

William Burns	Jared Trammel
William Lancaster	Jn° Butler
Edward Bazor	William Hunt
Robt Day	Henry Hall
Wm Hamilton	Turner Harwood
Benjamin Hall	Allen Cook

Who returned the following Verdict, viz. We, of the Jury, find Not guilty.

William Lancaster, foreman

Saturday 4th March 1797 [152]

The Adm^{rs} of Hamilton }
   vs   } Debt
Robert Montgomery }

In this Case, Judgm^t having gone against the def^t yesterday, he he craves an Appeal, whereupon John McKenzie came into court and entered himself security, on this Condition, to wit, that if said Robert Montgomery shall be cast in this Appeal, he will pay the eventual condemnation Money, or surrender himself into Court as the Law directs, or I (john McKenzie) will do it for him. Taken and acknowledged in Open Court the 4th March 1797.

Before Mar Martin, Clk   Robert Montgomery
             John McKenzie

The State   }
  vs   } Indictm^t for selling a free Negro & for deceit
William Braswell }

Noli prosequi. Entered by order of Court & consent of Solicitor General.

       Signed   P. Alen, S. G.

rec^d 25 Ct^s for cons^{ble} who attended the G^d Jury.

The State   }   [153]
  vs   } Indictment for Cattle Stealing
Thomas Pickard }

The Defendant acknowledged himself indebted to his Excellency the Governor and his successors in office in the sum of 4,000 dollars & Isham Hogan & Loyd Kelly in the sum 2,000 dollars Each, to be levied on their Several and respective goods and chattels, lands and tenement, but to be void on Condition that said Thomas Pickard shall appear at Court during the present term, to answer all such matters and things as may be objected against him and not depart without leave of the Court.

Taken and acknowledged in Open Court 4th March 1797.

Before Mar Martin, Clk   Thomas X Pickard, his mark
                                Isham Hogan
                                Loyd Kenley

The Court adjourned until Monday Morning ten o'Clock.

                                Ben Taliaferro

James Goodtitle, ex }
dem of John Kelley }
        vs   } Ejectment
W[m] Stiles &   }
John Mapp, tenants }

On Motion of Def[ts] Att[y], Ordered that Sam[l] Phillips be made Co Def[t], he having entered into the [illegible]

                Monday 6th March 1797   [154]

The Court met according to adjournment. Present, the Honorable Judge Taliaferro.

Jesse Thompson }
       vs   } Case for Words
Julius Sanders }

Dismissed.

Richard Mills }
      vs   } Case
Nathan Culver }

Dismissed.

John Heath }
  vs   } assault
Thomas Johnson, et al }

Witnesses plff, A. Borland, Thos Heath

Def^t, Job Jackson, Stephen Jackson

This day the parties came into court by their attornies and thereupon Came a Jury, to wit.

  William Bivins   Benjamin Hall
  William Lancaster   Jarrard Trammel
  Edward Bazor   John Butler
  Robt Day   William Hunt
  William Browne   Salathiel Culver
  William Hamilton   Miles Rachels

Who returned the following Verdict, to Wit. We, the Jury, find for the plaintiff eighty five dollars & Cost.

          Wm Hunt, foreman

Exon iss^d 3rd Jany 1798.

      Monday the 6th March 1797   [155]

Patrick Hays }
  vs   } Case
Henry Jernigan }

The death of the pltff Suggested in usual form.

William Turner }
  vs   } Case Referred
Levin Smith }

The Referees returned their award, Which is ordered to entered of Record and made the Judgement of the court and is as follows.

Hancock County

Whereas, the honorable the Superior Court of said county last Sept[r] term did appoint us, the Subscribing Arbitrators, in a Case Wherein William Turner is Pltff & Levin Smith Def[t], and after taking said case into consideration, We do hereby agree & award that each party pay their own Lawyer and also each to pay an equal part of the Cost that have arrisen on on Said Suits. given under our hands this 28th day of Feb[y] 1797.

        Signed   Charles Abercrombie
               David Dickson
               P. Boyle
               Jn[o] Bailey

Monday 6th March 1797   [156]

John Kelly   }
  vs   } Ejectment
Samuel Phillips &   }
John Mapp, Ten[t] in possession }

The following Jury sworn to wit.

    Joseph Turner   Isaac Vaughan
    Tho[s] Trammill   William Lawson
    Jn[o] Justice   Turner Harwood
    Azariah Butts   James Turner
    Wimburn Dickinson   Hugh Montgomery
    Samuel Dent   Harris Nicholson

Who returned the following Verdict, to wit. We, the Jury, find for the plaintiff.

          Sam[l] Dent, foreman

Appeal Entered 13th March 1797. Sam[l] Braswell, Sec[y]

William Street }
  vs   } attc[t]
William Thompson }

The same Jury as in the case of Heth vs Johnson, et al, who returned the following Verdict, to wit.

We, the Jury, find for the plaintiff three hundred and ninety eight dollars.

Wm Hunt, foreman

Exon iss^d 16th May 1797.

and James Wood, the garnishee, acknowledged that he was indebted to the said William Thompson the amount of the said Verdict after deducting the sum of thirty six pounds, of which leaves the balance of two hundred and [blot] dollars [blot] I acknowledge bound with the [blot] for the Judgement & Stay of Execution sixty days from this date.

[smear]

Monday 6th March 1797 [157]

Jesse Thompson }
  vs } Debt
Stephen Horton }

Settled & cost paid.

Isaac Vaughan }
  vs } Debt
William Morgan }

Settled.

Michael & Laurence }
  vs   } Debt
Aron Wood }

I do hereby Confess Judgement to the plaintiff for the Sum of Sixty dollars and ninety cents & cost of Suit & Stay Six months 7th ~~January~~ March 1797.

P. L. Van Alen, Def^{ts} Att^y

Exon iss^d for cost 26th July 1798.

William Leneer }
    vs   } case
Thomas Stephens }

Settled & cost paid.

Christian Treutten, Exo[r] }
of John A. Treutten   }
    vs   } Debt
John & Aaron [smear] }
Adm[rs] of Philip [smear] }

Non Suit.

Exo[n] iss[d] 1st May 1797.

                Monday 6th March 1797   [158]

Ralston & Nesbit }
    vs   } Case
Thomas Credenton }

The same Jury as in the case of Kelly vs Mapp, Who returned the following Verdict. We, the Jury, find for the plaintiff fifty eight Dollars & thirty five cents.

                        Sam[l] Dent, foreman

Exon iss[d] 27th March 1797.

Fanny Forsyth }
    vs   } Ejectment
Cha[s] Abercrombie }
& And[w] Borland }

Dismissed.

Rich[d] Shipp, Att[y] & Ass[ee] }
    vs   } Two Cases
Job Allen & James Cowden }

~~The following Jury sworn~~

~~Willm Burns, Wm Lancaster~~

The same Jury as in the case of John Heath vs Thos Johnson, et al, who returned the following Verdict, to wit. We, the Jury, find for the Plaintiff three Hundred and twenty six Dollars and seventy eight Cents, ~~with costs~~ on both obligations, with Cost.

Wm Hunt, foreman

Monday 6th March 1797   [159]

George Hearndon, Assn^ee }
       vs   } Case
Danl Muse & John Bond }

In this case, the def^t, Danl Muse, came into Court with Charles Abercrombie, who acknowledged himself (and signed for John Waller according to his instruction) Special bail, on this condition, to wit, that if said def^t shall be cast in this action, they will pay the condemnation Money, or surrender themselves into Court as the Law directs, or we (Chas Abercrombie & John Waller) will do it for them.

Taken & acknowledged in Open Court the 5th March 1797.

Before Mar Martin, Clk   Chas Abercrombie
                                     for him Self and
                                       John Waller

Azariah Butts, one of the original pannel of the Petit Jury, being indisposed, was discharged of Service as Petit Juror for the present term.

The Court then adjourned till 10 O'Clock tomorrow.

Ben Taliaferro

Tuesday 7th March 1797   [160]

The Court met according to Adjournment. Present, his Honor Judge Taliaferro.

Wallace & wife, et al}
       vs   } debt
William Weeks   }

The following Jury were sworn, to wit.

William Bivins	John Butler
William Lancaster	William Hunt
William Bearden	Salathiel Culver
Robt Day	Turner Harwood
William Hamilton	Thomas Trammell
Jared Trammell	John Justice

Who returned the following Verdict. We, the Jury, find the plaintiff seventeen hundred and Ninety Nine Dollars and twelve Cents.

William Hunt, forman

It is agreed that execution in this Case Bail be Stayed six months and benefit of appeal waived.

Jno Mathews, Att^y for Plff

John Heath }
    vs   } Assault
Thomas Diknson }

[161]

Verdict for Eighty five Dollars & Cost.

John Lamar came into Court & acknowledged himself bound with the above Defendant for the payment of the Verdict aforesaid.

John Lamar

Whereupon, the plaintiff in the said Case consents to a stay of levy until the first day of December next.

John W. Devereux }
    vs   } Case
Abram Reddick }

The following Jury sworn.

Stephen Horton	William Lawson
Saml Dent	Wimburn Dickinson

Edwd Bazor
William Brown
Ben^j Hall
Miles Rachels
John Lamar

Mich^l Gilbert
John Hamilton
Julius Sanders

Who returned the following Verdict. We, the Jury, find in favor of plaintiff thirty five dollars sixty two & an half Cents.

Saml Dent, foreman

Exo^n iss^d 28th March 1797.

Satisfied as by Rec^t of John W. Devereux. Jno W. Devereux, Plff

Tuesday March 7th 1797 [162]

The State }
   vs } Riot
Thomas Johnston }
Zephaniah Johnston }
Job Jackson and }
Stephen Jackson }

By consent of the prosecutors and the Defendants, it is ordered that a Nol pros be entered in the above case and Judgement against the Defendants for the following Costs, to wit.

To the Solicitor General		$7.500
To the Clerk		3.000
To John Heath (Pros^r)		5.000
To Thomas Heath (a Wtns^s)		5.000
	Total	20.5000

Exon iss^d 2nd Jany 1798.

William Reily }
   vs } Case
William Owsley }

~~I do hereby confess Judg~~

Judgment confessed for the sum of fifty five dollars, with costs. Stay of Execution two months.

Test. T. P. Carnes   Wm Owsley, 2nd March 1797

5th June 1797 rec^d fifty six dollars in this case for principal. Mr Martin, Clk

I am satisfied for the above Judgment Reily vs Owsley 2nd Septr 1797 for Peter Harris.

T. P. Carnes

Tuesday 7th March 1797 [163]

E. Wambersie }
    vs   } Case
John Spencer }

The same Jury as in the Case of Devereux vs Reddick, Who returned the following verdict. We, the Jury find for the plaintiff thirty eight Dollars fifty six & an half cents.

Saml Dent, foreman

Resa Howard }
    vs   } Assumpsit
Job Jackson }

Dismissed.

The Grand Jury returned the following Bill, viz.

The State }
    vs   } Ind^t for selling liquor without license
Jesse Ellis }

A True Bill.   Jesse Grigg, foreman

Brown & Co }
    vs   } Debt
Wm Brown }

Judgment confessed for the Sum of thirty seven dollars & cost of Suit.

William Brown

Tuesday 7th 1797   [164]

Benedix, Leon & Co }
     vs   } Case
William Cureton   }

The following Jury sworn.

Davis McGehee	Lewis Barnes
Ralph Low	James Thomas
Isham Hogans	Joseph Turner
Wm Barksdale	Abner Bankston
Austin Morris	Hugh Montgomery
Jno Pound	
Isaac Vaughan	

We, the Jury, find for the Plaintiff Sixty two Dollars & four Cents.

Hugh Montgomery, foreman

Exo^n iss^d 28th March 1797.

William Barksdale }
     vs   } Case
Elisha Whatley   }

The following Jury Sworn.

Stephen Horton	William Lawson
Saml Dent	Wimburn Dickinson
Edwd Bazor	Mich^l Gilbert
Wm Brown	John Hamilton
Ben^j Hall	Julius Sanders
Miles Rachels	Marshall Turner

Who returned the following Verdict. We, the Jury, find for the plaintiff one hundred & ninety one Dollars & twenty five cents.

Saml Dent, foreman

appeal entered.

March 7th 1797   [165]

George Thompson, Ass^{ee} }
    vs   } debt
George Vest   }

The same Jury as in the Case Benedix, Leon & C° vs William Cureton. We, the Jury, find for the Plff forty Dollars.

Hugh Montgomery, foreman

Exoⁿ iss^d 28th March 1797.

Andrew King }
    vs   } Case
James Works }

The same Jury as in the case of Wallis & wife vs Weeks. We, the Jury find for the plaintiff one hundred and six Dollars & twenty five cents.

Wm Hunt, foreman

Execution not to issue untill the first day of Decr next by order of Plff. 22 March 1797

Exoⁿ iss^d 1st January 1798.

James B. Oliver }
    vs   } Debt
James Shorter }

In virtue of a Warrant of Att^y to me with others directed, I do appear and confess Judgement against the Def^t, James Shorter for the Sum of ninety six Dollars & [smear] with In^t according to Specialty & cost of suit.

G. Walker, Att^y

Exon iss^d.

James Hutcherson }
     vs   }
Thadeus Beal   }

Dismissed.

Tuesday 7th March 1797   [166]

The adm^{rs} of John Lawson }
     vs   } [illegible]
William Lawson, Sn^r }

William Lawson, Sn^r }
     vs   } Ejectment
J. Thomas &   }
William Horton   }

J. Thomas   }
     vs   } Trespass
William Lawson, Sn^r }
Francis Lawson   }
James Lawrence & }
Thomas Lawson   }

The parties in the above Cases have mutually agreed that they shall be withdrawn, each party paying their own cost, and the said William Lawson, Sn^r agrees and obliges himself to give unto the heirs of John Lawson one negro, either Jane or Harry, now in the possession of the said William Lawson, the choice to be made by the adm^{rs} of John Lawson, which negro is to be made of equal value to a certain negro, to wit, named Abram

formerly in possession of John Lawson, and William Lawson, Sn^r is also   [167] at his death to give to the heirs of John Lawson, Dec^d one other likely negro,

117

between the age of twelve & twenty years. And further, the said William Lawson, Sn^r agrees to let William Horton have the use of the plantation whereon John Lawson formerly lived untill the first day of January next. This agreement to take effect from this day, so far as respects the plantation, and negro to be made Choice of by the Adm^{rs} of John Lawson, Dec^d.

In witness whereof, We have hereunto Set our hands and seals this 7th day of March 1797.

Teste. B. Hall   Wm Horton
                                          Wm Lawson
                                          Josiah Thomas

Sanders Walker for   }
the use of J. Coleman }
        vs   } Cov^t
John Perkins   }

Settled & Cost paid.

                    Tuesday 7th March 1797   [168]

John Torrence   }
      vs   } Case
John De Yampert }

The same Jury as in the case of Benedix, Leon & Co vs Wm Curton.

We, the Jury, find for the plaintiff one hundred and twenty five Dollars.

                                              Hugh Montgomery, foreman

Robt Watkins   }
John C. Walton   }
      vs   } Case
Moses Harris &   }
James Wood   }

The following Jury Sworn.

William Bivins John Butler
William Lancaster Wm Hunt
William Bearden Salathiel Culver
Robt Day Turner Harwood
William Hamilton Thos Trammil
Jarrard Trammil

Who returned the following Verdict (to wit). We, the Jury, find for the Pltff forty eight Dollars.

Wm Hunt, foreman

Tuesday 7th March 1797 [169]

James Martin }
    vs   } Case
Stephen Horton }

The same Jury as in the Aforegoing case. We, the Jury, find for the Pltff forty two Dollars & Seventy Cents.

Wm Hunt, foreman

Appeal Entered, And^w Borland, Sec^y.

The Court then adjourned till 10 O'Clock tomorrow.

Ben Taliaferro

Wednesday 8th March 1797

The Court met according to adjournment. Present, his Honor Judge Taliaferro.

James Nisbet }
    vs   } Debt
Aaron Wood }

I do hereby confess Judgment to the plaintiff for the sum of sixty dollars & ninety Cents & Costs of Suit & Stay Six Months.

8th March 1797   P. Alen, Def^{ts} Att^y

Wednesday 8th March 1797 [170]

The Grand Jury made the following presentments (to wit).

Hancock County 1st March 1797

We, the Grand jury present the Commissioners or the Overseers of the road, as the case may be, leading from the piney woods House to Mitchell's Bridge on Ogechee.

We present the commissioners or the Overseers of the road, as the case may be, leading from the Greensborough Road by James Harvey's to Poweltown.

We Present the commissioners or Overseers of the road, as the case may be, leading from the piney Woods House to Stith's Mill on Ogechee as far as Hickory Nut Creek.

We present the Commissioners or Overseers of the road, as the case may be, leading from Town Creek by Nathaniel Waller's to Sparta.

We recommend that a road be laid out from Where the Reverend W. Cunningham formerly taught School on the Accademy to the Piney woods House, the most convenient way.

We present Samuel Felps as a Vagrant.

Wednesday 8th March 1797 [171]

We present Jesse & Benjamin Sanford for keeping open doors on the Sabbath & trading with negroes without permits from their Masters.

We present Aaron, Abraham, & William Woodward for trading with negroes without permits from their Masters and keeping open doors on the Sabbath. Secondly for selling spiritous Liqours without Licence.

We present William Clark for preventing his negro Dorse from making an open confession When on trial for theft.

We present each and every Capt in this County for not puting the patrole law in execution.

We present Benjamin ~~Newsome~~ Anderson & William Cureton, jn[r] for their profanity and rioting in the Court yard in time of Court and for the Horse racing through the Streets of Sparta on public days.

We present Charles Parks as a Vagrant.

We present William Stewart, the Soldier, who gave testimony against Milirons this Term for willfull profane perjury.

Wednesday 8th March 1797 [172]

We present James Hill as a vagrant, not seeking a proper Support for his family.

We present Benjamin Waller for blasphemy of the most heinous and attrocious kind.

We present William Morgan for false swearing.

We present the Commissioners or overseers of the road, as the case may be, leading from Sparta to Georgetown.

We present Joseph Henry as Overseer of the Road leading from Sparta by Needham Jernigan's to Powelton.

We present as a grievance that the Militia of this County are not paid for their services on the frontiers.

We return to his Honor Judge Taliaferro our unfeigned thanks for his great attention in discharge of his duty when on the seat of Justice, and his Judicious charge, and recommend that his charge with these our presentments be made public.

March 8th 1797 [173]

John Haynes   }
    vs   } fi fa
Etheldred Wood }

Ordered, that the Exo[n] go on.

Robert Flournoy }
    vs   } Attachment
Ulyssis Rogers }

William Pentecost, one of the Garnishees summoned in the above Attachment, being therein Solemnly called, failed to appear, and on Motion it is ordered that Judgment be entered by default against the said Garnishee.

Michael & Laurence }
    vs   } fi fa Sheriff's Report
Barnaby Pope   }
& W^m McGehee }

Dismissed.

                  Wednesday 8th March 1797   [174]

Joseph White }
    vs   } fi fa & Sheriff's Report
Isham Hogan }

The court on hearing argument ordered the Execution to go on.

The following Jury Sworn.

        William Bivins   William Hamilton
        William Lancaster   Ben^j Hall
        William Bearden   Jarrard Trammil
        Saml Dent   Salathiel Culver
        Robt Day   Turner Harwood
        William Browne   Miles Rachels

Who returned the following Verdict.

[blank]

Absolem Jackson }
    vs   } fi fa Sheriff's Report
William Low   }

Continued.

Mathew Hubert }
    vs   } fi fa See fi em
Thomas Pickard }

The claim of Defend^ت discharged.

Wednesday 8th March 1797   [175]

The State   }
    vs   } Indictment for Cattle Stealing
Thomas Pickard } Verdict of guilty

The prisoner having been convicted was brought forward to the bar, whereupon the Judge demanded of him if he had anything to say, why the Court ought not upon the verdict aforesaid proceed to pass Judgement against him and having nothing to say the Court proceeded to pronounce the following Sentence. See page 144.

(to Wit) You are to be Set in the Pillory by the Sheriff of this County, or his deputy, for the space of two hours. You are to be commited to the common Jail of this County, where you are to remain untill the Sixteenth day of this present instant (March). And before you are discharged from thence, you are to be publicly Whiped on your bear back three several times and receive at each time thirty nine lashes, Which shall be executed and done at the hours of twelve O'Clock on the 14th, 15th, and 16th of this present instant. (March) You are then to be branded on your Shoulder with the letter **R** and then discharged, the sentence to be executed by the Sheriff or one of his deputies.

Wednesday 8th March 1797   [176]

Nathaniel Waller }
    vs   } Trespass Refered
William Bazor, Sn^r }
John Bazor and   }
Edward Bazor   }

The arbitrators returned their award which was ordered to be entered of record and made the Judgement of the Court & is as follows.

Georgia   }
Hancock County } Agreeable to an order of the Honorable the Superior Court of

the said County to us directed, being independently Chosen by Nathaniel Waller, plaintiff, William Bazor, Sn^r, John & Edward Bazor, Def^{ts}, for trespass to settle & determine. We do award and decree as follows (to Wit) that the dividing line or land mark between Nathl Waller & the said William Bazor, Sn^r. Beginning at a dog wood corner agreeable to the said Waller's Plat, from thence along the old Marked line up a branch to a post Oak Station on the South side of the same, being opposite the head thereof and a small distance to the west of the said line, or the course that the Original plat called for, thence along the said old marked line on the out side of Bazor's improvement

Wednesday 8th March 1797   [177]

the said William Bazor's corner shall be the dividing line. and we consider and award that the said William Bazor, Sn^r and John Bazor have not trespassed on the premises of the said Nathaniel Waller, but that the said Edward Bazor shall pay to the said Nathl Waller one Dollar and all Cost of Suit. Given under our hands this 23 day February 1797.

> John Harbirt
> Jno Bailey
> James Thweatt
> Thos Mitchell
> John Cook
> Mark Saunders
> Thos Mathews
> Stephen Kirk

Witnesses in the following on the part of the State, John Whitney, Joel McClendon, Hubert Terrel, Francis Beard, George Simpson

Defendant's, Andrew O. Kelly, Jones Sherly, Wm Carson

The State   }
    vs   } Indictment for Grand Larceny
William Stewart }

The following Jury sworn.

William Lancaster	Miles Rachel
William Brown	Jarrard Trammel
William Hamilton	William Barns

John McKenzie   Salathiel Culver
Robert Day   Turner Harwood
William Brown   Abraham Borland

Who returned the following verdict, to wit. We, the Jurors, find the prisoner not guilty.

John McKenzie, Foreman

Wednesday 8th March 1797 [178]

West Jones }
    vs   } Ass^t & Battery
Isham Hogen}

In this cause, the parties in the above Suit have agreed to submit all matters in dispute between them to the final award and arbitrament of James Miller ~~and~~ James Turner and William Turner, whose award When made Shall be final and Conclusive, provided the same is Returned to the Next Superior Court, Which award is to be made the Judgment of the Court.

West X Jones, his mark
Isham Hogan

The Grand Jury made the following presentments, to wit.

We present Isham Hogan for profane swearing & for offering to fight a duel.

We present as a grievance that William Fitzgerald has not been detected for false swearing, agreeably to a presentment of the last Grand Jury.

Wednesday 8th March 1797 [179]

We present Joseph Patterson, William Grantham, & Moses Harris as a nuisance to Society, and Joseph Patterson & William Grantham for false swearing.

We recommend that a Road be laid off from Cooper's Mill the most convenient and direct way to Sparta and that Alexander Reid, John Studdivant, & Joseph Cooper be appointed commissioners & that James Huckaby be appointed Overseer of said Road.

~~The Court then adjourned till 10 O'Clock tomorrow.~~

~~Ben Taliaferro~~

[What appears to be a list of some 18 names follows, apparently the members of the grand jury, but the image is too faint to read.]

Thursday 9th March 1797 [180]

The Court met according to adjournment. Present, his honor Judge Taliaferro.

Ja^s Wood, Appell^t }
     vs   } Case
Mich^l & Laurence, Resp^t }

Settled.

Danl Whatley, Appel^t }
     vs   } Case
Andrew Borland, Resp^t }

Settled.

Levi Lancaster, Appel^t }
     vs   } Case
Michael & Laurence, Resp^t }

Judgment confessed for the sum of Seventy six dollars & Seventy nine cents, with costs & stay of execution two months.

Levi Lancaster

Exon iss^d 17th May 1797.

William Low, App^t }
     vs   } Case
[faint] Resp^t }

Settled.

Exon iss^d 20th June 1797.

Isaac Daniel, Appl^t }
    vs   } Case
Robt Montgomery, Resp^t }

Settled at [faint]

                    Thursday 9th March 1797   [181]

The State }
    vs   } Indictment for Larceny
William Stewart }

Nol pros.

The State }
    vs   } Indictment for Larceny
William Stewart }

Nol pros.

John Burge, App^t }
    vs   } debt
John Robertson, Resp^t }

The following Special Jury Sworn, viz.

Jesse Grigg	Thos Cooper
Jecamiah Moore	Wm Owsley
George Lee	Danl Mitchell
David Felps	W^m [faint]
Randolph Rutland	Jarard Burch
Moses Powell	John Halcomb

Who returned the following verdict, to wit. We, the Jury, find for the Respondent [faint]

                              Jesse Grigg, foreman

James Hogg, Appel^t }
    vs   } Case
Joel McClendon, Resp^t }

Settled.

Thursday 9th March 1797   [182]

John Whatley &   }
John Pounds, Apl^t   }
    vs   } Debt
Joshua Williams, Resp^t }

The following Special Jury Sworn, to wit.

Jesse Grigg	Thomas Cooper
Jecamiah Moore	Wm Owsley
George Lee	Wyatt Collier
David Felps	Danl Mitchell
Randolph Rutland	Jarrard Burch
Moses Powell	John Halcomb

Who returned the following Verdict, viz. We, the Jury, find for the Respondent one hundred and twenty five dollars & eighty four Cents, with lawful interest from the within date.

Jesse Grigg, foreman

The State }
   vs   } Indictment for selling liquor without licence
Jesse Ellis }

Witness for State, William Turner

Def^{ts}, James Turner, Abram Potter

The following Jury Sworn.

Miles Rachels	William Burns
Salathiel Culver	Wm Hunt
William Browne	Ben^j Hall
William Hamilton	Robt Day
William Beardth	Jarard Trammel
Turner Harwood	Wm Lancaster

Who returned the following Verdict, to wit. We, the Jury, find the def^t not guilty.

Wm Hunt, foreman

Thursday 9th March 1797 [183]

Moses Harris & }
James Turner, Apl^t }
    vs } Case
William Turner, Resp^t }

Appellant's Witness, Austin Morris, Josiah Dennis

For Resp^t, Larkin Turner

The following Special Jury Sworn.

Jesse Grigg	Thos Cooper
Jecamiah Moore	William Owsley
George Lee	Wyatt Collier
David Felps	Danl Mitchell
Randolph Rutland	William [faint]
Moses Powell	Jarard Burch

Who returned the following Verdict. We, of the Jury, find for the Respondent one hundred & forty eight dollars & seventy five cents, with lawful Interest from the date of the Note.

Jesse Grigg, foreman

Execution iss^d 22nd March 1797, returned no property shewn & 2 ffi ffa iss^d 17th Octr 1797.

Joshua L. Acee, App^l}
    vs } Slander
William Street, Resp^t}

Resp^{ts} Witnesses, John McKenzie 8 day paid, Robt Simms 4 days paid, John Shackleford 7

Appellant's Witness, Abram [faint] William Cain, James Wood

The above Special Jury Sworn, Who returned the following Verdict, viz. We, the Jury, find for the Respondent fifty dollars & Cost of suit.

Jesse Grigg, foreman

5th June Satisfaction rec^d for the principal according of a receipt given to John Day.

Ge° Walton

Thursday 9th March 1797   [184]

John Jack, Appel^t }
    vs   } Case
Joseph Cooper, Resp^t }

Page 99

Appeal withdrawn. The original Judgment Confirmed and stay of levy sixty days and four dollars and fifty cents for Witnesses claims.

Exon iss^d See page 99

Moses Harris, Appel^t }
    vs   } Case
John Lindsey, Resp^t }

Dismissed.

Richard Hamlin, Appl^t }
    vs   } Case
Hezekiah Johnston   }
& Evan Harvey, Resp^t }

The same Jury as in the case of Turner & Harris, who returned the following Verdict, to wit. We, of the Jury, find for the Appellant one hundred & twenty seven dollars ten Cents against Johnston, with lawful interest.

Jesse Grigg, foreman

Ca Sa iss^d the 26th Octr 1797.

The Court then adjourned until ~~ten~~ nine O'Clock tomorrow.

Ben Taliaferro

Friday 10th March 1797 [185]

The Court Met according to adjournment. Present, his Honor Judge Taliaferro.

Joseph Turner, Appl^t }
      vs   } Case
Lewis Barnes, Resp^t }

The following Special Jury Sworn.

Jesse Grigg	William Owsley
Jecamiah Moore	Danl Mitchell
George Lee	Jarrard Burch
David Felps	John Halcomb
Randolph Rutland	Jacob Gore
Thos Cooper	Absolem Harris

We, the Jury, find for the Respondent one hundred Dollars, with Lawfull Interest from the date.

Jesse Grigg, foreman

[writing obscured by seam] one hundred & twenty six Dollars principal & Interest.

Lewis Barnes

Richard Bonner, appl^t }
      vs   } Eject.
John Lamar, Resp^t }

Respondent's Witness, Ben^j Thompson

The same Jury as in the above case. We, the Jury, find for the Appellant the Land.

Jesse Grigg, foreman

Friday 10th March 1797 [186]

John Robison }
    vs   } Case
James Huckaby }

Richd Smith, ex dem }
& John Robison   }
    vs   } Ejectment
[smear] Stith   }
tenant in possession }
James Huckaby   }

In the above causes, the parties have agreed to submit all matters in controversy to the final end and arbitrament of Henry Mitchell, Risdon Moore, Edward Butler, Jerard Burch, Needham Jernigan, Senr, Henry Graybill, Alexander Reid, Tully Choice, John Hamilton, John Sturdivant, & Joseph Cooper, Junr, or a majority of them, whose award shall be final & conclusive, & made the Judgment of the next Court.

                                    G. Walker, Att^y
                                    P. Alen, Def^{ts} Att^y

Robt Flournoy }
    vs   } Attachm^t
Ulysses Rogers }

Charles Abercrombie, Esqr [smear] as Garnishee in an Attachment of Robert Flournoy vs Ulysses Rogers [smear]

hath no property belonging to said Rogers in his possession.   [187]

[An entire line crossed out and illegible.]

Henry Parrish }
    vs   } Case
Moses Harris }

In this case, James Wood, the original Bail, came forward and entered himself special bail, on this condition, that if said defendant shall be cast in this suit, he will pay the condemnation money, or surrender himself into Court as the law directs, or I (James Wood) will do it for him. Taken & acknowledged in Open Court the 10th March 1797.

Before Mar Martin, Clk   James Wood

The Court then adjourned till Court in course.

                                    Ben Taliaferro

The Jury List corrected, and Jurors drawn for next term.   [188]

Grand Jurors

Robert Cunningham	John Shackleford, Senr
Miel Monk	Edmond Butler, Senr
Saml Goode	Dixon Hall
Saml Slaughter	Jonas Shivers
Andrew Baxter	Brice Gaither
Ge^o Hargraves	Jessee Veazy
Alex^r Reid	Sterling Cato
Saml Dent	Moses Wilie
Jessee Battaile	Peter Coffee
John Rispess	Charles Statam
Wm Lord	Stephen Evans
Benj^a Whitfield	Davis Long
James Wilson	James Bishop
Robert McGinty	John Sturdivant
Peter Dent	Francis Traywick
John Talbot	William Wright
John Greer	Moses Miles

Petit Jurors

Demsey Harden	Charles Simmons
John Crouch	Robt Moreland
Wm Huddlestone	James Wadsworth
Isaac Jackson	Isaac Carter
Saml Reid	Wm Morgan
Ralph Low	Ge^o Thompson
Jacob Earnest	James Prichet
Benjⁿ Bryant	James Butts

Jefry Barksdale　　　　　　Abner Abercrombie
　　　　　　　　　　　　　　John Scarlet

John Sweat　　　　　　　　Edward Brooks　　　[189]
John Manor　　　　　　　　James Montgomery
Wm Graves　　　　　　　　Zack Madox
Chas Hoskins　　　　　　　Malone Mullins
Isaac Brewer　　　　　　　John Thompson
Edward Brown　　　　　　　Zack Nowles
Wm Harvie　　　　　　　　Jeremiah McCarter
Robert Blackney　　　　　　Isham Brooks
Green Lee　　　　　　　　　Nicholas Hughs
Mathew Stroud　　　　　　　John Huster
Henry Jernigan　　　　　　Henry Lanier
Wm Barns　　　　　　　　　James Philips
John Harvie　　　　　　　　Joshua Jacobs
Isaac Dennis　　　　　　　Hugh Horton
Henry Mitchell　　　　　　Joel Kinny
Philip Pricket　　　　　　Wm Washington
John Pollion　　　　　　　Jeremiah Spiller
Edmund Welch　　　　　　　Mose Spear
John Boice　　　　　　　　Ge^o Bagby
John Ward　　　　　　　　　Aaron Wood
Joshua Turner　　　　　　　James Wilkins
Thomas Vicars　　　　　　　Micajah Harris
John Boyd　　　　　　　　　John Hamlin
Zadoc Bonner　　　　　　　John Marcus
Abijah Tumons　　　　　　　Wm Brown
Henry Low　　　　　　　　　James Roan
Mordicai Jacobs

　　　　　　　　　　　　　　Ben Taliaferro

[blank page]　　　　　　　　　　　　　　　　　　[190]

At a Superior Court begun and held in and for the County of Hancock on　[190]
Friday the 1st September 1797, Present His Honor Judge Stephens.

His Honor's Commission & the clause of the Judiciary Act that [smear] the Judges to preside alternately [illegible]

134

The following persons attended and after having retired and chosen Robert Cunningham as their foreman came into Court and were sworn of the Grand Jury, viz.

Robert Cunningham	Edmond Butler, Sn[r]
Mial Monk	Dixon Hall
Andrew Baxter	Brice Gaither
George Hargraves	Jesse Veazey
Alexander Reid	Sterling Cato
Jesse Battle	Moses Willey
John Rispas	Davis Long
Benjamin Whitfield	James Bishop
Robert McGinty	John Sturdivant
Peter Dent	Francis Traywick
John Greer	William Wright

John Shackelford, Sn[r], one of the Original pannel of the Grand Jury, having made oath that he was above the age of sixty years, was excused of serving.

Friday 1st September 1797 [191]

George Bagby, Esquire, one of the original pannel of the Petit Jury was excused from Service at this term on account of his indisposition of body.

Henry Lanier also excused on account of indisposition.

Jacob Ernest excused untill monday morning.

Richard Smith, on the dem of }
the Exo[rs] of James Adams, dec[d] }
        vs } Ejectment
William Stiles and }
Edmond Noles, tenants in }
possession }

By consent of parties, It is ordered that in this case Solomon Sutton be admited a Co defendant agreeably to the established practice.

Susannah Moor }
    vs } Case
Jordan Bonner }

In this case, Thomas Bonner and Zadok Bonner came into court and acknowledged themselves Special Bail, on this condition, that if the defendant shall be cast in this action, he will pay the eventual Condemnation Money, or we will do it for him, or surrender his body as the law directs.

Taken and acknowledged in Open   Thos Bonner
Court before Mar Martin, Clk   Zadok Bonner

Friday 1st September 1797   [192]

Judkins Hunt }
     vs   } Case
Jeremiah Bonner }

The following Jury Sworn (Viz.)

1. Saml Reid
2. Ralph Low
3. Jeffery Barksdale
4. Robt Moreland
5. George Thompson
6. Abner Abercrombie
7. Matthew Stroud
8. William Barnes
9. Philip Pritchett
10. Thomas Vickars
11. Mordecai Jacobs
12. James Montgomery

Who returned the following Verdict, to wit. We, the Jurors, find for the plaintiff one hundred & seventy dollars & twenty five Cents.

Robert Moreland, foreman

Exon iss^d 14th Septr 1797.

Andrew Borland }
     vs   } case
William Minor }

Settled by Report of Plaintiff's Attorney.

Henry Gaither }
     vs   } assumpsit
William Minor }

The death of the defendant Suggested in the usual form.

James Garrett }
    vs   } case
George Smith }

Settled by information of Anderson Comer, Esqr, Plff^s Att^y

                Friday 1st September 1797   [193]

Jonas Shivers }
    vs   } attachment
Harris Spear }

Settled by information of the deputy Sheriff and the property released by order of the plaintiff.

Joshua L. Acee   }
    vs   } case
Benjamin Thompson }
& Joseph Thompson }

Dismissed by Plf.

Joseph Smith }
    vs   } case
Joseph Cooper }

Settled by information of Hines Holt, Esqr, D. S. [blot]

The Court then adjourned untill tomorrow Nine O'Clock.

                Saturday 2nd September 1797   [194]

Court met according to adjournment. Present, his honor Judge Stephens.

Thomas Wilcoxon }
    vs   } Case
James Hogg, jun^r }

Settled at defendant's Costs.

Exon iss^d for Costs 26th June 1799.

James Shakelford }
    vs   } Case
John McCullock }

Settled by information of the Clerk.

James Butts, one of the original pannel of the petit Jury, excused on account of indisposition.

Patrick Hayes   }
    vs   } Case
Henry Journegan }

The Death of the Defendant Suggested & ordered that the suit proceed in the name of John Willson, the Adm^r.

Michael & Laurence   }
    vs   } debt
Lewis, Halcomb & Bankston }

Discontinued.

                      Saturday 2nd September 1797   [195]

William Wallace & Co }
    vs   } case
William Walker   }

Judgement confessed for the amount due on the note and interest, with a stay of levy five months.

Teste. Jno Griffin   W. Walker

Exon iss^d 25th Ap^l 1798.

George Hearndon, ass^e }
of Harman Runnels   }
    vs   } case
Daniel Muse &   }
John Bond   }

The following Jury sworn, to wit.

Robt Moreland	Malone Mullins
Matthew Stroud	Ralph Low
Mordecai Jacobs	Samuel Reid
William Barnes	Nicholas Hughes
Philip Pritchett	Isaac Dennis
Abner Abercrombie	Thomas Vickars

Who Returned the following verdict, to wit. We, the Jurors, find for the Plaintiff two hundred and fourteen dollars and seventy cents, with cost.

Robert Moreland, foreman

Appealed from.

Saturday 2nd September 1797 [196]

Jacob Williams }
    vs   } Slander
James Miller }

Jacob Williams }
    vs   } assault and battery
James Miller }

Witnesses Subpoenaed, John Williams, Richard Castlebery, Asa Castlebery, Paul Williams, Mark Gander, Thomas Saterwhite, Robert Flournoy, Lloyd Kelley, Thomas Mason, & Samuel Pope

It appearing on affidavit that the above persons were duly Subpoenaed and not attending to give evidence in the causes, it is ordered that they shew cause on Tuesday 10 O'Clock why an attachment of Contempt should not issue against each & every of them.

William Minor }
    vs   }
John McKinsey }

Death of the Plaintiff suggested & Ordered that the Suit proceed in the name of John Minor & William Minor, Executors of the last Will & Testament of the Dec^d.

Saturday 2nd September 1797 [197]

Robert Flournoy }
    vs } attachment
Ulysses Rogers }

The following persons sworn of the Jurrry, Viz.

1. Jeffery Barksdale
2. George Thompson
3. James Montgomery
4. John Thompson
5. Isaac Carter
6. John Butler
7. William McGaughey
8. Andrew Maddox
9. James Pritchett
10. Hugh Hall
11. Samuel Holley
12. Henry Muppett

Who Returned the following verdict, to wit. We, the Jurors, find for the plaintiff One hundred and fifty five dollars and fifty seven cents.

Saml Holley, foreman

Joseph Smith }
    vs } case
John C. Mason }

Settled at def^s cost. Pltff^s Att^y Present.

Saturday 2nd September 1797 [198]

Robert Flournoy }
    vs } attachment
Ulysses Rogers }

Verdict for the sum of One hundred and fifty five dollars and fifty seven cents. and it appearing to the Court that Judgement by default had been entered against William Pentecost, a defaulting Garnishee, it is therefore ordered final Judgement be entered against the said defendant and garnishee for the amount of said verdict.

The State }
    vs } Indictment for Larceny
Moses Harris }

The defendant Came into Court with James Wood & James Turner, his Securities, who acknowledged themselves bound unto his Excellency the Governor & his successors in Office, the said Moses Harris in the sum of two hundred and fifty dollars & the said Wood & Turner in the sum of one hundred & twenty five dollars each, to be void on condition that the said Moses Harris will make his personal ~~attendance~~ appearance from day to day during the present term & not depart without leave of the Court.

Taken & acknowledged	Moses Harris
in open Court	James Wood
attest. Mar Martin, Clk	Ja^s Turner

Saturday 2nd September 1797 [199]

The State }
    vs } Riot & Assault
Charles Abercrombie }
and others }

Ordered, that the Sheriff bring up the body of John Gan, a prisoner confined for Horse Stealing, to give evidence on the part of the state before the Grand Inquest on the above charge for a riot.

The State }
    vs } Negro Stealing
Robert Clary }

Ordered, that the recognizance in this case be extended to Greene, the Prosecutor, and prisoner Consenting thereto.

Mary Barnett }
Saml Barnett & }
Robt McAlpin, Exo^{rs} }
    vs } Case
Edward Hunter }

Dismissed.

Saturday 2nd September 1797 [200]

Joel McClendon }
    vs } case
James Hogg, jn^r }

Settled at df^{ts} cost.

Absolem Jackson }
    vs } 2nd fi fa Sheriff's Report
William Low }

Exceptions filed to the legality of the Exon. Sustained.

Court adjourned until Monday Morning 10 O'Clock.

                        W. Stephens

Monday 4th September 1797 [201]

Court met according to adjournment. Present, his Honor Judge Stephens.

Philip Howell }
    vs } Trover for Negroes
Abraham Womack }

The death of the defendant was suggested, and a question was made to the Court on the ground Whether the action survived or not, & a Motion Made to abate the writ and proceedings.

On Argument, the Court were clearly of Opinion that the Action does survive, for altho the wrong or Trespass is alledged to be the personal act of the defendant. yet it may so happen, that a recovery would prove the fact, and of consequence the estate of the deceased supposed to have benefited by this conversion of property.

As to abating the process, the cause of action surviving, the Court are positively <u>restrained</u> by the Judiciary Law.

By prosecuting the Suit in its <u>present form</u> against an Exo^r or Adm^r, it cannot be done with Justice to either plaintiff or the representatives of the deceased.

The petition must be so amended and notice given thereof to such representatives as to enable them not only to plead to the cause of the Original action, but to defend themselves from the consequences that may follow.

Monday 4th September 1797 [202]

Should a recovery in damages take place, however simple the mode of proceedings are allowed to be, yet they must not be made more so, or suffered by the Court to proceed in the present shape to the injury of individuals.

Let the cause continue on the doquet and the proceedings amended. if the party plaintiff sees fit.

Philip Spiller }
    vs   } case
Robert McGinty }

Jury Sworn and case withdrawn by consent.

        Robert Moreland   Malone Mullins
        Matthew Stroud   Ralph Low
        Mordecai Jacobs   Samuel Reid
        William Barns   Nicholas Hughs
        Philip Pritchett   Isaac Dennis
        Abner Abercrombie   Thomas Vickars

On Motion, it is ordered that the petition be amended by adding a count of money had and received and a Copy thereof served on the defendant, or his attorney, in ten days from this date and that the cause do peremptorily come to trial next court.

Hezekiah Johnson }
    vs   } debt
Martin Armstrong }

Discontinued.

Monday 4th Septr 1797 [203]

James Upright, ex dem }
of Stith Parham }
    vs } Ejectment
Abraham Lawless }
Jesse McKinney Pope, Exor }
of John Tripp, decd }

On Motion of Mr Anderson, Atty for the plaintiff in this case.

It is ordered, That the County Surveyor do go upon the premises in question & make an Accurate survey and platt of the same and make report ~~of~~ thereof ~~same~~ to the next Superior Court held in and for this County on the first day of March next.

Provided ten days notice be given to the defendant of the making of said survey and that the pltff and Dft be each of them entitled to carry with them a Surveyor at the time Such Survey is made.

Constant Right, ex dem of }
the heirs of Alexander Miller }
    vs } Ejectment
Brazer Wrangler, tenant in possession }
William Burns }

Discontinued.

Monday 4th Septr 1797 [204]

Andrew Willson }
    vs } Cont Special Bail
Robert Middleton }

In this case, William Ousley & Jesse Carrel Came into Court and entered themselves Special Bail for the defendant, on this Condition, that if said defendant is cast in this case, he will pay the eventual condemnation money, or surrender himself as the law directs, or we, William Ousley and Jesse Carrel, will do it for him.

taken and acknowledged William owsley
in open Court Jesse Carrel
Attest. Mar Martin

Richard Haddock }
    vs   } Case in deceit
James Miller }

Pltff^s Witness, Paul Williams

Jury Sworn

Robert Moreland	Malone Mullins
Matthew Stroud	Ralph Low
Mordecai Jacobs	Samuel Reid
William Barnes	Nicholas Hughs
Philip Pritchett	Isaac Dennis
Abner Abercrombie	Thomas Vickars

Verdict. We, the Jurors, find for the defendant.

                    Robert Moreland, foreman

Appeal Entered.

Monday 4th September 1797   [205]

James Scurlock }
    vs   } Trover
Arthur Danielly }

Witnesses for Pltff, Russel Massey, Joel Patterson, John Kirk, Ben^j Brantly

for Def^t, Mial Monk, Levin Hudson

Jury Sworn

Jeffery Barksdale	John Thompson
George Thompson	Levi Daniel

James Pritchett	John Butler
Henry Jernigan	John Sweat
John Harvey	Isaac Morgan
James Montgomery	Zephaniah John

Verdict. We, the Jurors, find for the defendant.

                                          Henry Jernigan, foreman

Abraham Upright, ex dem }
of Robert Middleton }
      vs } Ejectment
James Lawless, tenant in possession }
James Golightly }

In this Action, the Substantial parties, to wit, Robert Middleton and James Golightly, submit all their differences in and about the premises to the final award and arbitrament of John Bailey, James Thweatt, David Dickson, Jesse Grigg, Francis Moreland, Saml Hall, Sn^r, Obadiah Richardson, Jesse Sanford, William Dent, James Evans, James Bynam, & Jaret Burch, said arbitrators mutually chosen by the parties [smear] of said award be unanimous according to law, so as to be legally made a judgement of court.

                Monday 4th September 1797   [206]

The Grand Jury brought in the following bills, Viz.

The State }
   vs   } Indictment for Trespass
James Cathel }

True Bill.   Robert Cunningham, foreman

The State }
   vs   } Indictment for Misdemeanor
Jeremiah Bonner }

No Bill.   Robert Cunningham, foreman

The State }
    vs   } Indictment for Horse Stealing
John Gann }

True Bill.   Robert Cunningham, foreman

The State   }
    vs   } Indictment for Nuisance
Jesse Thompson }

True Bill.   Robert Cunningham, foreman

Abram Borland   }
    vs   } [faint]
Abner Bankston }

Settled at the Cost of the Defendant.

Adjourned until Nine O'Clock to Morrow.

                              W. Stephens

                  Tuesday 5th Septr 1797   [207]

Court met according to adjournment. Present, his Honor Judge Stephens.

Patrick Hays   }
    vs   } ffi ffa levied on property of Price
John Price &   }
William Hutcherson }

It appearing from the Original record that Price never was served and was not a party to the case. Ordered, that the execution be set aside as to the said John Price.

The State   }
    vs   } Indictment inveigling & giving a Pass to Negro
James Marony }

True Bill.   Robert Cunningham, foreman

The State }
    vs   } Indictment inveigling a Negro
James Merony }

True Bill.   Robt Cunningham, foreman

                 Tuesday 5th Septr 1797   [208]

William Stark }
    vs   } Trover
Jeremiah Bonner }
& Robert Bonner }

Witnesses for Pltff, Joseph Bonner, James Thweatt

~~Jury Sworn~~

Action Discontinued.

Henry Rogers, Appl^t }
    vs   } Case
Matthew Hawkins, Respd^t }

Appl^{ts} Witness, William Bivins, Reuben Mobley

Respd^{ts} Witness, Robert Rivers

                 Special Jury Sworn

        Miel Monk   Benjamin Whitfield
        Andrew Baxter   Robert McGinty
        George Hargraves   Peter Dent
        Alexander Reid   John Greer
        Jesse Battle   Edmond Butler, Sn^r
        John Rispess   Dixon Hall

Verdict. We, the Jurors, find for the Respondent one hundred and thirty one dollars and fifty six cents, with costs of suit.

                                     Andrew Baxter, foreman

Rec[d] [illegible] full Satisfaction of the above Verdict, Together with my Law Fee.

P. Alen, Att[y] for Hawkins

Tuesday 5th September 1797 [209]

Joel McClendon, Appl[t] }
   vs   } Appeal
Henry Gaither, Respd[t] }

The Appellant McClendon had notified the Respondent Gaither's Atty that he should apply for a Rule to bring a certain Award or umpirage into Court as necessary to Support the action. And the Court being of Opinion that such award or umpirage is pertinent to the issue.

It is ordered, that said award or umpirage be produced at next term or trial of the cause (if good cause is not shewn) to the Contrary. On the default thereof, let the defendant be subject to the regulations made by the Statute in such cases.

The plaintiff also making affidavit that he cannot proceed to trial with safety without such award or umpirage. The cause is, under the special circumstances of the case, continued.

The State   }
  vs   } Indictment Riot & assault
Charles Abercrombie }
& others, et al }

True Bill.   Rob[t] Cunningham, foreman

Tuesday 5th September 1797 [210]

Aaron Wood, one of the Original Pannel of the Petit Jury, being indisposed, is excused from Service at this term.

Peter L. Van Alen, Appel[t] }
   vs   } Case
William Ousley, Respondent }

Appeal Withdrawn & original Verdict Confirmed.

Nancy Creswell }
     vs   } Spec^l Action on the case
William Bivin }

In this case, Robert Rivers came into court and entered himself Special for the defendant, to be void on condition that, if the said Df^t is cast in this case, he will pay the eventual condemnation money, or surrender himself as the law directs, or that he, the said Robert Rivers, will do it for him.

Taken and acknowledged
in Open Court Before   Robert Rivers
Mar Martin, Clk

Adj^d till tomorrow 9 O'Clock.   W. Stephens

                Wednesday 6th September 1797   [211]

Court met according to adjournment. Present, his Honor Judge Stephens.

Paul Williams, one of the witnesses subponaed in the cases of Williams vs Miller, having appeared agreeably to the Rule of Court to shew cause why an attachment for contempt should not issue against them, having made satisfactory excuse to the Court, is exonerated from the penalties of said Rule.

Benjamin Porter for   }
the Exo^{rs} of Peter Carnes }
     vs   } assumpsit
Jesse Thompson &   }
Robert Middleton   }

Settled at the df^{ts} cost.

Benjamin Porter for   }
the Exo^{rs} of Peter Carnes }
     vs   } assumpsit
Jesse Thompson &   }
Robert Middleton   }

Settled at the defendant's cost.

Wednesday 6th September 1797 [212]

Jacob Williams, appl^t }
      vs   } Slander
James Miller, Respd^t }

Witnesses for Respd^t, Henry Tounsend paid att^{ce}, ~~Henry~~ Francis Strauther paid att^{ce}, ~~Mary Stallings~~, to Henry Townsend, Esqr

Special Jury Sworn

Benjamin Whitfield	Moses Willey
John Rispess	James Bishop
Alexander Reid	John Sturdivant
Peter Dent	Francis Trawick
John Greer	William Wright
Starling Cato	Edmond Butler, Sn^r

Verdict. We, the Jury, find for the Appellant.

                                        Benjamin Whitfield, foreman

The State }
     vs   } Indictment for Trespass
James Cathell }

State Witnesses Sworn, Robert Middleton, Elizabeth Middleton, Potter Stallings, William Crosby, James Montgomery

for Df^t, Jesse Talbert, Prudence Daudle

Jury Sworn

Robert Moreland	Malone Mullins
Matthew Stroud	Saml Reid
Mordecai Jacobs	Nicholas Hughs
William Barnes	Isaac Dennis
Philip Pritchett	Thomas Vicars
Abner Abercrombie	Jeffery Barksdale

Verdict. Not Guilty.   Robt Moreland, foreman

Exon iss^d for costs 27th June 1799.

Wednesday 6th September 1797 [213]

Moses Harris, appl^t }
    vs } case
John Lindsay, Respd^t }

Appeal dismissed March Term 1797.

In this case, execution issued against the appel^t and Austin Morris, the Security. Whereupon, the said Security Came into Court and delivered up the principal, Moses Harris, in discharge of his recognizance.

Ordered, that the Sheriff receive the said Moses Harris into his custody and be Served with a copy of this Order.

Nathaniel Waller }
    vs } case
James Scarlett }

In this case, James Scarlett came into court with Brice Gaither, who entered himself Special Bail for said Scarlett, the Df^t, and acknowledged himself bound to the plaintiff in the full anount of the eventual condemnation Money, but to be void on Condition that, if the said Scarlett is cast in this case, he will pay the eventual condemnation Money, or surrender himself as the law directs, or that he, the said Brice Gaither, will do it for him.

Taken and acknowledged	Ja^s Scarlett
in Open Court Before	B. Gaither
Mar Martin, Clk	

Wednesday 6th September 1797 [214]

John Denn, on the dem }
of Robert Flournoy, Esqr }
    vs } Ejectment
Richard Fenn and }
James Evans, Tenants }

The same Jury as in the case of The State vs James Cathell.

152

Verdict. We find for the plaintiff.   Robert Moreland, foreman

In the above case, it is consented by the parties that an appeal be entered with costs or surites & that the whole Costs of both trials follow the final determination.

Reubin Harrison   }
    vs   } Debt
Adm^{rs} of John Wooten }

                    Jury Sworn

Robert Moreland	Malone Mullins
Matthew Stroud	Ralph Low
Mordecai Jacobs	Nicholas Hughes
Wm Barnes	Isaac Dennis
Philip Pritchett	Thos Vickars
~~Abner Abercrombie~~	James Pritchett
Saml Reid	

Verdict. We, the Jurors, find for the plaintiff one hundred and sixty five dollars & thirty two Cents, with interest from the twenty fourth day of March seventeen hundred and ninety six.

                      Robt Moreland, foreman

Exon Issued 14th Septr 1797.

                Wednesday 6th Septr 1797   [215]

Samuel Giles   }
    vs   } fi fa Sheriff's report
Harris Nicholson }

Exceptions Overruled.

Exon renewed 14th Septr 1797.

John Lindsay   }
    vs   } fi fa Sheriff's Report
Moses Harris &   }
Austin Morris   }

Execution Dismissed as to Morris.

Danl Muse }
vs } Special Action on the Case in the
Harman Runnels } Inferior Court of [blot] the County

A Rule to shew cause was moved for, to prohibit the Inferior Court from further Proceeding in this Cause, on a Suggestion that the Justices had exceeded their Jurisdiction in setting aside the Verdict.

Two ~~Points~~ points were made by the Court to be argued on, namely

First. Wether the Superior Courts have a controuling Jurisdiction over the Inferior Courts and can take cognizance of their proceedings so as to issue a Prohibition, or wether this Writ is issuable by the Superior Courts?

Second. If the Superior Courts have Jurisdiction, Wether this is a proper Case to exercise it in?

The following Facts appear from the Record of the Justices of the Inferior Court. That the Verdict was set aside for misbehavior in the Jury and the Party in whose favor they found, and the case considered a mistrial By

Wednesday 6th Septembr 1797 [216]

By the Judge (after special argument and time to consider)

As to the 1st point. The Superior Court is created by the Constitution and is the final resort in most cases; its powers are in some measure defined, enlarged, and abridg'd by the several Laws under which the Court sits. To suppose that a superior Tribunal can not controul the improper exercise of power in lesser Tribunals, is to carry the Idea too far and is not warranted by the nature of things; but to exercise it, where necessary upon principles of Justice and sound discretion, as committed that controuling Power in the Superior Courts, as not only necessary to support the Constitution and Laws as relate to the Judicial System, but authorises such Courts to prohibit or direct Inferior Tribunals to prevent, in cases where they exceed their Jurisdiction, or cease to do justice, by not exercising that Power the Law has committed to them. For the furtherance of Justice therefore and the greater security to the Lives and property of Individuals, it has been wisely devised that a controuling or superior power rests in this Court. the exercise of it must be according to Law and that legal discretion which necessarily attaches itself in the exercise of power.

As to the 2nd point. The Inferior Courts are warranted by the Constitution; they are created by Law and may be annihilated by Law. in their present formation, they have in all civil cases, except as to Land causes, a concurrant Jurisdiction with this Court, and in many cases an exclusive Jurisdiction as to the particular subjects refered to them. They are a special Jurisdiction erected for the benefit of the Citizens; are to be governed by the same rules and regulations as this Court and the Justices take the same oath that the Judges of the [smear] do. [faint] power to punish for contempt and default before them, and ought to exercise those powers with firmness, Justice

Wednesday 6th Septembr 1797   [217]

Justice, and moderation. The doctrine of new Trial in England depends in some measure on the opinion of the Judges, but in general it is admitted that it has been beneficial to the People. With us the power of the Judges ~~has been~~ is abridged and more granted to Jurors, who by their Oath Judge of the Law as well as Facts. Hence, the trial by Jury is preserved by an express article of the Constitution. And we find there powers extended to a great degree, as necessary to the security of Life, Liberty, and Property, but when we speak of Trial by Jury, it must be that kind of Trial which is honest, fair, open, and agreeable to Law, and the usages and practices of our Courts.

If there is not the basis on which Verdicts are found, they are liable to be shaken where Courts can get at them. And finding cause to vitiate such Verdict, it can only be done under ~~a~~ our Judicial System in two particular points, Viz. Contempt in the Jury, which is misbehavior, or breaking up without giving a Verdict, in either case, the Court may declare a <u>mistrial</u> and the cause is again reheard. It is true a new trial is a right granted by the Constitution, and it is equally true that that right is so modified by Law as to obtain it in certain terms only, and then the cause travels to the high tribunal of the County, the Superior Court, and a Special Jury taken from the Grand Inquest, which embraces the Equity of the Case, and so decides finally and conclusively.

A Verdict may be set aside for cause, either a Common Law Court or before a Special Jury.

There is nothing that can justify this Court to inhibit the Proceedings of the Justices of the Inferior Court in this Cause, they have, in the opinion of the Judge, exercised that power the Law has vested them with, and from the Record before the Court, it is concluded that declaring a Mistrial has taken place in the cause before us the Justices have acted according

Wednesday 6th Septembr 1797 [218]

to Law. Therefore let nothing be taken by the Motion.

For the Motion, Mr Stith, Mr Anderson, Mr Early, Mr Hamill

Against the Motion, Mr Solicitor Van Alen, Mr Hobby, Mr Elholm

Court adjourned until to morrow morning 9 O'Clock.

W. Stephens

Thursday 7th September 1797

Court met according to Adjournment. Present, his Honor Judge Stephens.

The State }
    vs   } Indictmt for Inveigling a Negro
James Marony }

Boling Cureton, His bail, Surrendered the body of said James Marony into Court. Whereupon, the Sheriff was ordered to receive him into his custody.

Thursday 7th Septr 1797 [219]

The State }
    vs   } Indictment for Horse Stealing
John Gann }

Bird Ferrill, Archelous Ferrill, Zealous Milstead, & William Jones came into Court and acknowledged themselves bound to his Excellency the Governor and his Successors in Office in the Sum of two hundred and fifty dollars each, to be levied on their goods and chattels, lands and tenements, to be void on Condition that they appear at the next Superior Court to give testimony on the above Indictment.

The State }
    vs   } Indictment for Horse Stealing
John Gann }

The prisoner demanding his trial and the State not being prepared and consenting that the prisoner be bailed on the Motion of his council.

It is Ordered. That bail be taken, the principal in fifteen hundred dollars and two or more sureties in an equal sum and Justify in open Court that they are worth the money.

Whereupon Charles Moore, Isham Hogan, Elisha Waller, and Levin Smith Came into Court and having Justified entered themselves

                Thursday 7th September 1797   [220]

his bail, agreeably to the foregoing Order, were bound.

The principal, Jn° Gann in fifteen hundred Dollars,
Charles Moore in the sum of seven hundred dollars,
Isham Hogan in the sum of three hundred dollars,
Elisha Waller in the sum of three hundred dollars, and
Levin Smith in the sum of two hundred dollars.

To be discharged if the said Jn° Gann shall appear at the next Superior Court for this County to answer to the above charge, or any other charge which may be exhibitedd against him, and that he shall not depart the Court without leave there of.

The State   }
    vs   } Indictment Riot & Assault
Charles Abercrombie }
& Wiley Abercrombie }
Henry Dixon   }
William Rabun   }
Jacob Gore &   }
Thaddeus Holt   }

Charles Abercrombie & Willie Abercrombie plead not Guilty.

Whereupon, Andrew Borland acknowledged himself bound to his Excellency the Governor and his Successors in Office in the sum of five hundred Dollars, to be void on Condition that said Charles & Willie Abercrombie will make the personal appearance at the next Superior Court and not depart without leave.

Thursday 7th September 1797 [221]

The State }
    vs } Indictment Riot & Assault
Charles Abercrombie et al }

~~John Gann~~, Jesse Ellis, Jane Vincent, Elizabeth Greer, Elisha Waller, Elizabeth Greer, jn[r], Mary Gann, Elisha Vincent, ~~Zebediah Briggs~~, ~~Benjamin Waller~~, Thomas Cairy, & William Maddox came into Court and acknowledged themselves bound to his Excellency the Governor and his Successors in Office in the Sum of two hundred dollars each, to be void on condition the said parties attend at the next Superior Court to give testimony on the above Indictment and not depart without leave of the Court.

John Mapp & Sam[l] Phillips, Appel[ts] }
    vs } Ejectment
John Kelly, Respondent }

On Motion of Respondent's Att[y], Ordered that the Surveyor of the County, on application of the party, proceed to Re-Survey the tract of Land in dispute between the parties, and that the said Surveyor return [blot] accurate plat of such Survey, Shewing the interferences, if any, and the pretentions of each party delineated under his hand to the Clerk of this Court on or before the first day of the Next Term. And it is

Thursday 7th Sept[r] 1797 [222]

is further ordered that the opposite party have fifteen days Notice of the time of such Re-Survey and that each party in Addition to the County Surveyor be at liberty to have a Surveyor at the time of Making Such Re-Survey.

The State }
    vs } Indictment Larceny
Moses Harris }

Witnesses for the State, Archelus Everett, Daniel McDowell

Defendant's Witnesses, Paul Williams

Jury Sworn

Isaac Dennis	Mordecai Jacobs
Abner Abercrombie	Ralph Low
John Sweat	Jeffery Barksdale
John Thompson	Aaron Wood
Thomas Vickars	Samuel Reid
Matthew Stroud	William Barnes

Verdict. We, the Jurors, find the criminal Not Guilty.

Saml Reid, foreman

West Jones }
    vs   } Assault
Isham Hogan}

We, the arbitrators appointed by Rule of Court, do award that the said Isham Hogan do pay unto the said West Jones the sum of five dollars damage and all Costs. This award to be final & conclusive. Given under our hands this [blank] day of [blank] 1797.

James Turner
James Miller
William Turner

Exon issued 6th Octr 1797.

Thursday 7th September 1797   [223]

Robert Flournoy }
    vs   } Debt
William Brown }

By virtue of a Power of Attorney to me as well as others directed & herewith filed, I do hereby appear for the defendant, and receive process, and confess Judgment for the sum of one hundred and sixty six dollars and fifty Seven Cents, releasing all errors and misprision of errors.

Th⁰ Flournoy, def^{ts} att^y

Exon iss^d 1st Jany 1798.

Robert Flournoy }
    vs   } debt
Ephraim A. Salmons }

By virtue of a power of Att^y to me as well as others directed & herewith filed, I do hereby appear for the defendant, Receive process, and confess Judgement to the plaintiff for ninety nine dollars & forty four Cents, relinquising all errors & Misprision of errors.

Thos Flournoy, Df^s Att^y

Exon iss^d 1st Jany 1798.

Rec^d of the above Judgm^t 114$9.

paid Shff 3$00

paid plff in full receipt on Exon.   B. Hall

Thursday 7th September 1797   [224]

William Tuplen ag^t of   }
William Washington   }
    vs   } Ejectment
John & Philip Cook   }

On Motion of the plaintiff's Att^y, it is Ordered,

That the Surveyor of the County attend and make an accurate survey of the disputed premises, and that he return an exact platt of the same on or before the first day of the next term, with a designation of any lines, Marks, butings, and bounds in which the parties differ, and that the said surveyor give at least twenty days notice to the parties, or their agents, so that if either of them think fit they may Appoint one person to attend said surveyor in the execution of this order.

The Grand Jury returned the following bill.

The State }
    vs   } Assault
Thaddeus Holt }

True Bill.   Robert Cunningham, foreman

Asa Alexander }
    vs   } Case
John Mapp   }

Settled by Report of the Clerk.

Isaac Downs   }
    vs   } Trespass
James M. C. Montgomery }

Settled.

Thursday 7th September 1797   [225]

The State   }
    vs   } Indictm^t Inveigling a Negro
James Merony }

The Same }
    vs   } Ind^t for Inveigling &c
The Same }

James Marony, the defendant, came into Court with Boling Cureton & Daniel McDowell, his Securities, who acknowledge themselves indebted to his Excellency the Governor and his Successors in Office, the said James Marony in the sum of two hundred dollars and the said Surities in the sum of one hundred dollars each, to be levied on their goods and chattels, lands and Tenements, but to be void on Condition, the said Merony will make his personal Appearance at the next Superior Court for the County of Hancock and not depart without leave.

The State   }
    vs   } Indictment for Nuisance
Jessee Thompson }

The Df came into Court with Wm Owsley, his Surety, who acknowledged themselves bound to his Excellency the Governor in the sum of two hundred dollars, to be levied on their goods &c, but to be void on Condition that the said Jesse Thompson will appear at the next Superior Court for the County of Hancock and not depart without leave.

Thursday 7th September 1797 [226]

The State }
    vs   } Contempt
Jesse Ellis }

Jesse Ellis acknowledges himself bound in One hundred dollars to appear at the next Superior Court to shew cause why an Attachment should not issue against him for a Contempt in obstructing the process of this Court in the Service of a Subpona on Jane Gann.

Thomas Cairy, Hines Holt, and Willie Abercrombie acknowledge themselves bound unto his Excellency the Governor and his Successors in Office, ~~to be void on Condition~~ the said Thomas Cairy in the sum of one hundred dollars, Hines Holt and Willie Abercrombie in the sum of twenty five dollars each, to be void on Condition the said Thomas Cairy will keep the peace to Levin Ellis until the next term of the Superior Court.

John Denn, ex dem }
of Obadiah Richardson }
    vs   } Ejectment
Richard Fenn & }
Thomas Breedlove, Tenants }

On Motion of the Pltff^s Att^y, it is

Ordered, that the county surveyor attend and make an accurate survey of the premises in dispute and return an exact Platt of the same on or before the first day of the next term, with a designation of any lines, marks, buttings, & boundings in which the parties differ, and that the said surveyor give at least twenty days notice to the parties, or their agents, so that if either of them think fit, they may appoint one person to attend said surveyor in the execution of this order.

Thursday 7th September 1797 [227]

James Evans, Appl^t }
    vs } Ejectment
Robert Flournoy, Respd^t }

On Motion of the respondent & by consent of parties

It is Ordered, that Bolling Hall, Esqr be directed to re-survey the tract of Land in question and that the said Bolling Hall, Esqr return an Accurate Platt of such new survey, shewing the interferences, if any, & that the claims of each party be delineated and return thereof made under his hand to the Clerk of this Court on or before the first day of the next term, and that the appl^t have at least ten days notice of the time of making such Survey.

                    W. Stith, jn^r, for Respd^t
                    Jno E. Anderson, for appl^t

Peter L. Van Alen }
    vs } case
William Ousley }

An appeal from the Inferior Court.

Mr Van Alen, the appl^t, withdrew his appeal in this Court, he had a right to do so. It appears from the Certificate of M. Hall, Clerk of the Inferior Court, that Ousley, the Df^t, intended to have appealed, but was prevented by the Clerk, on a supposition that as one party had appealed, the other need not. From this circumstance, no appeal from Ousley was entered, this is a hard case, and a failure of justice. the Court have in this instance no power over the records, or Clerk of the Inferior Court, so as to order an appeal nunc pro tunc. If the plaintiff however will proceed to issue Execution, the case may be examined in that way.

Thursday 7th Septr 1797 [228]

Presentments of the Grand Jury

1st We the Grand Jury of Hancock County present as a grievance the want of confidence in the greater part of the trustees of the Academy Lands. Their apparent Contempt of his Excellency's proclamation of July last, and also the irreparable damage sustained by the public in consequence of the shameful prostitution of their Sacred trust.

2nd We present as a grievance the want of some specific Law to ascertain the criminality of those, who in a private and concealed manner, keep in their possession Moulds, Stamps, & dyes for the coinage of base Metal.

3rd We present as a grievance that the Militia of this State are not paid for services rendered on the Frontiers in times of imminant danger. Soldiery being Kept out of their pay destroys that Milatary alertness which in all well regulated free governments is the chief pillar in the political structure.

4th We present Martin Johnson for profane swearing at the window of the Court house, As well as immodest & immoral conduct in the court yard.

5th After viewing the state of the finances of this County, we find that legal and accurate appropriations have been made.

We request that his Honor Judge Stephens will accept our thanks for his Judicious charge delivered to us at the opening of the Court. And that his

Thursday 7th Septr 1797 [229]

his Charge, together with these Presentments, be published in the State Gazette.

Robert Cunningham	Edmond Butler
Miel Monk	Dixon Hall
Andrew Baxter	Brice Gaither
George Hargraves	Jesse Veazey
Alexander Reid	Starling Cato
Jesse Battle	Moses Wiley
John Rispess	Davis Long
Benjamin Whitfield	James Bishop
Robert McGinty	John Sturdivant
Peter Dent	Francis Traywick
John Greer	William Wright

It is Ordered, That the Solicitor General turn as many of the presentments into Indictments as the nature of the case will admit. And these presentments and the Charge be published.

Ordered, that all defaulting Jurors be fined, unless good cause be shewn Court as the Law directs.

The Grand & Petit Jurors were then discharged and thanked by the Judge for their attendance.

W. Stephens

Grand Jury for March Term 1798 [230]

1. Robert Tate
2. John Bond
3. Nathaniel Tatum
4. Charles Abercrombie
5. Richard Shipp
6. Saml Barron
7. Levi Lancaster
8. John Hamilton
9. Samuel Barron, jun^r
10. David Adams
11. William Dent, jun^r
12. Jeremiah Nelson, M. D.
13. James Walker
14. Zephaniah John
15. William Pigg
16. John Mitchell
17. Stephen Bishop
18. John Brewer
19. Eppes Brown
20. Barthol^w Wyche
21. Thomas Mitchell
22. Robt Raines
23. Randolph Rutland

Petit Jurors

1. Isaac Hall
2. William Buckner
3. John Spear
4. John McKessack
5. George Brewer
6. John Coleman
7. Nehemiah Scoggan
8. Nathan Barrington
9. Joseph Cooper
10. Anderson Harwell
11. John Dennis
12. James Yarborough
13. Francis Moreland
14. George Medlock
15. John Dunn
16. Jacob Keaner
17. Absalom Trailer
18. Malachi Brantley
19. Thomas Wynn
20. Benjamin Braswell

Petit Jurors Continued [231]

21. John Spencer
22. Benjamin Jones
23. Robt Finch
35. Jesse McKinney Pope
36. Ezekiel Smith
37. Mark Nowles

24. Richard Fretwell
25. James Rogers
26. Moses Fuquay
27. John Stembridge
28. Matthew Durham
29. Thomas Wynn, jun^r
30. Robert Bonner
31. Elijah Runnels
32. John Hansel
33. Benjamin Parker
34. William Chandler

38. James Thomas
39. John Ward
40. Charles Parker
41. John K. Candler
42. Jacob Holcomb
43. James Cowden
44. John Wallace
45. James Darby
46. Thomas Paramour
47. Thomas Trammell
48. John Buckner

Court adjourned until Next Term.

W. Stephens

Georgia [232]

At a Superior Court begun & held in and for the County of Hancock on the first day of March 1798, pursuant to the adjournment of the last Court. Present, his honor Judge Carnes.

His Honor's commission being read, the following persons attended & were sworn of the Grand Jury, viz.

1. Charles Abercrombie, foreman
2. John Bond
3. Saml Barron
4. Levi Lancaster
5. John Hamilton
6. Saml Barron, jun^r
7. William Pigg
8. Eppes Brown
9. Bartholomew Wyche
10. Thomas Mitchell

11. Robert Raines
12. Randolph Rutland
13. Jonas Shivers
14. Henry Moffatt
15. Martin Armstrong
16. Reuben Jones
17. Joel McClendon
18. Littleton Reese
19. Andrew Maddux
20. Zephaniah John

John Brewer, Senr, one of the original pannel, excused as being over the age required by Law for service as Grand Juror.

Absalom Trailer excused from service as a Petit Juror. John T. Spencer excused on account of indisposition. Nehemiah Scoggan excused on account of the indisposition of his wife & his frontier situation.

James Thomas excused on account of indisposition. John Ward excused on account of the ill health of his family.

Thursday 1st March 1798 [233]

Robert Wynne }
    vs   } Slander
John Champen }

Settled.

Jane Browne }
    vs   } Case
Israel Johnson }

Settled & Cost paid.

George Clower }
    vs   } Case
Thomas Wynne }

The defendant came into Court with Robt Montgomery, who entered himself special bail on this condition, that if the def^t is cast in this Action, he will pay the Condemnation money, or suurender himself in discharge thereof, or I (Robt Montgomery) will do it for him. Taken & acknowledged in open Court.

Before Mar Martin, Clk   Thos X Wynne, his mark
                                          Robert Montgomery

Court adjourned till to morrow morning 9 O'Clock.

Thos P. Carnes

Friday 2nd March 1798 [234]

Court Met according to adjournment. Present, his Honor Judge Carnes.

Jonathan Nisbet }
    vs   } debt
Martin Armstrong }
& Richard Shipp }

Settled.

Patrick Hays }
    vs   } Case
Henry Jernigan }

Continued by consent.

William F. Booker }
    vs   } 2 Cases
Robert Flournoy }

Continued by consent.

Turner Harwood }
    vs   } Spec^l Case
Thomas Deal }

Thomas Deal Came into Court with John Deal, Who entered himself Special Bail for the defendant, On this Condition, that if he is cast in this suit, he will pay the Condemnation Money, or sur^d himself in discharge thereof, or I (John Deal) will do it for him. Taken and acknowledged in Open Court.

Before Mar Martin, Clk   Thomas X Deal, his mark
                                         John X Deal, his mark

                      Friday 2nd March 1798   [235]

Jacob Williams }
    vs   } Slander
James Miller }

Plaintiff's Witness, Lloyd Kelley, Thos Saterwhite, Mark Gander, Paul Williams, John Williams, Robert Flournoy

Jury Sworn

1. Isaac Hall
2. William Buckner
3. John Spier
4. Anderson Harwell
5. Thomas Wynn
6. Richard Fretwell
7. John Stembridge
8. Robert Bonner
9. Benjamin Parker
10. Jesse McK. Pope
11. John Wallace
12. Thomas Paramour

Verdict. We, the Jury, find for the Plaintiff fifty dollars, with cost.

Jesse McKinney Pope, foreman

Appeal Entered, Josiah Dennis, Sec^y.

The Grand Jury returned the following Bills.

The State }
   vs   } Indictment Misdemeanor
William Waller }

A true Bill.   Chas Abercrombie, foreman

The State }
   vs   } Indictment for Larceny
John Pruitt, Junr }
Charles Pruitt }
James Pruitt }

A true Bill.   Chas Abercrombie, foreman

Friday 2nd March 1798

The State }
   vs   } Assault
Jacob Williams }

A true Bill.   Chas Abercrombie, foreman

The State }
    vs   } Assault
Paul Williams }

A true Bill.   Chas Abercrombie, foreman

Matthew Durham excused from service as a Petit Juror on account of indisposition.

Jacob Williams }
    vs   } Assault
James Miller }

Plaintiff's Winesses, Thomas Mason, Saml Pope, Gabriel Hubert p^d

Jury Sworn

1. Francis Moreland   7. Saml Pope
2. Britain Rogers   8. Nathl Waller
3. John Humphries   9. Willis Whatley
4. William Harper   10. William Brown
5. Peter Grammer   11. John Grammer
6. John Dennis   12. Zorobabel Williamson

Verdict. We, the Jurors, find for the plaintiff twenty five cents and cost of suit.

                                            Nathaniel Waller, foreman

Exon iss^d the 28th March 1798.

Friday 2nd March 1798   [237]

Handy Waller }
    vs   } Covenant
Abraham Smith }

Dismissed by the plaintiff's counsel.

The Grand Jury returned the following bill.

The State }
    vs   } Indictment Perjury
Robert Day }

A true Bill.   Cha[s] Abercrombie, foreman

William Smith }
    vs   } Case
Daniel Whatley }

Non-Suit.

William Glass }
    vs   } debt
William McKenzie }

dismissed.

Jordan Bonner }
    vs   } Case
Benjamin Gilbert }

The same Jury as in the Case of Jacob Williams vs James Miller for Slander.

Verdict. We, the Jury, find for the plaintiff two hundred & two dollars & fifty Cents [illegible]

                                    Jesse Quinae Pope, foreman

                Friday 2nd March 1798   [238]

James B. Oliver }
    vs   } Exon
James Shorter }

Ordered, that the Sheriff show cause on Monday morning nine o'Clock (if any he has) why the money by him collected on the above Execution be not paid to the Executors of William Minor, deceased.

The State   }
    vs   } Indict Assault
Paul Williams }

Noli prosequi.   Sol Genl paid

The State   }
    vs   } Indictmt Assault
Jacob Williams }

Noli prosequi.   Sol Genl paid

Peter B. Terrill, for the }
use of Edward Stevens }
    vs   } Case
John Reid   }

Jury Sworn

    Nathl Waller   Willis Whatley
    Thomas Wilcoxon   John Grammer
    Francis Moreland   Zorobabel Williamson
    William Harper   William Hurt
    Peter Grammer   Alexander Dunn
    John Dennis   Jecamiah Moore

Verdict. We, the Jury, find for the plaintiff four hundred Dollars, with cost of suit.

                                    Nathl Waller, foreman

Exon issd 28th March 1798.

The Court then adjourned till to morrow morning 9 O'Clock.

                                      Thos P. Carnes

Saturday 3rd March 1798

Court met according to adjournment. Present, his Honor Judge Carnes.

Samuel Givins }
    vs   } Case
Joseph Patterson }

Def[ts] Witness, Joshua Miller, Nath[l] Waller

Plff[s] Witnesses, Manning Bolling, P. L. V. Alen

Jury Sworn

1. Isaac Hall
2. William Buckner
3. John Spears
4. Anderson Harwell
5. Thomas Wynne
6. Richard Fretwell
7. John Stembridge
8. John Buckner
9. Ben[j] Parker
10. Jesse McK. Pope
11. John Wallace
12. Tho[s] Paramour

Verdict. We, the Jury, find for the plaintiff ninety dollars, interest included.

                              Jesse McKinney Pope, Foreman

Appeal entered, Nath[l] Waller, Sec[y].

George Goodright, ex dem }
William Triplett, agent   }
of William Washington   }
    vs   } Ejectment
Richard Noright &   }
John & Philip Cook   }

Continued until Monday next.

Matthias Maher & C[o] }
    vs   } Case
John E. Scott &   }
Mary S. Scott   }

Jury Sworn

1. Francis Moreland
2. William Harper
7. John Grammer
8. Zorobabel Williamson

3. Peter Grammer	9. Isham Reid
4. John Dennis	10. Richd Lockhart
5. Nathl Waller	11. Manning Bolling
6. Willis Whatley	12. Mark Saunders

Verdict. We, the Jury, find for the plaintiff one hundred sixty six dollars & twenty five cents, including interest & cost of suit.

Nathl Waller, foreman

Appeal Entered, Thos Scott, Sec^y.

Saturday 3rd March 1798 [240]

Matthias Maher & Co }
     vs   } Case
Robert Flournoy }

The same Jury as in the Case of Maher & Co vs Jno & Mary Scott. Verdict. We, the Jury, find for the plaintiff three hundred & seventy eight dollars, including interest and cost of suit.

Nathl Waller, foreman

The 8th March 1798 Rec^d of the def^t seventy eight dollars & Rec^d from George Walker, Att^y for Plff, for three hundred dollars, in full of this Verdict.

Satisfied.   Mar Martin, Clk

Jordan Bonner }
     vs   } Case
John McKenzie }

The defendant came into Court with Robert McGinty, who entered himself special bail on this condition, that if the defendant shall be cast in this Action, he will pay the condemnation money, or render himself in discharge thereof, or I (Robert McGinty) will do it for him. Taken & acknowledged in Open Court.

Before Mar Martin, Clk   Jno McKenzie
                                                            Robt McGinty

The Court adjourned till monday morning 9 O'Clock.

Thos P. Carnes

Monday the 5th March 1798   [241]

Court met according to adjournment. Present, his Honor Judge Carnes.

William Lawson, jun^r }
    vs   } Case
Thomas Cooper, et al }
Exo^{rs} of Thomas Cooper, dec^d }

Plff^s Witnesses, John Shackelford, Stephen Daniell

Defend^{ts} Witnesses, Edmund Butler, Senr, Henry Graybill, Esqr, Henry Long

Jury Sworn

1. Isaac Hall   7. Ben^j Parker
2. William Buckner   8. Jesse McK. Pope
3. Anderson Harwell   9. Thos Paramour
4. Thomas Wynne   10. James Yarborough
5. Richard Fretwell   11. John Buckner
6. John Stembridge   12. John Dennis

Verdict. We, the Jury, find for the Defendant.

Jesse McKinne Pope, foreman

The State }
    vs   } Indictment Larceny
Samuel Hunter }

A true Bill.   Chas Abercrombie, foreman

Monday the 5th March 1798   [242]

Robert Montgomery, App^l }
    vs   } debt
The Adm^{rs} of Hamilton, Respd^t }

Appeal withdrawn & Original Verdict confirmed.

Elisha Whatley, Appell^t }
   vs   } Case
William Barksdale, Resp^t }

Settled & cost paid, plff^s Att^y present.

Philip Spiller }
  vs } Case
Robert McGinty }

Plaintiff's Witnesses, Ja^s Fail, Mrs Lucy Pruitt

      Jury Sworn

  1. Robert Bonner   7. Wm Gilleland
  2. Fra^s Moreland   8. Laurence Smith
  3. John Spear   9. John Kelly
  4. Michael Gilbert   10. Robt Chambers
  5. Hugh Hall   11. Wm Maddox
  6. Wm Yarborough 12. Henry Townsend

Verdict. We, the Jurors, find for plaintiff two hundred dollars, with cost of suit.

           Hugh Hall, foreman

Appeal entered, Joel McClendon, Sec^y.

John Spear, one of the original pannel of the Petit Jury, excused from further service at this term on account of the indisposition of his family.

      Monday 5th March 1798

The State }
  vs } Indictm^t for Larceny
John Gann }

Continued until next Term.

Whereupon, Matthew Rabun, Esqr, Zealous Milstead, Archelous Terrill, Jacob Gore, Bird Terrill, & Henry Moffatt came into Court & acknowledged themselves bound to his Excellency the Governor and his successors in Office in the sum of one hundred dollars each, to be void on condition that they will severally attend at the next Superior Court to be held for the County of Hancock to give testimony in the above case. Taken and acknowledged in open Court.

Before Mar Martin, Clk   Matt^w Rabun
                                           Zealous X Milstead, his mark
                                           Archelous Terrell
                                           Jacob Goar
                                           Byrd Terrell
                                           Henry Moffet

And the defendant John Gann came into Court with Isham Hogan and Joshua Kinney, his security, who acknowledged themselves bound in like manner, the def^t in one hundred & fifty dollars & his securities in seventy five dollars each. Taken & acknowledged as aforesaid.

Before Mar Martin, Clk   John X Gann, his mark
                                             Isham Hogan
                                             Joshua X Kinney, his mark

Monday the 5th March 1798   [244]

John Spencer, Appel^t }
          vs   } Case
Emanuel Wambersie, Resp^t }

The following Special Jury Sworn, viz.

       1. Charles Abercrombie   7. Randolph Rutland
       2. Saml Barron   8. Jonas Shivers
       3. Levi Lancaster   9. Martin Armstrong
       4. Saml Barron, jun^r 10. Reuben Jones
       5. William Pigg   11. Andrew Maddux
       6. Thomas Mitchell   12. Zephaniah John

Verdict. We, the Jury, find for the Respondent thirty eight Dollars & fifty seven Cents, Interest from the 29th October 1785, & cost of suit.

                                                       Chas Abercrombie, Foreman

Sparta 18th Apl 1798 Recd full Satisfaction for this Judgment, Principle & Interest.

J. L. Dixon for P. J. Carnes, Atty

The State }
    vs   } Indict Perjury
Robt Day }

The Defendant came into Court with David Adams & Etheldred Wood, who acknowledged themselves bound to his Excelly the Governor & his successors in Office, the deft in the sum of three hundred dollars & his securities in one hundred & fifty dollars each, to be void on Condition the said Robt Day will make his appearance at the next Superior Court & not depart without leave. Taken & acknowledged in Open Court.

Before Mar Martin, Clk   Robert day
                                      David Adams
                                      Ethd Wood

Monday the 5th March 1798   [245]

Richard Smith, ex dem of }
the Exors of Jas Adams, decd }
        vs   } Ejectment
William Stiles, Tenant in possession }
Edmund Nowles, Senior }

On Motion of the Plaintiff's Attorney, it is Ordered That an accurate survey & view of the Premises in dispute be made by the County Surveyor, or any other person legally authorized by him, and that a true return be made before or at the next Superior Court to be holden for the County of Hancock, first giving ten days notice to the parties who are entitled to attend the said survey or view.

Susanna Moon }
    vs   } Case
Jordan Bonner }

Settled.

Matthias Maher & C⁰ }
    vs   } Case
Joseph Bryan   }

Settled.

James Upright, ex dem }
of Stith Parham   }
    vs   } Ejectment
Abram Lawless &   }
Jesse McKinny Pope Exo^rs }
of John Trippe, Tenants }

Dismissed.

Monday the 5th March 1798   [246]

John Scarlett, Appellant }
    vs   } Case
Stephen Horton, Respd^t }

Settled at appellant's costs.

Joel Dickinson }
    vs   } debt
William Dent & }
Robert Simms   }

Dismissed.

Richard Smith, ex dem }
of John Pinkston   }
    vs   } Ejectment
William Stiles &   }
Richard Bonner, Tenants }

Settled, Says plaintiff's Counsel.

Jordan Bonner }
    vs   } Case
John Kelley   }

In this case, Charles Stewart and Isham Hogan came into Court & entered themselves Special bail on the following condition, viz. that if said John Kelly is cast in the Suit, he will pay the condemnation money, or render himself in discharge, or we (Chas Stewart & Isham Hogan) will do it for him. Taken & acknowledged in Open Court.

Before Mar Martin, Clk   Charles Stewart
                                           Isham Hogan

Adjourned until to morrow 9 O'Clock.

                                                             Thos P. Carnes

Tuesday the 6th March 1798   [247]

The Court met according to adjournment. Present, his Honor Judge Carnes.

Robert Flournoy }
       vs   } debt
Jesse Clements }

I do hereby appear for the defendant & confess Judgment to the plaintiff for one hundred & nine dollars.

                                                       Early, Def^{ts} Att^y

March 23rd 1798 Rec^d the principal & In^t of the above Judgment in full.

                                                       R. Flournoy, Plff

The State   }
      vs   } Indict^t for Inveigling a Negro
James Merony }

The defendant being thrice solemnly called & not appearing & the bail Bolling Cureton and Daniel McDowell being called to produce his body and failing so to do, it is

Ordered, that their Recognizance be Estreated.

Sci fa iss^d 12th day March 1798.

John Denn, ex dem }
of Jeremiah Bonner }
     vs } Ejectment
Richard Fenn, Ten^t in }
possession }
David McAlister }

On Motion, Ordered that James M. Simmons be made Defendant in & of the said McAlister, the Tenant in possession, he having entered into the usual [faint]

               Tuesday the 6th March 1798   [248]

The State }
   vs } Indictm^t Misdemeanor
William Waller }

Noli prosequi. Fees paid.

Richard Smith, ex dem }
of Lesley Coats }
     vs } Ejectment
William Stiles, Ten^t in }
Possession }
Francis Moreland }

On Motion of Augustus Christian George Elholm, of Consel for the defendant, it is Ordered that the County Surveyor be directed to make an accurate survey of the premises contended for by the above parties and return the same to the Clerk's Office of this Court on or before the first day of the next Superior Court, each party having ten days notice previous to Survey.

Joel McClendon, Appell^t }
    vs } Case
Henry Gaither, Resp^t }

Appellant's Witnesses, Saml Slaughter

               Special Jury Sworn

    1. John Bond   7. Thomas Mitchell
    2. Saml Barron   8. Robert Raines

3. Levi Lancaster
4. Saml Barron, jun^r
5. Eppes Brown
6. Batt Wyche

9. Randolph Rutland
10. Jonas Shivers
11. Henry Moffatt
12. Martin Armstrong

Verdict. We, the Jury, find for the Appellant two hundred Dollars, with cost of suit.

Robt Raines, Foreman

Exon issued 28th March 1798.

Tuesday 6th March 1798 [249]

Richard Smith, ex dem }
John Robertson }
    vs } Ejectment
William Stiles, Ten^t in }
possession }
James Huckaby }

On Motion, Ordered that a view & Survey be made of the Lands in dispute between the parties by the County Surveyor, upon the Application of the plaintiff, he giving the defendant ten days notice of the time of making such view & Survey, and that the said Surveyor return the same duly qualified.

The State }
    vs } Indictm^t Assault
Andrew Maddux }

Fees paid & Def^t discharged.

John Denn, ex dem }
of Robert Raines }
    vs } Ejectment
Richard Fenn, Ten^t in }
possession Richd Bonner }

On Motion of A. C. G. Elholm, of counsel for the Plaintiff, it is Ordered that the County Surveyor be directed to make an accurate Survey of the land & premises contended for by the parties, & return the same to the Clerk's Office of this Court on or before the first day of the next Superior Court, each party having ten days notice previous to the Survey.

[faint] 7th May 1798

Tuesday 6th March 1798   [250]

Daniel Whatley, Appel^t }
       vs   } Assumpsit
William Nuoman, Resp^{dt} }

The same Special Jury as in the Case of McClendon, Appell^t vs Gaither, Respondent. By consent of the parties, a Juror was withdrawn & the cause continued until next term.

Aaron Woodward & Co }
       vs   } Attachment
James Shorter   }

In this case, the defendant came into Court with Henry Shorter, who entered himself Special bail on the following Condititions, viz. that is, if the defendant is cast in this Action, he will pay the condemnation money, or render himself in discharge thereof, or I (Henry Shorter) will do it for him. Taken & acknowledges in open Court.

Before Mar Martin, Clk   James Shorter
                                        Henry Shorter

John Torrence   }
       vs   } fi fa Sheriff's Report
John De Yampert }
& James Wood   }

Exon Dismissed on account of illegality.

Tuesday the 6th March 1798   [251]

The State   }
      vs   } Indictment for Larceny
Samuel Hunter }

The said Samuel Hunter appeared in Court and acknowledged himself indebted to his Excellency the Governor and his Successors in Office in the Sum of six hundred dollars and Chas Abercrombie, David Dickson, Benjamin Thompson, David Walker, and John Hunter Walker, his securities, in the sum of One hundred & ~~fifty~~ twenty five dollars each, to be levied on their several & respective goods & Chattels, rights and credits, to be void on Condition that the said Samuel Hunter appear to answer the said Indictment at the next term and not depart without leave of the Court. Taken & acknowledged in Open Court.

before Mar Martin, Clk   Sam Hunter
                                          Chas Abercrombie
                                          David Dickson
                                          Ben^j Thompson
                                          David Walker
                                          John H. Walker

Whereupon, James Thweatt, Duke Hamilton, Isham Rees, & Williamson C. Rees Came into Court & ack^d themselves bound to his Excellency the Governor, for the time being, and his Successors in Office each in the Sum of one hundred dollars, to appear at the next Term of the Superior Court to prosecute the said Saml Hunter and not depart without leave. acknowledged in open Court before Mar Martin, Clk

[blank]

Tuesday the 6th March 1798   [252]

The State   }
     vs   } Indictment for Larceny
John Pruett }
Charles Pruett }
James Pruett }

The said John Pruett, Charles Pruett, & James Pruett appeared in Court and acknowledged themselves indebted to his Excellency the Governor and his Successors in Office in the sum of Six hundred dollars, & Hardy Smith Jacob Pruett, his securities, in the sum of three hundred each, to be levied on their serveral and respective properties, good & Chattels, rights and Credits, to be void on Condition that the said John Pruett, Charles Pruett, & James Pruett appear to answer the said Indictment at the next Term & not depart without leave of the Court. Taken & acknowledged in open Court.

Before B. Hall for Mar Martin, Clk   John X Pruett, his mark
                                           Charles 8ᵖ Pruett, his mark
                                           James X Pruett, his mark
                                           Hardy X Smith, his mark
                                           Jacob Q Pruett, his mark

Moses Lloyd   }
      vs   } Cas
Henry Butler &}
Henry Garrett }

Settled.

Tuesday the 6th March 1798   [253]

Robert Watkins }
      vs   } Case
James Shorter }

In this Case, the Defendant came into court with Henry Shorter, his Special bail, who acknowledged themselves bound to the plaintiff in the sum of three hundred and twenty eight dollars, on this Condition, that if the def^t is cast in this Action, he will pay the condemnation money, or render himself in discharge thereof, or I (Henry Shorter) will do it for him. Taken & acknowledged in open Court.

Before Mar Martin, Clk   James Shorter
                                Henry Shorter

John Jack   }
    vs   } Case
James Shorter }

In this Case, the defendant came forward with the same bail, who acknowledged themselves bound to the plff upon the above condititions. Taken and acknowledged in open Court as above.

Before Mar Martin, Clk   James Shorter
                                Henry Shorter

John Denn, ex dem }
of Thomas Atkinson }
    vs } Ejectment
William Fenn, Ten^t in }
possession John Booth }

On Motion of Mr Van Alen, Ordered that John Booth, Senr be made Defendant with John Booth, Tenant in possession, he having entered into the common rules.

            Tuesday the 6th March 1798   [254]

Abraham Upright, ex dem }
of Robert Middleton }
    vs } Ejectment
James Lawless, Ten^t in }
possession James Golightly }

On Motion of Augustus C. George Elholm, of council for the defendant, it is Ordered that the County Surveyor be directed to make an accurate survey of the land and premises contended for by the above parties and return the same to the Clerk's Office of this Court on or before the first day of the next Superior Court, each party having ten days notice previous to the Survey.

James Hogg, Senr, Appel^t }
    vs } Slander
William Yarborough, Resp^t }

Settled.

The Grand Jury returned their presentments which were as follows, viz.

Georgia }
Hancock County } We, the Grand Jurors for the County aforesaid, upon our Oaths, present as a grievance of no small magnitude that no particular attention known to us has been paid by our Senators and Representatives in General Government to a Remonstrance of the Legislature of this State of the year one thousand Seven hundred and ninety Seven, which Remonstrance appears

Tuesday the 6th March 1798 [255]

appears not only to contain, but fully exhibit, the mind of the people respecting a cession of lands Southwest of the Oconee River. We sincerely regret that, notwithstanding the State of Georgia was among the first that gave birth to the Federal Government, she would be so uniformly & deliberately neglected, while her youngest neighboring Sister has all her complaints officially and constitutionally heard and her wrongs speedily redressed, in consequence of the patriotism and zealous exertions of her Representatives in Congress.

We present Elizabeth Greer, Senr & Mary Gann for false swearing.

We present it as a grievance that the public roads in this County are not kept in good repair.

Lastly, we present our thanks to his Honor Judge Carnes for his judicious charge to us at the opening Session, & recommend that it, with our presentments, be published in the next Gazette.

Chas Abercrombie, foreman
Samuel Barron
Levi Lancaster
John Hamilton
Samuel Barron, jun^r
William Pigg
Eppes Brown
Ba^t Wyche
Thos Mitchell
Robt Raines

Randolph Rutland
Jonas Shivers
Henry Moffatt
Martin Armstrong
Reuben Jones
Joel McClendon
Littleton Rees
Andrew Maddux
John Bond

Tuesday the 6th March 1798 [256]

The following persons were drawn, empannelled, Summoned, and returned to serve as Petit Jurors at this term, not attending in obedience to the authority of Law, are fined in the sum of ten dollars each, unless they and each of them shall shew good & sufficient cause of excuse, agreeably to Law. the names of the aforesaid defaulting Jurors are as follows, George Brewer, John Coleman, Joseph Cooper, Senr, Benjn Jones, Robert Finch, John K. Candler, James Cowdon, and Thomas Trammill.

John Spear, one of the Petit Jurors, who absented himself without leave during the sitting of this Court, is fined five dollars, unless he shall excuse himself as the Law directs.

ors 29th Octr 98 Exons iss^d for this.

It is further ordered, that a transcript of the foregoing be posted up at the door of the Court house and at three or more of the most public places within the County.

After the Judge had returned the Grand and Petit Jurors his thanks for their faithful attendance and discharge of their duty, they were dismissed from further service at this term.

The following persons were drawn to serve as Grand Jurors for next term, viz. [257]

1. Thomas Wilcoxon
2. Martin Armstrong
3. Robt Buchannan
4. Zephaniah Harvey
5. Matthew Rabun
6. Saml McGehee
7. James Greene
8. Joel Reese
9. Abraham Myles
10. John Veazey
11. Elijah Freeneau
12. Thos Mercer
13. Jesse Grigg
14. Francis Ross
15. Samuel Johnson
16. Richd Shipp
17. Mark Saunders
18. Stephen Horton
19. James Thweatt
20. Henry Moffatt
21. James Reese
22. James Lucas
23. Abner Atkinson
24. Richard Lockhart
25. Jesse Sanford
26. Wyatt Collier
27. Joshua L. Acee
28. John Taliaferro
29. Jerard Burch
30. Thomas Lamar

Petit Jurors

1. Thomas Moore
2. James Askey
3. Joel Dickinson
4. David Kelly
5. Robt Knight
6. Th^o Kilbee
9. Ben^j Trice
10. Salathiel Culver
11. James Kerr
12. Chas McKay
13. Levi Daniel
14. Jesse Harwood

7. George Evans
8. Willie Burge
15. William Rigby
16. Saml Weeks

Petit Jurors Continued [258]

17. J. Lary
18. Danl Conner
19. Richd Harwell
20. Nathan Saunders
21. Th^o Lancaster
22. James Cathell
23. Hardy Jernigan
24. Fred^k G. Thomas
25. Robt Gray
26. John C. Armstrong
27. Aaron Boron
28. William Clark
29. Michael Peavy
30. William Grimmer
31. B. Rachels
32. Matt Walker
33. William Butler
34. John Bazer
35. Allen Rogers
36. Joel Buckner
37. James Naylor
38. Thomas Chappell
39. John Butts
40. Nathan Breedlove
41. D. Jackson
42. William Evans
43. William Weeks
44. Abr^m Hilton
45. John Wilson
46. John Freeneau
47. William Wright
48. James Youngblood
49. John Pardue
50. James Works
51. Saml Noble
52. Abr^m Myles, jun^r
53. Saml Hart
54. Moses Robertson
55. John Cobb
56. Ject Hall
57. William Barnes
58. Th^s Bradford
59. P. Gay
60. John Stanbanks

The Court then adjourned until Court in Course.

Thos P. Carnes

Georgia Hancock Superior Court September First 1798 [259]

At a Sup^r Court began and held in and for the County & State aforesaid, Pursuant to adjournment at last Court. Present, his Honor Judge Mitchell.

His Honor the Judge's Commission being produced and read.

The following persons appeared and were sworn of the Grand Jury, Viz.

1. Matt Rabun, foreman	11. James Reese
2. Zephaniah Harvey	12. Abner Atkinson
3. Samuel McGehee	13. Richard Lockhart
4. James Greene	14. Wyatt Collier
5. Joel Reese	15. Joshua L. Acee
6. John Veasey	16. Jerard Burch
7. Jesse Grigg	17. Thomas Wilcoxen
8. Francis Ross	18. Thomas Mercer
9. Samuel Johnson	19. Elijah Freeney
10. Mark Saunders	

Thomas Bradford, one of the original pannel of the Petit Jury, excused from service on account of his age, he being over sixty years.

A petition was presented by Thaddeus Holt praying to be admitted a practititioner of Law on the common principles of admission.

Saturday 1st September 1798 [260]

Whereupon, Ordered that Mr Griffin, Mr Early, & Mr Skrine be a committee to examine the petitioner and report to the Court.

Court adjourned till Monday morning 9 o'Clock.

D. B. Mitchell

Monday 3rd September 1798 Court met according to adjournment. Present, his Honor Judge Mitchell.

Richard Ship, Martin Armstrong, Henry Moffat, Stephen Horton, & Thomas Lamar, being of the original pannel of the Grand Jury, attended and were sworn. Samuel Johnson, having been sworn on the Grand Jury, is excused from further service during this term.

The Venire of the Petit Jury being called, the following persons attended and were empanneled and sworn, viz.

Jury N° (1)

1. Joel Dickinson
2. George Evans
3. Levi Daniell
4. Nathan Saunders
5. Hardy Jernigan
6. William Clark
7. William Grimmer
8. Joel Buckner
9. Thomas Chappel
10. William Evans
11. James Works
12. William Barnes

Monday 3rd September 1798 [261]

John Willson, Adm^r }
of Patrick Hays }
    vs } Casse
Henry Jernigan }

Non Suit.

William F. Booker }
    vs } Spec^l Case
Robert Flournoy }

William F. Booker }
    vs } Case
Robert Flournoy }

Plaintiff's Witnesses sworn. Thaddeus Holt 15 days. Wm Brown by T. Holt in open court. Rec^d my fees. Thad^s Holt.

Jury N° (1) sworn and the above Cases Consolidated by consent of parties.

Verdict. We, the Jury, find for the plaintiff Sixty eight thousand five hundred and Seventy One dollars and forty three Cents.

                          James Works, foreman

Henry Parish }
    vs   } Case
Moses Harris }

Settled.

Jury N° (2) Sworn, to wit.

1. Salathel Culver
2. John C. Armstrong
3. Drury Jackson
4. Obadiah Richardson
5. Edmond Abercrombie
6. Jecamiah Moore
7. Noah Dodridge
8. James Hogg, jn^r
9. Michael Gilbert
10. James Willson
11. William Bivins
12. Thomas Moore

Monday 3rd September 1798   [262]

Henry Gaither }
    vs   } assumpsit
William Minor & }
John Minor, Exo^{rs} }
of William Minor, dec^d }

Plaintiff's Witness, Jn° McClendon

Jury N° (2) Sworn.

Verdict. We, the Jury, find for the plaintiff twenty seven dollars and fifty two cents, with cost of Suit.

                                             Obadiah Richardson, foreman

Paid Attorney.

3rd Novr 1796 paid the principal & to P. L. V. Alen, Esqr.

Philip Howell }
    vs   } Trover
Sherwood Wamack }
& Mancel Wamack }
Exo^{rs} of Abraham Wamack, dec^d }

Jury Nº (1)

~~Verdict~~.

Non Suit.

The Grand Jury returned the following Bills.

The State }
   vs   } Indictm^t Assault
Thomas King }

True Bill.   Matt Rabun, foreman

The State }
   vs   } Indictm^t Assault
Thomas King }

True Bill.   Matt Rabun, foreman

The State }
   vs   } Indictm^t Assault
George Strother }

True Bill.   Matt Rabun, foreman

Monday 3rd September 1798   [263]

The State }
   vs   } Indictm^t Assault
George Strother }

No Bill.   Matt Rabun, foreman

The State }
   vs   } Indictm^t Forgery
James Shorter }

True Bill.   Matt Rabun, foreman

Richard Smith, ex dem }
John Robertson }
    vs } Ejectment
William Stiles, Ten.^t in }
possession James Huckaby }

Jury N.º 1 Sworn.

Non Suit!

James Harvey, Henry Graybill

Turner Hunt & Anderson Harwell were sworn in the place of William Bivins & James Willson on Jury N.º (1).

Ordered, That William Bivins & James Willson, defaulting Jurors, be fined in the sum of one dollar each for non attendance.

                Monday 3.rd September 1798   [264]

John Robertson }
    vs } Case
James Huckaby }

Continued.

Isaac Daniel }
    vs } Debt
Robert Montgomery }

Settled.

Cou

Joshua L. Acee, one of the original pannel of the Grand Jury, excused from further service at this Term.

Court adjourned until tomorrow 9 O'Clock.

                              D. B. Mitchell

Tuesday 4th September 1798 [265]

Court met according to Adjournment. Present, his Honor Judge Mitchell.

John Denn, ex dem }
O. Richardson }
  vs } Ejectment
Richard Fenn }
Thomas Breedlove }

~~Non Suit.~~

Upon Motion of M{}^r Griffin, Att{}^y, it is ordered that Mary Breedlove be Made defendant upon the usual Rule.

Harris Coleman, Exo{}^r et al }
  vs } Case in Deceit
David Dickson }
Thomas Gorden and }
Benjamin Gorden }

Non Suit.

Witness for the Plff, Hezekiah Kindrick 5 days [blot]

    Jury Sworn N° (3)

1. Joel Dickinson 7. William Grimmer
2. George Evans 8. Drury Jackson
3. Levi Daniel 9. John C. Armstrong
4. Nathan Saunders 10. William Evans
5. Hardy Jernigan 11. James Works
6. William Clark 12. William Barnes

William Bivins, a defaulting Juror, who was yesterday fined for non attendance, on rendering an excuse, was exonerated by the Court.

Tuesday 4th September 1798 [266]

Abraham Lawrence }
    vs } Case
John Swepson & }
Peter Coffee }

Defendant's Witness, Samuel Alexander

Jury N° (3)

Verdict. We, the Jury, find for the Plaintiff eight hundred and ninety one dollars & seventy cents.

                              Ja^s Works, foreman

Appeal entered.

John Denn, ex dem }
Turner Hunt }
    vs } Eject
Richard Fenn }
Tenant in possession }
David Jackson }

Settled at Mutual Cost.

Christian Trutten Exo^r }
of John A. Treutten }
    vs } Debt
John & Aaron McKenzie }
adm^{rs} of Philip Howell }

Dismissed.

State tax	$1.50
Att^y	4.00
Shff	1.50
Clk	3.00
	$10.00

196

Exon iss^d 29th Octr 1798.

Thomas H. Langham }
Adm^r of Tobias McClure }
    vs } Case
James Wood }

I confess Judgment to the Plaintiff for the Sum of forty dollars eighty nine & three fourths cents, with a deduction of an half the above costs.

S. M. Goode   James Wood

            Tuesday 4th September 1798   [267]

Middleton Pool }
    vs } Cov^t
Jonathan Miller }

Plaintiff's Witnesses, Benjn Evans

                 Jury Sworn

    1. Thomas Chappell   7. Edmund Corley
    2. Joel Buckner   8. Noah Dodridge
    3. Willie Burge   9. James Hogg, jn^r
    4. Salathiel Culver   10. Michael Gilbert
    5. Thomas Moore   11. James Wilson
    6. Jesse Q. Pope   12. William Bivins

Verdict. We, the Jury, find for the Defendant.

                      Edm^d Corley, foreman

Abraham Lawrence }
    vs } Case
John Swepson & }
Peter Coffee }

[The clerk crossed out an entire paragraph, rendering it illegible.]

This was an appeal entered by the Clk & agreed by order of the presiding Judge.

Tuesday 4th September 1798 [268]

The State }
    vs }
Dennis McCue }

The prisoner, having been yesterday apprehended and commited to prison on Suspicion of having been concerned in burning the Spanish Vessel in the River Savannah on the fourth last month, is now brought up for further examination, and the affidavits upon which he was apprehended & committed being before the Court and duly considered, and upon the Strictest examination of the prisoner, the Court is of opinion that the fact with which he stands charged does not appear sufficiently clear to warrant his detention. He is therefore discharged.

                        D. B. Mitchell

Court adjourned untill tomorrow morning nine O'Clock.

                Wednesday 5th September 1798

Court met according to adjournment. Present, his Honor Judge Mitchell.

Nathaniel Waller }
    vs   } Case
James Scarlett }

Plff[s] Witness, p[d] Willis Whatley 8 days proven P, p[d] Nath[l] Waller 7 days att[ce] proven paid, Duke Hamilton

def[ts] Witness, John Ragan, John Marbert

                    Jury Sworn

1. Joel Dickinson	7. John C. Armstrong
2. George Evans	8. William Evans
3. Nathan Sanders	9. William Barnes
4. Hardy Jernigan	10. Willie Burge
5. William Clark	11. Joel Buckner
6. William Grimmer	12. Thomas Moore

Verdict. We, the Jury, do find for the plaintiff three hundred and seventeen dollars & fourteen and a quarter cents.

       William Evans, foreman

Appeal entered, Ab^m Borland, Sec^y.

    Wednesday 5th Septr 1798   [269]

John Price   }
 vs   } Case
Robert Chambers & }
John Jones, Exo^rs of the }
last Will & Testament of }
Meredith Price, deceased }

By consent of the parties, it is agreed that all matters relative to the above suit be referred to the award & determination of Jesse Pope, Jesse McKinney Pope, Hugh Horton, Jonas Shivers, & Joel McClendon, their award to be returned at this term & made the Judgment of Court.

The Grand Jury returned the following bills, to wit.

The State }
 vs   } Indc^t Misdemeanor
David Clements }

True Bill.   Matt Rabun, Foreman

The State }
 vs   } Indc^t Libell
Robert Day }

No Bill.   Matt Rabun, foreman

The State }
 vs   } Indc^t Larceny
David Tidd }

True Bill.   Matt Rabun, foreman

The State }
    vs   } Indc^t Selling liquor without licence
John Telmund }

No Bill.   Matt Rabun, foreman

Wednesday 5th Septr 1798   [270]

Joshua L. Acee }
    vs   } Case
Jesse Thompson, Exo^r }
of Ben^j Thompson, dec^d }
& Joseph Thompson }

By consent of parties in this Case, it is Ordered that the subject matter in dispute be referred to the arbitrament of Henry Graybill, Jesse Bunkley, James Lucas, & Ransom Harwell, whose award, or the award of a majority of them, shall be returned to the next Superior Court Court & made the Judgment thereof.

John Denn, ex dem }
of Samuel Hart }
    vs   } Ejec^t
Richard Fenn, ten^t in }
possession John Baits }

It is agreed by the above parties to the suit, that all matters in dispute shall be left to the reference of John Rogers, Ben^j Whitfield, James Alford, Peter Coffee, & Jesse Battle, whose award shall be made the Judgement of the court, provided the same be returned to the Clerk's Office on or before the first day of the next Term.

The State }
    vs   } Indic^t for Larceny
John Pruett, jn^r }
Charles Pruett }
James Pruett }

Witness for the State, Clement Mullins, George Gray prov^d 6 days att^{ce} in Op Ct p^d, Malone Mullins in Court to Gray

Def^{ts} Witnesses, James Davis

Jury

1. Salathiel Culver
2. Drury Jackson
3. Thomas Chappel
4. James Works
5. Jesse Thompson
6. Joseph Cooper
7. James Askey
8. Thomas Lancaster
9. Henry Townsend
10. William Thornton
11. Edmond Corley
12. James Thomas

Verdict. We, the Jury, find the prisoners guilty.

James Works, foreman

Wednesday 5th September 1798 [271]

John Shackleford }
    vs   } Case
Ezekiel Smith }

Witness for plff, Robert Abercrombie, Reuben Jones proves 3 days Op Ct paid, Matt Rabun

Def^{ts} Witnesses, Henry Moffatt, Aaron Smith

Jury Sworn, the same as in the case of Waller vs James Scarlett.

Verdict. We, the Jurors, do find for the plaintiff One hundred and twelve dollars & twenty five Cents.

Appeal enetered.   William Evans, foreman

27th Feby 1800 Rec^d the Am^t of principal & In^t on the above Verdict.

Test. John Adams   John Shackelford

John Price }
    vs   } Case
Robert Chambers & }
John Jones, Exo^{rs} of }
the last Will & Testam^t }
Meredith Price, dec^d }

We, the Arbitrators, mutually chosen by the parties to decide on the subject of the above Suit, do award that the Exo^{rs} Robt Chambers and John Jones pay unto the Plaintiff three hundred & forty six dollars forty seven & a quarter cents.

Satisfied   Joel McClendon
                                    Jesse Pope
                                    Jesse McKinney Pope
                                    Hugh Horton
                                    Jonas Shivers

Satisfied as p^r R^t in process & Clk's Office of the Court of Ordinary.

Whereupon, On motion of Mr Griffin, Att^y for plff, & the Def^{ts} not gainsaying, it is Ordered that the above award be made the Judgment of the Court.

Wednesday 5th Septr 1798   [272]

John Denn, ex dem }
of Thomas Atkinson }
         vs   } Ejec^t
William Fenn, tenant in }
possession John Booth }

On Motion of Mr Walker, Council for the plaintiff. Ordered, that a Survey be made of the Land in dispute between the parties by the County Surveyor, & that he make Special report to the next Court, with a platt designating the boundaries & the manner in which the Lands interfere, the said Surveyor giving the parties ten days notice of the time of making Such Survey.

issued.

George Evans, one of the original Pannel of the Petit Jury, excused from further service during this Term.

Abraham Upright, ex dem }
of Robert Middleton   }
         vs   } Ejectment
James Lawless   }
Tenant in possession   }
James Golightly   }

Dismissed.

Court adjourned until to morrow morning 9 o'Clock.

D. B. Mitchell

Thursday 6th September 1798

The Court met according to adjournment, present his Honor Judge Mitchell.

William Minor, Appl* }
     vs   } Case
Henry Gaither   }

Appeal withdrawn and the original verdict Confirmed.

Jesse Sanford, one of the original Pannel of the Grand Jury, attended & was excused from service at this term on account of indisposition.

The State   }
    vs   } Grand Larceny
John, Charles, & }
James Pruitt   }

The prisoners, John Pruett, jn^r, Charles Pruett, and James Pruett, having been found guilty of Grand Larceny during the present Term, were again brought to the Bar, When it was moved by Mr Solicitor Genl, that they severally receive the Sentence which the Law affixes to the crime of which they have been found guilty. Whereupon, it being demanded of them severally, whether they had anything to say, wherefore sentence of death should not now be pronounced against them, they each of them severally claim the benefit of Clergy. It is therefore Considered by the Court, that they, the said John Pruett, jn^r, Charles Pruett, and James Pruett, be each and every of them, severally and immediately, in the presence of and at the Bar of the Court, Burnt in the Brawn of the left thumb with a hot iron, & then be discharged on payment of Costs.

Thursday 6th September 1798

William Henson, Appl^t }
     vs   } Case
John Robertson, Resp^t }

Appl^ts Witness, Joseph Cooper proves 4 days, James Christopher proves 33 days attendance & 200 Miles riding in this case pro app^l.

Special Jury Sworn, to wit

1. Matt Rabun
2. Zephaniah Harvey
3. Samuel McGehee
4. James Greene
5. John Veasey
6. Jesse Grigg
7. Mark Saunders
8. James Rees
9. Abner Atkinson
10. Richard Lockhart
11. Wyatt Collier
12. Jarerd Burch

Verdict. We, the Jury, find for the appellant the sum of twenty seven dollars eighty five cents & Costs.

Matt Rabun, foreman

Ca Sa issued 4th Octr 1798.

The State }
    vs   } Indic^t for Horse Stealing
John Gann }

State's Witness, Bird Terrel, Archelous Terrel, Zealous Milstead, Jacob Gore, Joseph Burges, James Turner, Nathan Culver

Rec^d com fee 25 Ct^s paid to Jno Whitehurst.

Defendant's Witnesses, Richard Ship, jun^r, Mary Gann, Elizabeth Grier, Jesse Ellis, Philip Allen

Jury Sworn, Viz.

1. James Askey
2. Joel Dickinson
3. Salathiel Culver
4. Joel Buckner
5. Thomas Chappell
6. Drury Jackson
7. William Evans
8. Hardy Jernigan
9. William Barnes
10. Thomas Johnson
11. Joseph Cooper
12. Michael Gilbert

Verdict. We, the Jury, find the prisoner not guilty.

          Jo^s Cooper, Foreman

Court adjourned until to morrow morning 9 o'Clock.

          D. B. Mitchell

    Friday the 7th Spetember 1798   [275]

Court met according to adjournment. Present his Honor Judge Mitchell.

Stephen Horton, Appl^t }
  vs   } Case
James Martin, Respd^t }

Appeal withdrawn and original Judgement Confirmed.

Sparta 7th Septr 1798 Rec^d full satisfaction of the above Judgment & a Rec^t given by Clk to Appel^t.

        J. Minor, Exo^r Wm Minor

Daniel Whatley, Appl^t }
  vs   } Assumpsit
William Nuoman, Respd^t }

Appeal withdrawn & original verdict confirmed.

Exon iss^d 24th Octr 1798.

Isham Hogan, Appl^t }
  vs   } Case
Benjamin Thompson, Respd^t }

Appl^{ts} Witnesses, Charles Abercrombie, John Dennis, 3 days att^{ce} Proven by Dennis

      Spec^l Jury Sworn

  1. Zephaniah Harvey   7. Thomas Lamar
  2. Samuel McGehee   8. Stephen Horton

3. James Greene
4. John Veazey
5. Jesse Grigg
6. Mark Saunders
9. Wyatt Collier
10. Elijah Freeney
11. Martin Armstrong
12. James Reese

Verdict. We, the Jury, do find for the Respondent the Sum of seventy three dollars and forty Seven Cents & costs of suit.

James W. Greene, forman

Ca Sas iss^d 10th Decr 1798.

Friday 7th Spetember 1798 [276]

Charles McDonald, Appl^t }
vs } Case
Charles Abercrombie & }
James Scarlett, Respd^{ts} }

Appeal withdrawn by consent of parties and Original Verdict confirmed.

Exon iss^d 16th July 1799.

Richard Smith, ex dem of }
the Exo^{rs} of James Adams }
vs } Ejectment
William Stiles, tenant in }
possession Edmond Knowles }

Upon Motion of Mr Griffin. It is Ordered, That Solomon Jaxon be made defendant in this case upon the usual Rule.

Jury Sworn

1. Thomas Moore
2. Willie Burge
3. Drury Jackson
4. Salathiel Culver
5. Thomas Chappel
6. Joel Buckner
7. Nathan Saunders
8. William Barnes
9. Joel Dickinson
10. William Grimmer
11. William Evans
12. William Clark

By consent of parties, a Juror withdrawn and the Case continued.

Richard Smith, ex dem }
of Lesley Coats }
     vs } Ejectment
William Stiles, Tenant in }
possession Francis Moreland }

Settled by information of the Clerk.

                Friday 7th Spetember 1798   [277]

The State }
     vs } Indict[t] assault
Thomas King & }
George Strauther }

Continued until next term. Whereupon, The defendants came into Court with Richard Strother and Matthias Dennis, their securities, woh acknowledged themselves bound to his Excellency the Governor and his successors in Office in the sum of twenty five dollars each, to be levied on their respective goods, chattels, lands, and tenements, but to be void on condition that, the said Thomas King and George Strother will make their personal appearance at the next Superior Court for the County of Hancock and not depart without leave. Taken and acknowledged in Open Court this 7th Sept[r] 1798.

Before Mar Martin, Clk   Thomas King
                                            George Strother
                                            Richard Strother
                                            Matthias Dennis

George Herndon, ass[e], Appl[t] }
     vs } case
Daniel Muse & }
John Bond, Respd[ts] }

The same special Jury as in the case of Isham Hagan, Appl[t] vs Thompson, Respd[t].

Verdict. We, the Jury, do find for the Appellant the sum of four hundred and twenty seven dollars & Costs.

James W. Greene, foreman

Exon iss^d the 24th Octr 1798.

Shff's fee on appeal p^d.

Paid.

Friday 7th Spetember 1798 [278]

James Upright, ex dem }
of Stith Parham }
vs } Ejectment
Abraham Lawless, tenant in }
possession Jesse McKiney Pope }

On motion of Mr Anderson, Att^y for plaintiff, Ordered, that the County surveyor, or his deputy, do go upon the demised premises in Company with two or more persons of the neighborhood selected by the parties, and make an accurate admeasurement of the same, marking in a fair Platt the courses, Stations, and interferences, and return the same in person to the next Superior Court to be held in the County aforesaid. A Copy of this Order to be served on the tenant in possession at least ten days before such Survey is made.

issued.

John Denn, ex dem of }
Robert Flournoy, Respd^t }
vs } Ejectment
Richard Fenn, Tenant in }
possession James Evans, Appl^t }

Resp^{ts} Witnesses, Bolling Hall

Appellant's Witnesses, Henry Graybill, Robt Tate, Ben Thompson, Thomas Gordon

This case being called in order for trial and the Action involving in it a Question, in the decision of which Several of the original pannel of the Grand Jury were interested, and it appearing to the Court that after such interested Jurors were withdrawn, there would not be a sufficient pannel out of which to strike a Jury, the Clerk was ordered to produce the Original list. Whereupon, the following Special Jury were empannelled and Sworn, Viz.

1. Thomas Wilcoxon
2. Zephaniah Harvey
3. Saml McGehee
4. James Greene
5. Elijah Freeney
6. Thomas Mercer
7. Jesse Grigg
8. Mark Saunders
9. Henry Moffatt
10. James Reese
11. Wyatt Collier
12. Edmund Abercrombie

who returned the following Verdict. We, the Jury, do find for the Respondent.

James W. Greene, foreman

Friday 7th Spetember 1798 [279]

Thomas McDonald }
    vs   } Sci fa Enquiry
John Pound }

claim withdrawn.

Alexander Guthrie }
    vs   } Sci fa Shff's Report
William A. Burton, et al }

Stopped by Affidavit. Settled.

Joshua Williams }
    vs   } Sci fa enquiry
John Whatley & }
John Pound }

Claim withdrawn.

Jacob Williams }
    vs   } fi fa Sheriff's Report
James Miller }

Stopped on Aff^t of illegality. Exceptions overruled.

19th Sep^t 1798 Satisfied.

Reuben Harrison   }
    vs   } fi fa Sheriff's Report
The Adm^{rs} of John Wooten, dec^d }

Stopped on aff^t of illegality. Execution ordered to proceed for balance.

West Jones }
    vs   } fi fa Shff's Report
Isham Hogan}

Aff^t of illegality. Exon to proceed for Balance due.

Court adjourned until tomorrow morning 9 o'Clock.

                                        D. B. Mitchell

                     Saturday September 8th 1798   [280]

Court met according to adjournment. Present, his Honor Judge Mitchell.

John Burge, ass^{ee} }
of Hartwell Jones }
    vs   } Debt
Richard Bonner }

By consent of parties, Ordered that all matters in controversy between the parties in the above case be referred to the arbitrament and award of Jesse Grigg, Peter Boyle, Myles Greene, John Chappell, and James Thweatt, or any three of them, to meet at Sparta on Saturday week, with a power to Sit on their own adjournment, to decide on all matters between them upon the principles of Equity and justice, their award to be made in writing, returned to the next Court, and made the Judgment thereof.

Richard Bonner
John X Burge, his mark

The State }
    vs   } Indictm^t Assault
Thaddeus Holt }

State's Witnesses, Mary Gann, Elizabeth Grier, Elizabeth Waller, Thomas Lancaster.

Defend^{ts} Witnesses, Wm Rabun, Willie Abercrombie

Jury Sworn

1. Joel Dickinson
2. Nathan Saunders
3. William Clark
4. William Grimmer
5. William Barnes
6. Willie Burge
7. Joel Buckner
8. Drury Jackson
9. Thomas Moore
10. Thomas Chappell
11. James Askey
12. Thomas Lancaster

We, the Jury, have found the defendant guilty of an assault.

William Barnes, foreman

Saturday 8th September 1798   [281]

Hubbard Sykes }
    vs   } Deceit
Isham Hogan }

Death of the plaintiff suggested and the action to proceed in the name of John Comer Peak, the administrator.

The committee to whom was referred the examination of Mr Thaddeus Holt, beg leave to report to the Court that they appointed a time for his examination and that he failed to attend, that he informed the committee this morning that he had made up his mind to withdraw his petition & defer the time of his examination to some future period.

> John Griffin
> Ben^j Skrine
> Peter Early

The Grand Jury returned the following Bills, viz.

The State }
    vs   } Indictment Perjury
William Thompson }

True Bill.   Matt Rabun, foreman

The State }
    vs   } Indictm^t Perjury
Jesse Thompson }

True Bill.   Matt Rabun, fore^n

Saturday the 8th September 1798   [282]

Richard Haddock, Appel^t }
        vs   } Case for Deceit
James Miller, Respondent }

App^{ts} Witnesses, Harmon Runnels

Respond^{ts} Witnesses, Ja^s Miller, jun^r 4 days att^{ce} proven. Paid to Ja^s Miller 28th Sep^t 98.

Special Jury Sworn

1. Matt Rabun   7. James Reese
2. Zephaniah Harvey   8. Abner Atkinson
3. Saml McGehee   9. Richard Lockhart
4. James Greene   10. Wyatt Collier
5. John Veazey   11. Thomas Lamar
6. Jesse Grigg   12. Thomas Mercer

Verdict. We, the Jury, find no cause of Action.

Matt Rabun, foreman

William Turner }
    vs   } fi fa Sheriff's Report
Moses Harris & }
James Turner }

property claimed by Robt Tate.

plff^s Witnesses, John Kirk, John Hansel 4 days 140 Miles p^d, James Stringer, Joseph Thompson

Defendant's Witnesses, Peter Boyle, Esqr, Henry Townsend, Esqr 7 days, Wm Mangham 2 days att^{ce} p^d, [illegible] rec^d of Wood, days att^{ce} proven

Jury Sworn

1. Joel Dickinson
2. Nathan Saunders
3. William Clark
4. William Grimmer
5. William Barnes
6. Willie Burge
7. Joel Buckner
8. Drury Jackson
9. Thomas Moore
10. Thomas Chappell
11. Salathiel Culver
12. Thomas Lancaster

A Juror withdrawn & Exon Satisfied.

Ezekiel Smith, nat^l Guardian & }
nearest friend to John C. Smith }
    vs   } Slander
Robert Day   }

Dismissed.

Saturday the 8th September 1798   [283]

The State }
    vs   } Larceny
David Tidd }

The defendant, David Tidd, being three solemnly called and failing to appear, and his security, Isham Hogan, being likewise three solemnly called and failing to produce his body, it is thereupon ordered that the Recognizance be estreated & Scire facias issue.

The State }
    vs   } Indictm^t Larceny
Samuel Hunter }

Recognizance continued.

Samuel Dent }
    vs   } Case
Jesse Connel }

Settled at Plaintiff's cost.

Stiles, ex dem   }
William Washington   }
    vs   } Ejectment
Thos Fields & Martin Shivly }

Ordered, that a Survey be made in this case by the County Surveyor, attended with any Surveyor who may be choosed by the Plaintiff, upon the Plaintiff giving the adverse parties ten days notice of the time of making such survey. And that he return a plat and report specially as to the land in dispute at the next term.

issued 9th July 1799 when called for.

                    Saturday the 8th September 1798   [284]

The State }
    vs   } Indictment Perjury
Robert Day }

The defendant discharged.

The State   }
    vs   } Scire Facias on an Indictment
Bolling Cureton }

Judgment is hereby entered up against the defendant for one hundred dollars, being the amount of his recognizance estreated last term, as one of the securities of James Maroney, who made default to appear.

Joshua L. Acee }
    vs   } Case
Robert Flournoy }

Settled at Defendant's costs.

Joel McClendon, Appel^t }
    vs   } Scire Facias to Brice Gaither Special Bail
Henry Gaither, Respond^t } for Henry Gaither

Dismissed.

Philip Howell   }
    vs   } Sci Facias
Shearwood & Mancel Womack }
Exo^{rs} of Abraham Womack, Dec^d }

Decided. See Minutes of Monday the 3rd ins^t.

                Saturday the 8th September 1798   [285]

Henry Gaither }
    vs   } Scire Facias
William Minor }

This Sci Fa was issued to John & William Minor, Exo^{rs} of William Minor, deceased, and was decided on Monday last by Gaither's obtaining a Judgment ag^t the def^t Minor. See Minutes of Monday the 3rd ins^t.

Harris & John Spear, Appel^{ts} }
    vs   } Debt
Jonas Shivers, Responent }

Appeal withdrawn by Appellants' Att^y & original Verdict confirmed.

James Hogg, Appellant }
      vs   } Case
Daniel Muse, Resp^t }

Appeal withdrawn by Appellant's Att^y & original Verdict confirmed.

George Cotton }
      vs   } Case
Risdon Moore, jun^r }
& Isaac Vaughan }

Settled at Plaintiff's costs.

Saturday the 8th September 1798   [286]

William Wallace & Co }
      vs   } fi fa Sheriff's Report
William Walker }

Stopped on affidavit of illegality.

In this case, it appeared that a Judgment had been confessed for a certain quantity of Tobacco and that the Execution had issued directing a levy against that Article, upon which the Defendant filed an affidavit of illegality of such a Writ. It is ordered, that an Issue be made up and submitted to a Jury at the next term to ascertain the value of Tobacco.

The State   }
      vs   } Indictment Riot & Assault
Charles Abercrombie, et al}

The defendants in the above case, having at the last term plead "Not guilty" and traversed, come now into Court by Mr Skrine, their Attorney, withdraw their said plea, plead "guilty," and submit to the mercy of the Court, with affidavits of exculpation.

By the affidavits filed, it does appear that a foul Murder was committed and that strong suspicion of guilt fell upon the prosecutor. the Court therefore considers that the said Charles Abercrombie, Willie Abercrombie, Henry Dixon, William Rabun, Jacob Gore, and Thaddeus Holt do each and every of them severally pay a fine of five dollars and costs and then be discharged.

Fine paid 17th Novr 1798 Recd Con 25th.

Saturday the 8th September 1798 [287]

The State }
   vs   } Indictment Assault
Thaddeus Holt }

The defendant, having been convicted of an Assault during the present term, it is considered by the Court that he do pay a fine of two dollars and costs and then be discharged.

Judge Mitchell's charge to the Grand Jury

Gentlemen of the Grand Jury,

The present being the first opportunity I have had of addressing you in a Judicial capacity, it might be expected that I should give you a charge of some length on the nature of your duties as a Grand Jury, but those duties have been so frequently described to you by my predecessors, and you have been, no doubt, so frequently employed in them, that were it not the first circuit after so important an event to the State as the revision and establishment of our Constitution on a permanent basis, I should sup

Saturday the 8th September 1798 [288]

suppose it unnecessary to take up any of your time with my observations, but on this event, so interesting to every Citizen, I beg leave to trespass on your patience, whilst I congratulate you and my fellow citizens at large on its accomplishment. Too many Conventions and too many alterations the result of them have been held and taken place since the Revolution in this State for the Citizens to know what the Constitution really was, and the evils of those changes connected themselves with the Laws and prevented permancy in either. The Scene is now changed, and the mode of alteration is now so happily adopted, that without the most evident necessity joined with Utility in the change combine, no breach can be made in any part of that valuable instrument, and the great whole as it is now established must permanently remain.

I am well aware that local objections cane be made – No Human traits – No Sublunary works were ever perfect, and we have no right to think they ever will be. An Assemblage of Delegates drawn together from different parts of the

Government, from the frailty of human nature, unfortunately for Society, carry with them their local wishes & ideal Interests, of course these wishes and Interests clash, and some local wishes fail. But favor tracing

Saturday the 8th September 1798 [289]

tracing Society, we find this is unavoidable, at the very entrance into which, Man gave up a considerable portion of his natural inherent rights, to secure protection for the remainder. We must copy from our dawn of Society and be content with the great whole. We must give and take, and if the upper country complain of one part, they must consider that their Eastern Brethren complain of other parts.

If we Philosophically, and with good temper however, consider those ideal Interests, they will vanish like a Shadow. The Merchant of the East is supported by the Planter of the West, whilst the planter in return would see the labor of his hands waste and his produce perish, were it not for the Market the Merchant finds to vend it.

It matters little, Gentlemen, from what spot, from what quarter an additional Representative comes, when it is so much the Interest of every part to protect the whole. But supposing the ideal and visionary Interests to exist, there is more to be apprehended from the Eastern part of the community than the Western. The representative member is decidedly with the West and that and the Senatorial also must increase. New Counties cannot be expected from the Sea, and Florida

Saturday the 8th September 1798 [290]

on one hand, and South Carolina on the other, banish every idea of an increase to the East, whilst in the West, in considering the rapid population of the Western Circuit, a few years since a Wilderness, the contemplative mind is lost in astonishment at the immense numbers another half Century must add to their present strength.

I have called the Constitution a valuable Instrument, because many much to be admired additions have been made, and one not of the least respecting Religion. Every man has the privilege of worshipping his God in his own peculiar manner. He is not bound to maintain any Minister without his own consent, and in this happy Land, where the pernicious principles of the opposers of the Christian Religion, or rather of all Religion, have had too little influence to be dwelt on, there is no danger in the latitude which Conscience is allowed.

It is further valuable in having settled down by a fundamental principle the feuds, the convulsions, and disturbances occasioned by the Act of the 7th of January 1797, commonly called the Yazoo Law. I conceive States as well as individuals bound by Moral Contracts, but should the Contract be immoral [faint] of individuals to procure a bargain, a Suggestion of false hood as suppression of the truth, whereby the Public may

Saturday the 8th September 1798   [291]

may be deceived or defrauded, upon the principles of <u>Eternal</u> <u>Justice</u>, the Sovereign power is warranted in executing its authority to render such a contract a Nullity.

This was done by the Legislature, after due deliberation on the methods taken to obtain the Act, & the same declared void by the Rescinding Act of the 13th February 1796, recognized by the 24th Section of the 1st Article of the existing Constitution, and therefore to be considered a part thereof. The fixing this fundamental principle in the Constitution effectually prevents any further Speculations on the public Territory, as no sale thereof to Individuals can take place. A Sale to the United States, which is permitted, is rational and proper, our Citizens will Stand on an equality with other Citizens of the United States, either to purchase or settle those Lands as their Laws may direct. and if sold by Congress, this solid advantage takes place, the monies arising therefrom will equally benefit this State with others, by affording the means of protection and contributing to the discharge of the Public debt, a portion of which we must expect to pay. The

Saturday the 8th September 1798   [292]

The Judiciary Sytem, which I think a much better ground-work than the former, requires the hand of the Legislature to put it in motion. Little inconvenience can result, until the next Session when, no doubt, this important subject will occupy much of their deliberation.

A number of other salutary Principles have been ingrafted in the Constitution, which would take up too much of your time to attend to. I will only mention that a Digested Code of our Laws is directed to be arranged and promulgated within five years, for the want of which, Majistrates have often been at a loss and the Citizens injured. And further due arrangement to Seminaries of learning is ordered. A people thus Zealous to diffuse learning and enlighten the minds of the rising Generation may expect long to live happy & free. Ignorance and Tyranny have ever gone hand in hand, and when a people cease to understand their rights, Liberty will soon leave them.

The Grand Jury returned their presentments, which were as follows, viz.

We present as a grievance of a most aggravated nature that public Roads are not kept in good repair, and unless legal steps are speedily pursued to remedy this grievance, more coercive measures must inevitably be adopted.

We present as a Grievance of a most serious

Saturday the 8th September 1798 [293]

and alarming nature the great spread of Vice, to the great injury of our fellow Citizens in general, & of our rising youth in particular. This rise and progress of iniquity can be visibly traced up to the shameful and immoral prostitution of the Lord's day, and we humbly pray the next Legislature not to overlook this evil that is so extensive in its operation and detrimental in its consequences to Georgia.

As Agricultural commerce stands closely connected with not only inland, but foreign, Navigation, We earnestly solicit and invite the attention of the next Legislature to this object, and request them to extend their patriotic and liberal views to the opening and rendering Navigable the Oconee River, as far up as will be consistent with other objects of a public nature.

We cannot pass over in silence the important and interesting objects ebraced in the charge delivered by his Honor the Judge at the present term. With him and our fellow Citizens, we rejoice, that the political eclipse of Ninety five is beginning to veer off, and the Sun of Liberty and peace begins to shine with its native lustre, the jarring and discordant passions of the public mind begin to assume the more manly and uniform features of political maturity, for the truth of this observation, we may in some measure refer the public to the existing Constitution, which appears founded on as permanent and

Saturday the 8th September 1798 [294]

and immutable a basis as the rotatory nature of time things will admit.

We recommend to our next Legislature a partial cession of our Western lands, if the wish and expectation of the people cannot be gratified upon safer and better principles.

We return our thanks to his Honor the Judge for his judicious charge at the commencement of this term & his particular attention to the interest of the County, & request that his charge, together with these our presentments, be published in the State Gazette.

1. Matt Rabun, Foreman	11. Wyatt Collier
2. Zephaniah Harvey	12. Thomas Wilcoxon
3. Samuel McGehee	13. Thomas Mercer
4. James Greene	14. Elijah Freeney
5. John Veazey	15. Thomas Lamar
6. Jesse Grigg	16. Stephen Horton
7. Mark Saunders	17. Richard Ship
8. James Reese	18. Martin Armstrong
9. Abner Atkinson	19. Henry Moffat
10. Richard Lockhart	

The Judge having returned his thanks to the Jury, they were discharged from further services during this Term.

Court adjourned until Monday Morning 9 o'Clock.

D. B. Mitchell

Monday the 10th September 1798 [295]

Court met according to adjournment. Present, his Honor Judge Mitchell.

The State }
    vs   } Habeas Corpus
Samuel Roach }

The prisoner being brought up, it appeared that the State's Counsel had not been notified to attend, and the information upon which he had been committed not being before the Court, he is remanded until Wednesday next four o'Clock, when he will again be heard.

Grand Jurors drawn for next Term.

1. Jonathan Miller	19. William Selman
2. Andrew Borland	20. Risdon Moore
3. Alexander Reid	21. William Battle

4. William Rabun
5. William Cain
6. James Bishop
7. John Coulter
8. William Hamilton
9. Jecamiah Moore
10. Hugh Montgomery
11. John Montgomery
12. Ephraim Moore
13. Isham Reese
14. Zachariah Booth
15. Turner Hunt
16. Jacob Dennis
17. Archibald Smith
18. Jonathan Adams

22. Joel McClendon
23. Lewis Tyus
24. Thaddeus Holt
25. James Alford
26. James Scarlett
27. Absalom Harris
28. George Lea
29. Levi Daniell
30. Joseph Bryan
31. Francis Lawson
32. John Ragan
33. William Reese
34. Edmund Abercrombie
35. Thomas Raines
36. John Brown

Petit Jurors [296]

1. James Montgomery
2. Philip Barnhart
3. Zadok Stinson
4. Samuel Wilson
5. Edmund Harris
6. Reuben Mobley
7. James McCormick
8. B. W. Dent
9. Eli Hudson
10. William Bivin
11. Robert Rutherford
12. Henry Peak
13. John Reed
14. James Madaus
15. Alexander Steele
16. Enoch Seale
17. James Carter
18. Andrew Miller
19. Thomas Cooper
20. John McVay
21. Hardy Smith
22. John Johnson

29. Temple Lea
30. David Ship
31. Richard Parker
32. Francis Wall
33. James Wooten
34. Thomas Middlebroox
35. James Hardridge
36. Micajah Middlebroox
37. Peter Bird
38. Van Swaringame
39. John Harrison
40. William Sparks
41. Jephtha Strickland
42. Samuel Phillips
43. John Vinson
44. Elisha Brown
45. John Wilkinson
46. Bolling Cureton
47. Andrew Maddux
48. John Weymore
49. William Lawson
50. James Wood

23. William Taylor
24. Levin Turner
25. Thomas Lightfoot
26. William Mitchell
27. Edmund Bearden
28. Josiah Dennis

51. Martin Johnson
52. Eli Townsend
53. John Walker
54. Absalom Eiland
55. James Martin
56. Elijah Moore

Monday the 10th September 1798 [297]

Ordered, that all defaulting Grand Jurors at the present term, who have not been already excused, be fined forty dollars each, unless they make excuse agreeably to Law. And that all defaulting Petit Jurors be fined in the sum of twenty dollars each, unless they also make excuse agreeably to Law.

Ordered, That the presentments of the Grand Jury & the charge delivered at the commencement of the present Term be published in the State Gazette agreeably to their wish of this.

D. B. Mitchell

Court adjourned until Court in course.

Attest. Mar Martin, Clk

Georgia   Additional Rules   [298]
for the government of the Superior Court

For the purpose of carrying the Constitution as revised, amended, & compiled on the 30th day of May 1798 into as speedy and complete effect as possible under the existing circumstances, the Judges & Mr Solicitor Van Alen have and do hereby establish for the government of Practicioners & others in the Superior Courts of the said State the following as Additional Rules, that is to say

The mode of correcting errors in Inferior Judicatories shall be as follows.

The person entitled to a Writ of Certiorari to remove proceedings from the Courts below shall within four days after trial in the said Courts serve the opposite party or his counsel with a notice in writing, stating the grounds on which he means to rely, that he will on the first day, or as soon thereafter as counsel can be heard, move the presiding Judge of the next Superior Court of said County for a writ of Certiorari to remove the said proceedings.

On hearing the parties, if the Judge should grant the same, the proceedings shall brought up instanter, entered

Additional Rules 10th Septr 1798   [299]

entered on the Doquet and be tried at the next succeeding term of the Superior Court. The party obtaining the Writ of Certiorari shall, previous to Doqueting the proceedings for a new trial, enter into Special bail and pay costs, as has been usual heretofore in cases of Appeal.

In such cases as have been determined in the Inferior Courts and Appeals granted thereon since the adoption of the present Constitution & prior to the promulgation of these Additional Rules, the party so circumstanced, applying for a new trial, shall give notice in writing to the adverse party, or his counsel, stating the grounds on which he means to move on or before the first day of the next Superior Court of the County where the Appeal shall have been entered.

In Cases where application shall be made for a new trial after one had at common Law in the Superior Court, the party dissatisfied, after due notice in writing to the opposite party, or his Counsel, stating the cause on which the application is founded, may obtain a Rule to shew cause on or before the last day of the term in which the trial was had why a new trial should not be granted, and if such rule be made absolute, the party applying shall give security and pay costs as in Cases of Appeal

Additional Rules 10th Septr 1798   [300]

heretofore used, thereupon the same shall be Doquetted and stand for trial at the next Term.

That wherever a party in a cause shall make his election in issuing out a Subpæna to compel the attendance of a Witness residing out of the County where the cause may be depending, in preference to a commission, the party shall abide by such election.

That in all cases of Special bail, or where security hath been given, heretofore in Cases of Appeal, the Plaintiff shall, in order to make the bail answerable equally with the Principal, resort to his Ca Sa against Principal & Sci Fa against Bail, according to Rules laid down in the Books.

That Writs of Sci fa issued to revive Judgments shall be made returnable to the next Superior Court of the County where the defendant or Defendants reside, the party suing out such Writ shall procure the exemplification of the Record, to be sent to the Clerk of the County where the Writ is made returnable, on which such Judgment or Judgments may be revived.

That where presentments shall be made by a Grand Jury of an indictable nature, it shall be the duty of the State's Attorney & Solicitors to frame Bills of Indictment upon the Presentments, and the persons presented shall answer the Bill so framed, without preferring the said Bill to the same or second Grand Jury.

Extract from the Minutes of the Convention of the Judges. A true copy from the original.

Mar Martin, Clk J. L. Dixon, Clk 14th July 1798

Chambers 12th September 1798 [301]

Present, his Honor Judge Mitchell.

The State }
　　vs　　 } Cattle Stealing
Samuel Roach }

The prisoner being brought up aggreeably to the order of the 10th Instant, and after hearing Mr Elholm on the part of the Prisoner & Mr Solicitor General for the State.

Ordered, that he do give Bail for his appearance at the next term of the Superior Court of this County, himself in one hundred dollars & two Securities in fifty dollars each & be discharged on payment of fees.

Georgia　　　　　} At a Superior Court begun & holden in and for the County
Hancock County } aforesaid on the 1st day of March 1799

Present, his Honor Judge Carnes.

His Honor's commission being read, the following persons attended and were sworn of the Grand Jury, viz.

　　　1. Joseph Bryan, foreman
　　　2. Alexander Reed　　　　　　　14. Risdon Moore

3. William Rabun
4. James Bishop
5. Jecamiah Moore
6. John Montgomery
7. Isham Rees
8. Zachariah Booth
9. Turner Hunt
10. Jacob Dennis
11. Jonathan Adams
12. Archibald Smith
13. William Selman

15. William Battle
16. Lewis Tyus
17. Thaddeus Holt
18. Francis Lawson
19. William Reese
20. Edmond Abercrombie
21. Thomas Raines
22. John Browne
23. Absalom Harris

Hardy Wooten }
    vs } Case
Lewis & Mary Bailey }
& James Cathell }

Settled.

Ex^d Thos P. Carnes

Court adjourned till tomorrow morning 9 o'Clock.

Attest. Mar Martin, Clk

Hancock Superior Court Saturday 2nd March 1799   [303]

The Court met according to adjournment. Present, his Honor Judge Carnes.

Thomas Elliot }
    vs } Case
Joshua Scurlock }
& Sarah his wife }

Jury Sworn

Wm Bivins   Jeptha Strickland
Andrew Maddox   Jno Wilkinson
Wm Lawson   Saml Barron
Peter Bird   Jno Hudman

James Wood   Jonathan Calbert
Levin Turner   Laurence Smith

Verdict. We find for the plaintiff Sixty dollars, with Cost of Suit.

$\qquad$ Saml Barron, foreman

William Minor }
    vs   } Case
John McKenzie }

Settled.

John Robertson }
    vs   } Case
James Huckaby }

Dismissed.

Hancock Superior Court Saturday 2nd March 1799   [304]

Abner Atkinson }
    vs   } Trespass
Isham Hogan }

Witness for pltff, Robert Wedington prov^d in open court 3 days att^{ce}, Agrippa Atkinson 7 days proven

The Same Jury as in the Case of Thomas Elliot vs Joshua Scurlock & wife.

Verdict. We find for the plaintiff ten dollars, with Cost of suit.

$\qquad$ Saml Barron, foreman

Exon iss^d 2nd April 1799.

The Grand Jury returned the following Bills.

The State }
    vs   } Indictment forcible detainer
William Gay & }
Patience Gay }

True Bill.   Joseph Bryan, foreman

The State   }
    vs   } Indictment Assault
Ephraim Liles   }

True Bill.   Joseph Bryan, foreman

Richard Smith, ex dem of }
the Exo^rs of James Adams }
    vs   } Ejectment
William Stiles &   }
Edmond Nowles, Senr   }

Jury Sworn

Thomas Cooper	Henry Peak
Philip Barnhart	John Ousley
Absolom Eiland	William Weeks
Abner Atkinson	Aaron Benson
William Browne	George Weatherby
John Shackleford	Duncan Cammell

Verdict. By consent of parties, Refered to the Judges at Louisville.

Saturday 2nd March 1799   [305]

Joseph Jones & C° }
    vs   } Debt
Isham Hogan   }

I do hereby Confess a judgement to the plaintiff for the sum of one hundred and twenty six dollars thirty one Cents and a quarter, with interest till paid and Cost of suit.

Test. B. Hall   Isham Hogans

2 March 1799

It is consented that execution shall not issue before the first day of September next.

W. Stith, jn{r}, pltff{s} att{y}

March Term 1799

Exon iss{d} 19th Novr 1799.

The State }
    vs   } Indic{t} Cattle Stealing
Samuel Roach }

True Bill.   Joseph Bryan, foreman

Resa Howard }
    vs   } Assumpsit
Job Jackson }

Death of Plaintiff suggested and, on Motion, It is ordered that the case proceed in the name of William Few and John Howard, Administrators.

Duncan Campbell, a pettit Juror sworn, having left the Box without leave and refusing to attend when Called. It is Ordered, that for such his Contempt, he pay a fine of five dollars and be in custody till the fine is paid.

Saturday the 2nd March 1799   [306]

Robert Watkins }
    vs   } Case
James Shorter }

The Same Jury as in the Case of the Exo{rs} of Adams vs Knowles, except Richd Holmes in the room of Duncan Campbell.

Verdict. We, the Jurors, find James Shorter indebted to the plaintiff One hundred and Nine dollars seventy Six Cents.

Wm Weeks, F M

Exon iss{d}.   ☞   See Page 318.

Joseph Higgenbotham }
     vs   } Assault & Battery
Isaac Jackson, et al }

The matters in controversy in this suit are submitted to the Arbitrament and final award of Thomas Lamar, Robert Cunningham, and William Shelby, or any two of them, preferred mutualy by the parties, in any suitable place in the County of Hancock together to meet, and then and there to make up their award under their hands, and the same to return to the next term of the Superior Court of the said County, which are and without some legal objection to be made a Judgment of the said Court.

Duncan Campbell, having made his excuse to the Court for absenting himself as a petit juror and promising not to offend again, his fine of five dollars is hereby rescinded.

Saturday 2nd March 1799   [307]

Hezekiah Howell   }
& Joseph Howell, Appt[s] }
     vs   } Case
James Humphries, Resp[t] }

Settled at the Appellant's Cost. Att[y] 2 & Clk $1.25 paid.

William Walker }
     vs   } Trover
Martha Walker }

Dismissed & cost paid.

James Martin & James Hunter   }
              vs   } Special Case
Robert Fulwood, Jane Fulwood   }
E. Walker, J. H. Walker, Alex Hunter }

Non Suit.

Jorden Bonner }
     vs   } Case
John Kelley }

5th Septr 1798 I do Confess judgement to the plaintiff for the sum of One hundred & fifteen dollars & Stay of Execution till the fifteenth of January next & Costs.

Teste. John Griffin   John Kelley

Exon issd the 2nd April 1799.

239 fol

John E. Scott & Mary }
S. Scott, Appellants }
    vs } Case
Matthias Maher & Co, Respt }

Appeal withdrawn & original Judgment confirmed.

        Saturday 2nd March 1799   [308]

Jorden Bonner }
   vs } case
John McKenzie }

5th Septr 1798 I do hereby Confess judgement to the pltff for the sum of One hundred and fifty three dollars & fifty Cents & Stay of Execution nine Months & Costs.

Test. Jno Griffin   John McKenzie

Principal & Int paid pr a Rect from Plff.

George Clower }
   vs } Case
Thomas Wynn }

The Same Jury as in the Case of Exors of James Adams vs Knowles, except Richard Holmes in the place of Duncan Campbell.

Verdict. We, the Jurors, find for the pltff forty three dollars Seventy three & an half Cents, with Costs.

                William Weeks, foreman

22nd March 1799 rec^d $4 three in part of the Judg^t. Mar Martin, Clk First rec^d $8 in full 2nd Ap^l 1799 2.50 of am^t rec^d of this Judg^t. Wm Clower, ag^t for plff

Joshua L. Acee }
    vs } case
Jesse Thompson, Exo^{rs} of }
Benjamin Thompson, dec^d }
& Joseph Thompson }

This Case being referred at last Term, the Arbitrators returned their award. Whereupon, the parties not gainsaying, it was ordered to be entered of record and made the Judgment of Court, viz.

We, Henry Graybill, Jesse Bunkley, James Lucas, & Ransome Harwell, arbitrators appointed to settle and determine the above case, do give it as our Award, that the Exo^{rs} of Benjamin Thompson, dec^d pay unto Doct^r Joshua L. Acee the Sum of eighty dollars. Given under our hands this 10th of Novr 1798.

                              Henry Graybill
                              Jesse Bunkley
                              James Lucas
                              Ransom Harwell

Exon iss^d 18th June 1799.

                    Saturday 2nd March 1799

Joseph Cook }
    vs } Case
Frederick Tucker }
Exo^r of Edm^d Crowder }

Dismissed.

The State }
    vs } Indic^t forcible detainer
William Gay & }
Patience Gay }

William Gay & Patience Gay came into Court with John Gay & Allen Gay, their securities, who acknowledged themselves bound to his Excellency the Governor

& his successors in Office, the said William Gay & Patience Gay in the Sum of one hundred dollars each, and John & Allen Gay in fifty dollars each, to be levied on their several goods, chattels, lands, &c, but to be void on condition that the said William & Patience Gay will attend the Superior Court now sitting and not depart without leave.

Taken & acknowledged in open Court 2nd March 1799

Before Mar Martin, Clk   William Gay
                               Patience X Gay, her mark
                               John Gay
                               Allen Gay

Samuel Barron }
        vs   } debt
John Pound & }
Richard Pound }

We, John Pound & Richard Pound, do confess judgment to the plaintiff for the sum of thirty nine dollars, with Interest & Cost of Suit.

                               John Pound
                               Richard X Pound, his mark

Ex^d Thos P. Carnes

Court adjourned till Monday morning 9 o'Clock.

Attest. Mar Martin, Clk

Monday the 4th March 1799   [310]

Court met pursuant to adjournment. Present, his Honor Judge Carnes.

Thomas Flournoy }
        vs   } Case
Joshua L. Acee }

Settled at Defend^{ts} Costs.

Robt Flournoy }
    vs   } Case
John Talbert }

                        Jury Sworn

1. Henry Peak   7. William Lawson
2. Levin Turner   8. Peter Bird
3. Jephtha Strickland   9. William Hamilton
4. John Wilkinson   10. Dunkin Cambell
5. Andrew Madox   11. John Shackleford
6. James Wood   12. Aaron Benson

Verdict. We, the Jury, find for the Plaintiff Seventy Seven dollars and fifteen Cents, with Cost of Suit and Interest from the date untill paid.

                            Duncan Campbell, F M

William Clower }
    vs   } Debt
Caleb Bazor }

I, Caleb Bazor, do hereby confess a judgment for fifty seven dollars, that Sum being the principal & Interest of the plaintiff's, William Clower's, demand within expressed against me. Also for Costs. 4th day of September 1798, with Stay of Execution five months.

In open Court, Mar Martin, Clk   Caleb Bazor

[smudge] Rec^d the Judg^t in full.   Wm Clower, plff

               Monday the 4th March 1799

Elizabeth Thompson }
    vs   } Case
Isham Hogan }

The same Jury as in the case of Flournoy vs Talbert.

Verdict. We find for the plaintiff three hundred dollars, with cost of suit.

Duncan Campbell, foreman

Appeal entered, Hardy Jones, Secr^y.

Joseph Thompson }
    vs   } Trover
Jesse Thompson }

Georgia

Culverton 6th January 1798

We, the undersigned Arbitrators, to whom was referred a certain matter of Controversy depending between Joseph Thompson, plaintiff, and Jesse Thompson, Defendant, whereas said Joseph Thompson claims a certain Negro man named Harry and having not substantiated his right, we award said Negro to be the property of said Jesse Thompson, the defendant.

Peter Coffee
Hen Mitchell
Wm Lancaster
Solomon Jordan
B. Hall
James Shorter

The State   }
    vs   } Indic^t forcible detainer
William Gay &}
Patience Gay }

Recognizance cont^d till next term.

Monday the 4th March 1799   [312]

Uriah Askey }
    vs   } Case
Joseph Bryan }

Same Jury as in the case of E. Thompson vs Isham Hogan.

Verdict. We find for the Plaintiff Forty Six dollars and twelve & a half Cents, with Costs of Suit.

          Duncan Campbell, F M

William Wallace & C⁰ }
   vs   } Case
William Walker }

Enquiry as to the [faint] of Two fi fa.

Same Jury as in the above Case.

Verdict. We find for the plaintiff one hundred and fifty seven dollars and fifty cents, the price of Tobacco ascertained as currently sold at the rate of five dollars pr hundred weight at the time the enclosed judgment was obtained, with cost of suit.

          Duncan Campbell, foreman

Exon iss^d 18th June 1799.

John Candler }
   vs   } fi fa
William McInvaill }

Levy discharged.

John McKenzie }
   vs   } fi fa
Robert Middleton }
& William Owsley }

Property levied on claimed by William Clark.

Same Jury as in the last Case.

We, the Jury, find the property levied on subject to Execution.

          Duncan Campbell, foreman

Appeal entered.

Monday the 4th March 1799 [313]

Robert McGinty, Appel^t }
      vs   } Case
Philip Spiller, Resp^t }

App^{ts} Witnesses, William Rhodes

Resp^t Witnesses, Thos Fail, Lucy Pruitt 6 days proven

Special Jury Sworn

1. James Bishop	7. Jonathan Adams
2. John Montgomery	8. Arch^d Smith
3. Isham Reese	9. William Selman
4. Zach Booth	10. William Battle
5. Turner Hunt	11. Lewis Tyus
6. Jacob Dennis	12. William Reese

Verdict. We, the Jury, find in favor of the appllelant.

Wm Battle, foreman

Exon iss^d the 2nd Ap^l 1799.

John McKenzie, Appellant   }
      vs   } Case
Frederick Tucker, Exo^r of   }
Edmund Crowder, dec^d, Resp^t }

Appeal withdrawn & the original Verdict confirmed.

Cost paid & Rec^t in full for Judg^t inclosed in Process.

John Denn, ex dem   }
of Robert Raines   }
      vs   } Ejectment
Richard Fenn, ten^t in   }
possession Richd Bonner }

Settled & cost paid.

Jesse McKinney Pope }
    vs   } Case
John Cook   }

Death of the def^t suggested.

Monday the 4th March 1799   [314]

John Burge, Ass^{ee} }
of Hartwell Jones }
    vs   } Debt
Richard Bonner }

Richard Bonner, Ass^{ee} }
of Hartwell Jones   }
    vs   } Covenant
John Burge   }

Both cases referred at last term.

The Arbitrators returned their Award, which was made the Judgment of Court, and is as follows, viz.

Whereas, the Honorable the Superior Court of the County of Hancock did, on the eighth day of September last, order that all matters in dispute between John Burge and Richard Bonner be referred to the Arbitration of Jesse Grigg, Peter Boyle, Myles Greene, John Chappell, and James Thweatt, or any three of them. Therefore we, Jesse Grigg, James Thweatt, & Peter Boyle, three of the said Arbitrators, did meet at the time and place appointed by said order, and after duly considering the different matters in Controversy, do hereby award and agree as follows.

John Burge shall lay off and convey to the said Richard one hundred and forty three and three fourth Acres of land, being the same that is now in dispute, and in order to identify the same, Andrew Borland shall lay off said land in such manner and form as was originally agreed on by the parties in presence of him, the said Borland, when on the premises. And he, the said Bonner, shall pay to said Burge the sum of fifty four pounds Sterling money, subject first to a deduction of thirty dollars, as as a compensation for

Monday the 4th March 1799 [315]

for a Smoak house, Barn, & Stable. And Burge shall receive also, as an offset against the money to be paid him by Bonner, one hundred and twenty dollars in the hands of Robert Raines. Therefore the nett amount, after the above deduction, shall be eighty one dollars and forty three cents, due by said Bonner to said Burge.

Therefore we, the said Arbitrators, do hereby publish the above as our award & Arbitrament this 4th day of March 1799.

         Jesse Grigg
         James Thweatt
         P. Boyle

John Denn, ex dem }
of Samuel Hart   }
   vs   } Ejectment
Richd Fenn, Ten^t in }
possession John Bates }

The Arbitrators returned their Award, which was ordered to entered of Record & made the judgment of Court, viz.

Agreeably to an Order of the Honorable the Superior Court of Hancock County, directing us, the Subscribers, to determine on a certain matter of controversy now in dispute in the said Court, wherein Samuel Hart is plaintiff and John Bates defendant. After hearing what evidence was given, do Award & say that Samuel Hart is entitled to the land now in dispute, or five dollars for every Acre of the said land, with cost. In Witness whereof, we have hereunto set our hands this 15th September 1798.

      John Rogers   James Alford
      Ben^j Whitfield Peter Coffee
              Jesse Battle

Monday the 4th March 1799 [316]

John Denn, ex dem }
of Lewis Tyus }
    vs } Ejectment
Richard Fenn, Ten^t in }
possession William Turner}

On Motion of Peter L. Van Alen, Att^y for Def^t, it is Ordered that William Turner, Senr be made Defendant in the above action, on his entering into the Usual Rule of confessing, Lease, Entry, & Ouster.

The State }
    vs } Indictment Larceny
Saml Hunter }

Recognizance continued till next term.

Ex^d Thos P. Carnes

Court adjourned till tomorrow morning 9 o'Clock.

Attest. Mar Martin, Clk

Tuesday the 5th March 1799 [317]

The Court met pursuant to adjournment. Present, his Honor Judge Carnes.

Reuben Harrison }
    vs } fi fa
The Adm^{rs} of John Wooten, dec^d }

On Motion of Mr Walker, Attorney for plaintiff, it is Ordered, that the Sheriff do shew cause instanter why the money should not be paid into Court upon the above Exon. And no cause being shewn to the satisfaction of the Court, it is thereupon Ordered, that the money be forthwith paid into the Clerk's Office accordingly.

Joseph Patterson, Appel^t}
    vs } case
Saml Givens, Resp^t }

We confess Judgment for the sum of ninety seven dollars twenty Cents, with stay of Execution Seven months.

Ben^j Skrine, Att^y for def^t
Nathl Waller

Tuesday the 5th March 1799   [318]

Robert Watkins }
    vs   } Case
James Shorter }

306 fo^l

Whereas, Robert Watkins did, on the second day of March instant, obtain a verdict against James Shorter for the Sum of One hundred and nine dollars Seventy Six Cents & Costs. And now at this day cometh the said Robert Watkins, by John Harwell, his Attorney, and prays the judgment of this honorable Court. It is therefore Considered, that the said Robert Watkins recover against the said James Shorter his said debt of One hundred & nine dollars seventy six Cents and his Costs expended in recovering the said debt to twelve dollars twelve and a half Cents, by the Court here adjudged to the said Robert Watkins by his assent. And that the said James Shorter be in mercy &c.

J. Hamill, Pl^{ts} Att^y
5th March 1799

Att^y & Jury	$5.00	}
Clerk 3.12½ Shff 2.50	5.62½	}
State Tax	1.50	}
	12.12½	} the annexed costs rec^d the 30th Augt 1799

Mar Martin, Clk

The State }
    vs   } Indictm^t Trespass
Robt Flournoy }

True Bill.   Joseph Bryan, foreman

Tuesday the 5th March 1799 [319]

The excuses of Benjamin Jones, John Coleman, William Butler, & John Bazer, who were fined for non-attendance as petit Jurors at the last March and September terms, & against whom Executions had severally issued, were received and deemed satisfactory. The levies are therefore severally discharged on payment of costs.

The excuses of William Weeks, James Cathell, A. Miles, and Frederick G. Thomas, made on oath, for their non-attendance as Petit Jurors the last September term, were considered by the Court and deemed sufficient.

The excuse of Thomas Trammell, a Petit Juror summoned to last March term, was made on Oath and deemed sufficient.

Tuesday the 5th March 1799 [320]

The Grand Jury brought in the following presentments, viz.

We, the Grand Jury of Hancock County, do on our oaths present Joshua Kinney for retailing spirituous liqours without license, for trading with Negroes without permits from their Masters, and for keeping a disorderly house, especially on the Sabbath.

We present James Waller, James Dixon, Robt Rivers, John McCullers, John Butts, Osborn Brewer, Jesse Ellis, William Maddux, & Josiah Beall for selling liquors without license.

We present Nathaniel Waller for malpractice in Office as a Justice of the peace.

We return our most sincere thanks to Ensign McCall of the Federal troops at Fort Wilkinson for his independent and patriotic conduct in informing the Executive of the nefarious and more Savage conduct of Lieu^t Colonel Henry Gaither, in wishing those under his command to disguise themselves in Indian habits and to massacre the innocent citizens on the frontiers of this State, & think he deserves the most grateful acknowledgements of our fellow citizens in general.

We also take this method of expressing our entire approbation of the conduct of Governor Jackson and we do assure him that, notwithstanding the many daring attempts that have been made by the [faint] malicious fact[smear] in this State to lessen [blur] who esteem of the people, he will [blur] in a very

Tuesday the 5th March 1799 [321]

very high degree the confidence of this Grand Jury. It is therefore our fervent desire that he may long continue at the helm of the Government of this State, and by his wise and judicious administration finally bear down all those daring Usurpers that may pretend to trample on the constituted authorities therof. And

We further feel it a duty incumbent on us to return our sincere thanks to the last Legislature of this State for petitioning to the War Department of the United Sttes for the removal of Lieu^t Col^o Henry Gaither from the command of the Federal troops stationed on the frontiers of this State.

We return our thanks to his Honor the Judge for his strict attention to business the present term.

We request the foregoing to be published in the Augusta Chronicle.

>Joseph Bryan, foreman   William Reese
>William Rabun   Edmund Abercrombie
>Jecamiah Moore   Thomas Raines
>John Montgomery   James Bishop
>Jacob Dennis   Isham Reese
>Archibald Smith   Turner Hunt
>Jonathan Adams   Francis Lawson
>William Selman   Risdon Moore
>William Battle   Zachariah Booth
>Lewis Tyus

It is Ordered, that the foregoing presentments of the Grand Jury be published in the Augusta Chroncile agreeably to their request.

Tuesday the 5th March 1799 [322]

The following persons were drawn to serve as Grand & Petit Juroes at the next term.

Grand Jurors

1. John Burch   16. John Trice
2. Richd Rispess   17. William Pigg
3. John Herbert   18. Stephen Horton

4. Jonadab Reed
5. Wm Yarborough
6. Josiah Beall
7. John Henderson
8. John White
9. William Horton
10. Levin Smith
11. Charles Tate
12. Benjamin Reedy
13. Samuel Braswell, Senr
14. Robert Gray
15. Mathew Kinchen
19. Peter Dent
20. Benjamin Whitfield
21. William Hamilton
22. Francis Ross
23. James Bynum
24. Richard Shipp
25. James Green
26. Thomas Mercer
27. Joshua L. Acee
28. Gerard Burch
29. Robert Raines
30. Peter Coffee

Petitt Jury

1. Pleasant Potter
2. Zealous Milstead
3. Aaron Milstead
4. John Jones
5. John Stephens
6. Jno Youngblood
7. Philip Allen
8. Larkin Turner
9. Abram Womack
10. Thos Harris
11. Edwd Flowers
12. Robt Sims
13. Saml Turner
14. Robt Wilkinson
15. John Onear
16. Howel Braver
17. Henry Castleberry
18. Dempsey Battle
19. Saml Parker
20. John Harney
21. George Simpson
22. John Perkins
23. George Barnhart
24. William Foster
25. Stephen Evans
26. David Evans
27. William John
28. James Orrick
29. David Walker
30. Moses Brown
31. Drury Mitchell
32. Wm Magahee
33. Edm^d Butler, Junr
34. James Youngblood
35. Danl Nolley
36. John Byas
37. Jon^a Beall
38. James Taylor
39. Jacob Strickland
40. John Kelly
41. Levin Hudson

42. Levin Ellis
43. William Miles
44. Jno Moore
45. James Carr
46. John Buckner
47. Henry Jones
48. Wm Hearn
49. Richd Smith
50. Elisha Harris
52. James Huckaby
53. [blot] John McKay
54. Isham Humphries
55. Edwd McDonald
56. Joseph Thomas
57. Henry Clark
58. William Maddox
59. Dempsey Justice
60. Thomas Spencer

[323]

51. James Barksdale   61, Hezekiah Carter
                            62. Jesse Smith

The State   }
    vs   } Indictm^t Trespass
Robt Flournoy   }

The defendant came into Court with Daniel Low and John Shackelford, his securities, who acknowledged themselves bound to his Excellency the Gorvernor and his successors in Office, the said Robt Flournoy in the sum ~~of one~~ of one hundred and fifty dollars, and the said Daniel Low and John Shackelford in seventy five dollars each, to be levied on their respective goods, chattels, lands, and tenements, but to be void on condition that the said Robert Flournoy will make his personal appearance at the next Superior Court to be holden in & for the County of Hancock & not depart without leave. Taken & acknowledged in Open Court this 5th day of March 1799.

Before Mar Martin, Clk   R. Flournoy
                                    Daniel Low
                                    John Shackelford

Tuesday the 5th March 1799   [324]

Micajah Middlebrooks, one of the original pannel of the petit Jury, who made default to appear during the present term, is fined in the sum of ten dollars, unless he shall make sufficient excuse on Oath within the time required by Law.

Exon iss^d 26th June 1799.

Ex^d Thos P. Carnes

Court adjourned until Court in Course.

Attest. Mar Martin, Clk

At a Superior Court begun & held in & for the County of Hancock on   [325] the last Monday in August 1799, pursuant to an Act of the General Assembly passed at Louisville on the 16th day of February in the aforesaid year entitled an "An Act to revise & amend the Judiciary sytem of this State." Present, his Honor Judge Mitchell.

The pannell of the Grand Jury being call^d, the following persons appeared and were empannel^d & Sworn.

1. John Herbert, foreman
2. John Burch
3. Richard Rispess
4. William Yarborough
5. John Henderson
6. John White
7. William Horton
8. Matthew Kinchen
9. John Trice
10. William Hamilton
11. Francis Ross
12. James Bynum
13. James Green
14. Thomas Mercer
15. Joshua L. Acee
16. Jerard Burch
17. Peter Coffee
18. Stephen Horton

John Denn, Ex dem of}
Obadiah Richardson }
    vs   } Ejectment
Richard Fenn & }
Thomas Breedlove & }
Mary Breedlove, ex° }

Setled at mutual Costs.

Micajah Williamson }
    vs   } Case in Deceit
James Adams }

Setled.

Monday the 26th August 1799   [326]

The State }
    vs   } Sci fa
David Tidd }
& Isham Hogan }

In this case, Isham Hogan, the Surety, having surrendered up the defendant, he was received into custody accordingly & the Recognizance discharged.

Andrew Wilson }
    vs   } Covenant
Robt Middleton }

Plffˢ Witnesses, Eldridge Hargrove, Matthew Wood

Jury Sworn N° 1

1. Aaron Milstead
2. John Stephens
3. Philip Allen
4. Robᵗ Simms
5. Samˡ Turner
6. David Evans
7. William Maddux
8. Edmund Butler
9. John Kelley
10. Henry Jones
11. William Miles
12. Levin Ellis

Verdict. We, the Jury, find in favour of the Plaintiff four hundred dollars & Costs of Suit.

Robert Simms, foreman

Judgmᵗ signed 2ⁿᵈ Septʳ 1799. Exon issᵈ 24ᵗʰ Septr 1799.

The Grand Jury returned the following Indictment.

The State }
    vs   } Indictᵗ Assault
Edward Worsham }

A true Bill.   John Herbert, foreman

John Dent }
    vs   } Case
John Little }

On Motion of Mʳ Walker, counsel for plaintiff, founded on an Affidavit filed in the Clerk's Office [smear] witnesses on the part and behalf of Plaintiff be taken de bene esse before Martin Martin, Peter Boyle, & John Lucas, Esqʳˢ, or any two of them, & Interrogatories being filed in the Clerk's Office [smear]

Monday the 26ᵗʰ August 1799   [327]

The State }
    vs   } Indicᵗ Assᵗ
Samˡ Dent }

A true Bill.   John Herbert, foreman

William Triplett, Agent }
of William Washington }
  vs   } Ejectment
John & Philip Cook   }

On Motion of Mr Walker, It is Ordered That John L. Dixon be made a Co-defendant, he having entered into the Usual Rule.

Plaintiff's Witness, Jn° Ragan, Esqr

Jury Sworn, the same as in Case of Andrew Wilson vs Robt Middleton.

Verdict. We, the Jury, find in favour of the Plaintiff.

          Robert Sims, foreman

Appeal entered 27th Augt 1799.

John Denn, ex dem   }
of Thomas Atkinson   }
  vs   } Ejectment
William Fenn, Ten^t in   }
possession John Booth }

Settled at mutual Costs.

Henry Castlebury excused from further services as a petit Juror at the present term.

On the petition of John Shackelford praying to be admitted a practitioner of Law on the common principles of admission.

Ordered, That Mr Solicitor Genl, Mr Walker, & Mr Early be a committee to examine the petitioner & report to the Court.

      Monday the 26th August 1799   [328]

Ezekiel Smith }
    vs   } Special Case
Abner Bankston }
Rich[d] Lockhart }
Dan[l] McDowell & }
Etheldred Wood }

Settled, the defendant to pay all costs which may have accrued on this Case.

Costs paid. Exon iss[d] 2nd Sept[r] 1799.

Ex[d]   D. B. Mitchell

Court adjourned till to morrow morning 10 o'Clock.

Tuesday the 27th August 1799

Court met pursuant to adjournment. Present, his Honor Judge Mitchell.

Nancy Creswell }
    vs   } Special Case
William Biven }

discontinued.

James Cathell }
    vs   } Case
Robert Middleton }

Abated by the death of the Plaintiff.

Benjamin Gilbert }
    vs   } Case
Michael Gilbert }

Discontinued by the Plff[s] Att[y].

John Denn, ex Dem }
Jeremiah Bonner }
    vs } Ejectment
Richard Fenn, Ten^t in possession }
David McKester & James M. Simmons }

Non suit.

Tuesday the 27th August 1799   [329]

The Committee appointed by the Honorable the Superior Court to examine Mr John Shackelford, an applicant for admission to the Bar, beg leave to Report that they have made the proposed examination, & that they found Mr Shackelford well qualified to practice as an Attorney & Solicitor in the several Courts of this State, & recommend that he be admitted to the Bar accordingly.

Whereupon, he having taken the usual Oath, his name was ordered to be added to the list of Attornies, Solicitors, & proctors admitted to practice Law in the several Courts of Law & Equity within this State.

The State }
    vs } Indict^t Mahaim
Thomas Spencer }

A truse Bill.   John Harbirt, foreman

The Exo^{rs} of William Minor }
    vs } Special Case
John Freeman }

Plaintiff's Witnesses, And^w Borland, Hubbard Bonner

Defend^{ts} Witness, Jeremiah Bonner

Jury N° 1 Sworn as in the case of Wilson ag^t Robt Middleton.

Verdict. We, the Jurors, find in favor of the plaintiff the sum of five hundred dollars, with lawfull Interest thereon two years.

Robt Simms, foreman

Appeal entered, Joseph Baynes, Sec^y.

Tuesday the 27th August 1799 [330]

The State }
   vs } Indictm^t Mahaim
Thomas Spencer }

In this Case, the Defendant Came into Court with Nathaniel Waller & William Murphey, his securities, who acknowledged themselves bound to his Excellency the Governor & his successors in Office, the said Thomas Spencer in the sum of five hundred dollars, & the said Nathl & William Murphey in the sum of two hundred & fifty dollars each, to be levied on their respective goods, chattels, lands, & Tenements, but to be void on condition that the said Thomas Spencer shall make his personal appearance at the next Superior Court to be holden in & for the County of Hancock, & not depart without leave.

Taken & acknowledged in }   Thomas Spencer
Open Court the 27th Augt 1799 }   Wm Murfey
Before Mar Martin, Clk }   Nathl Waller

Sir Peyton Skipwith }
   vs } Cov^t
Etheldred Wood }
Matthew Wood }

Jury Sworn

1. Danl Nolly   7. Thos Pennington
2. William John   8. Lindsey Thornton
3. Stephen Evans   9. Pleasant Mowman
4. John Buyas   10. William Harper
5. John Peak   11. Thomas Seale
6. Joshua Kinney   12. Dempsey Justice

Verdict. We, the Jury, do find for the Plaintiff one hundred and eighty seven dollars & fifteen cents.

Dempsey Justice, Foreman

Tuesday the 27th August 1799 [331]

The Exo^{rs} of William Minor }
    vs   } Case
Jonathan Miller   }

Plaintiff's Witness, Hubbard Bonner, Henry Chapman

Def^{ts} Witness, Ben^j Miller 5 days att^{ce} proven, Moses Langford 11 days att^{ce} proven

The same Jury as in the Case of The Exo^{rs} of W. Minor vs Jno Freeman.

Verdict. We, the Jury, find in favor of the Defendant.

                              Robt Simms, foreman

Judgment filed the 30th Augt 1799.

Jesse McKinney Pope   }
    vs   } Debt
John Harbirt, et al   }
Adm^{rs} of John Cook, dec^d}

Ordered, that all matters in dispute between the parties in the above Cause & all other disputes existing between them be referred to the Arbitrament & award of Richard Fretwell, Hugh Horton, Britain Rogers, Stephen Horton, Abraham Womack, John Humphries, Gale Lewis, Charles McDonald, Jonathan Hosea, Matthew Kinchen, John Lamar, & Robt Buchannan, or a majority of them. Their Award to be made in writing, returned to the next Term, & made the judgment of Court.

The arbitrators to meet on the 15th day of January next at the house of Mr James Comer & sit on their own adjournment. & in case of an equal division of opinions, they to chose an Umpire.

John Jack   }
    vs   } Case
James Shorter }

The same Jury as in the [blot] Case of Skipworth ag^t Matthew & Ethel^d Wood.

Verdict. We find for the plaintiff one hundred thirty five dollars & Ninety five Cents, with costs of Suit.

Dempsey Justice, foreman

Judgment entered 27th Aug.t 1799.

Ca Sa iss.d 24th Sept.r 1799.

Tuesday the 27th August 1799   [332]

Joseph Higginbotham }
     vs   } Assault
Isaac Jackson, et al }

The Arbitrators returned their Award, which was ordered to be entered of Record & made the Judgment of Court, viz.

It is the judgment of the Referees that the plaintiff & defendants each pay their own costs & the Defendants pay ten dollars damages.

Rob.t M. Cunningham
Thomas Lamar
Sam.l Dent

The Executors of W.m Minor }
     vs   } case
Jonathan Miller   }

On Motion of M.r Anderson, Counsel for the plaintiffs. Ordered, that the said Jonathan Miller, by himself or Attorney, shew cause on to morrow, if any he hath to shew, or as soon thereafter as Counsel can be heard, why the Verdict rendered in this case should not be set aside & a non-suit awarded, the plaintiff's Attorney, upon the return of the Jury, having refused to answer.

Turner Harwood }
     vs   } Spec.l Case
Thomas Dent   }

Settled at Defendant's cost.

Court adjourned till tomorrow morning 10 o'Clock.

Ex^d D. B. Mitchell

Wednesday the 28th August 1799   [333]

Court met pursuant to adjournment. Present, his Honor Judge Mitchell.

The State   }
      vs   } Indictment Assault
Edward Worsham }

In this case, the defendant came into Court with Francis Lawson, his Security, who acknowledged themselves bound to his Excellency the Governor & his successors in Office, each in the sum of one hundred dollars, to be levied on their respective goods, chattels, lands, and tenements, but to be void on condition that the said Edward Worsham will make his personal appearance at the next Superior Court to be held in & for the County of Hancock, abide by the order of the said Court, & not depart without leave. Taken & acknowledged in Open Court the 28th Augt 1799.

Before Mar Martin, Clk   Edward X Worsham, his mark
                                           Francis Lawson

Clk p^d 50 Ct^s.

Jno Mapp & Saml Philips, App^l }
            vs   } Ejectment
James Goodtitle, ex dem Jno Kelly, Resp^t }

Resp^{ts} Witnesses, Robt Flournoy 30 days att^{ce} proven in Court paid Flournoy, Robt Kelley

Appellant's Witness, Jno Ragan, Esqr

Special Jury Sworn

        1. John Harbirt   7. Willm Horton
        2. John Burch   8. Matthew Kinchen
        3. Richd Rispes   9. John Trice
        4. Wm Yarborough   10. William Hamilton

5. John Henderson 11. Francis Ross
6. John White 12. James Bynum

Verdict. We find for the Respondent.

John Harbirt, foreman

Judgment filed the 30th Aug[t] 1799. Cost paid. Exon iss[d] 2nd Jan[y] 1800.

Wednesday the 28th August 1799 [334]

William Clarke, claim[t], Appellant }
    vs } Sci fi Enquiry
John McKenzie, Resp[t] }

Appeal withdrawn by consent of the parties.

John Williamson, Exo[r] }
    vs } Case
James Rease, jun[r] }

Discontinued.

James Upright, ex dem }
of Stith Parham }
    vs } Ejectment
Abraham Lawless, Ten[t] in }
possession Jesse McKinney Pope }

Dismissed by desire of Counsel.

Rich[d] Smith, ex dem }
of William Washington }
    vs } Ejectment
William Stiles, Tenant in }
possession Tho[s] Fields }
& Martin Stanley }

Dismissed by desire of Plaintiff's Counsel.

William Pentecost }
     vs   } Case
Robert Flournoy }

Plaintiff's Winess, Matthew Wood

Non Suit.

Wednesday the 28th August 1799   [335]

James Jackson, Appelant }
     vs   } Case
Charles McDonald, Resp^t }

Appellant's Witness, Robert Jackson

Resp^{ts} Witness, Jno Hamill, Esqr

Special Jury Sworn

1. John Herbert	7. John Trice
2. John Burch	8. William Hamilton
3. Richard Rispes	9. Francis Ross
4. John White	10. James Bynum
5. William Horton	11. Peter Coffee
6. Matthew Kinchen	12. Stephen Horton

Verdict. We find for the Respondent.

                        John Harbirt, foreman

Judgment entered 29th Augt 1799.

James Cathell, Appell^t }
     vs   } Case
Robt Middleton, Resp^t }

Death of appellant suggested.

James Miller, Appellant }
     vs   } Slander
Jacob Williams, Respond^t }

Settled by information of the Clerk at Miller's [blot]

Court adjourned till tomorrow morning 10 o'Clock.

Ex^d D. B. Mitchell

Thursday the 29th August 1799   [336]

Court met pursuant to adjournment. Present, his Honor Judge Mitchell.

Harmon Reynolds, Appell^t }
    vs   } Special Case
Daniel Muse, Respond^t }

Appel^{ts} Witnesses, James Stringer, Zadok Cook, Abner Atkinson

Respondent's Witnesses, Thomas Seale 22 days & 180 Miles proven $21.00, John Bond *, George Hearndon 18 days 80 Miles proven in C^t, John Bond proves 5 days sworn to in Open Court

This Case being called in order for trial & John White, one of the original pannel of the Grand Jury having been excused on account of indisposition, a sufficient number of the original pannel not being present, the Sheriff was ordered to summon by standers to complete the pannel. Whereupon, the following Special Jury were empannelled and Sworn, viz.

    1. Richd Rispes   7. Joshua L. Acee
    2. Matthew Kinchen   8. Peter Coffee
    3. Francis Ross   9. Stephen Horton
    4. James Bynum   10. Reuben Jones
    5. James Greene   11. Joseph Bryan
    6. Thomas Mercer   12. Thomas Cooper

Verdict. We, the Jury, find for the Respondent Seven hundred and eleven dollars, with costs of Suit.

            Joseph Bryan, foreman

Judgment filed the 30th Augt 1799.

Exon iss^d 6th Sep^t 1799.

Thursday the 29th August 1799 [337]

Benjamin Waller }
    vs   } Assault
Samuel Dent }

Settled at the Defendant's costs.

The State }
    vs   } Indictm^t Larceny
David Tidd }

The prisoner discharged.

On the petition of Thaddeus Holt, praying to be admitted a practitioner of Law on the common principles of admission.

Ordered, that Mr Solicitor General, Mr Griffin, & Mr Martin examine the petitioner & report to the Court.

Exam^d D. B. Mitchell

Court adjourned till tomorrow morning 10 o'Clock.

Friday the 30th August 1799 [338]

Court met pursuant to adjournment. Present, his Honor Judge Mitchell.

William Lawson, jun^r, Ap^l }
        vs   } Case
Thomas Cooper, et al Exo^{rs} of}
Thos Cooper, dec^d, Respond^{ts} }

Appel^{ts} Witness, Jno Shackelford 8 days proven, Edm^d Butler

Resp^{ts} Witness

                          Special Jury Sworn

      1. John Harbirt   7. James Bynum
      2. John Burch   8. James Greene
      3. Richard Rispes   9. Jerard Burch

4. William Yarborough
5. William Horton
6. William Hamilton
10. Stephen Horton
11. Reuben Jones
12. Joseph Bryan

Verdict. We find for the Appellant forty eight dollars Ninety eight cents and costs of Suit.

John Harbirt, foreman

Judgment signed the 30th August 1799. Rec^t in full enclosed in process for Judg^t 2nd Septr 1799.

John Denn, Ex dem }
of Lewis Lyas }
    vs } Ejectment
Richard Fenn, Tenants in }
possession William Turner, Senr }
& William Turner, jun^r }

On Motion of Mr Martin, Counsel for Plaintiff.

Ordered, that the County Surveyor, or his lawful deputy, do go upon the land in dispute And make an accurate Survey of the premises, Carefully delineating the interference (if any) and that he give the adverse party, or his Attorney, ten days previous notice of Such Survey so to be made, and return a plat thereof to the Clerk's Office on or before the first day of the next term.

Friday the 30th August 1799   [339]

The State }
    vs } Indictment forcible Detainer
William Gay & }
Patience Gay }

Recognizance continued.

The State }
    vs } Indictment Trespass
Robt Flournoy }

Recognizance continued.

Henry Mitchell, Ass^ee, Appel^t }
        vs   } Case
Allen Cook, Respondent   }

Appellant's Witness, Jonathan Hagerty

Resp^ts Witness, John Ragan, Nathl Waller

Special Jury Sworn

1. John Harbirt
2. John Burch
3. Richard Rispes
4. William Yarborough
5. John Henderson
6. William Horton
7. William Hamilton
8. Francis Ross
9. James Bynum
10. James Greene
11. Thomas Mercer
12. Jerard Burch

Verdict. We find for the Appellant Mitchell the sum of one hundred dollars & forty one cents, with costs of suit.

                        John Harbirt, foreman

Friday the 30th August 1799

The State   }
    vs   } Indictment Cattle Stealing
Samuel Roach }

State's Witness, John Booth, Senr, Archelous Farrell, Jonathan Colbert

Jury Sworn

1. Aaron Milstead
2. John Stephens
3. Philip Allen
4. Robert Simms
5. David Evans
6. Edmund Butler
7. John Kelly
8. Henry Jones
9. William Miles
10. Levin Ellis
11. Danl Nolly
12. Richard Smith

Verdict. We, the Jury, are of opinion that the Prisoner is not guilty agreeable to the charge.

Robt Simms, foreman

James Scarlet, Appel^t }
        vs   } Case
Nathaniel Waller, Resp^t }

Appellant's Witness, William Triplett

Resp^{ts} Witness, Nathl Waller, Junr, John Lamar, John Raglan, Joseph Patterson, Nathl Waller, jun^r 5 days att^{ce} proven in Court

Special Jury Sworn

1. John Harbirt
2. John Burch
3. Richard Rispes
4. William Yarborough
5. John Henderson
6. William Horton
7. William Hamilton
8. Francis Ross
9. James Bynum
10. James Green
11. Thomas Mercer
12. Jerard Burch

Verdict. We find for the Respondent three hundred and thirty Dollars & Eighty four Cents, with costs of suit.

John Harbirt, foreman

Judgm^t Signed 31st Augt 1799. Exon iss^d 24th Septr 1799.

Joseph Thomas, one of the original pannel of the Petit Jury appeared & ~~having~~ made satisfactory excuse for his non attendance the first of the present Term.

Friday the 30th August 1799   [341]

The State }
    vs   } Indictment Forgery
James Shorter }

The defendant discharged and the prosecutor, Sureties, & Witness exonerated from their Recognizances.

Daniel Parker for the }
use of Isham Hogan }
    vs   } Deceit
Abner Atkinson   }

Upon motion of Plaintiff's counsel, Ordered that the County Surveyor make an accurate Survey and plat of the premises in dispute, taking especial care to designate the several lines and interferences. And that he return the same to the Clerk's Office on or before the first day of the next term. And that he give the defendant twenty days previous Notice of the time of making such Survey. Each of the parties to be at liberty to take with them an assistant Surveyor, if they think proper so to do.

issued 28th January 1800.

                             D. B. Mitchell

Court adjourned till tomorrow morning 10 o'Clock.

                  Saturday the 31st August 1799

Court met pursuant to adjournment. Present, his Honor Judge Mitchell.

Ezekiel Smith, Reuben Jones, Joseph Bryan, John Ragan, William Chandler, being summoned as Talis men, were sworn as Grand Jurors to complete the pannel.

Mr Thaddeus Holt, an applicant for admission to the practice of Law, withdrew his petition for the present term.

The State   }
    vs   } Indictmt Assault
Moreton Gray }

A true Bill.   John Harbirt, foreman

George Naylor   }
    vs   } Deceit
Joseph Bryan & }
James Shorter   }

James Shorter not served with a Copy of the process & exceptions filed to the Writ as to Joseph Bryan & sustained by the Court.

Saturday the 31st August 1799   [343]

John Swepson &   }
Peter Coffee, Appel^{ts}   }
     vs   } Case
Abraham Laurence, Resp^t }

Special Jury Sworn

1. John Harbirt   7. William Hamilton
2. John Burch   8. James Greene
3. Richard Rispes   9. Thomas Mercer
4. Willm Yarborough   10. Reuben Jones
5. John Henderson   11. Joseph Bryan
6. William Horton   12. William Chandler

Verdict. We find for the Respondent four hundred & seventy four dollars thirty five cents & costs of suit.

John Harbirt, foreman

Judg^t filed 31st Augt 1799. $485.40½ paid 11th Sep^t 1799.

Rec^d this Judgment in full the 21st October 1799.

Abraham X Laurence, his mark
H. Lewis

Turner Hunt   }
    vs   } Ejectment
Stephen Evans }

On motion, it is Ordered that the County Surveyor proceed to examine & take a view of the disputed premises. & that the parties have the privilege of attending with one person chosen by each, if they think fit. That the said Surveyor make a correct return of the premises, with the interfering lines, on or before the first day of the next term of the Superior Court, the party proceeding to execute this order to give the adverse party twenty days Notice.

Issued.

Saturday the 31st August 1799 [344]

Zachariah Booth }
    vs   } Debt
John Cobbs   }

Judgment by default.

Julius Sanders }
    vs   } Case
Noel Mitchell }

Judgment by default.

John Dent }
    vs   } Case
John Little }

On motion, ordered that the declaration be amended.

Bird & Harriss }
    vs   } Special Case
Job Allen   }

The Defendant, having failed to appear & file his answer agreeable to Law, it is thereupon Considered that Judgment pass against him by Default, and that an enquiry be had at the next term.

J. Hamill, Plf^t Att^y

Rescinded.

Seth Kennedy &   }
James Ross   }
    vs   } In Equity
The Exo^{rs} of Ja^s Adams }

On Motion of Mr Walker, Solicitor for Defendants, Ordered that the said Defendants have four Months to plead, answer, or Demur, not demurring alone.

Bird & Harriss }
    vs   } Special Case
Job Allen   }

On motion of Mr Walton & by consent of Plff^s Att^y, Ordered that the Judg^t by Default be rescinded.

Saturday the 31st August 1799   [345]

The State   }
    vs   } Indictment Larceny
Samuel Hunter }

In this case, the Witnesses being called & failing to appear, on Motion, Ordered that the Defendant be discharged.

Turner Hunt   }
    vs   } Trespass
Stephen Evans, et al }

On Motion of Defendant's Attorney, it is ordered that, at the trial of this Suit, the plaintiff produce a paper purporting to be a Bond subscribed by Stephen Evans, with a penalty of two thousand dollars, for the performance of a certain condition, dated the 5th day of April 1796. The plaintif's counsel having been notified thereof or that the said Plaintif shew good cause why said Bond is not produced at the said trial in terms of the act.

John Barron   }
    vs   } fi fa Sheriff's report
Isham Hogan & }
Etheldred Wood }

Stopped by an affidavit of illegality. Ordered, that the Execution proceed for balance.

Saturday the 31st August 1799   [346]

Robert Hill   }
    vs   } Assault
John McGaughey }

Settled by information from the Clerk.

The Grand Jury returned the following Presentments, viz.

We, the Grand Inquest for the County of Hancock, being concious of the commercial State of our Country, and knowing it to be impossible for inland commerce to produce advantages equal to the wisdom of the institution, present as a grievance of the most inconvenient nature the want of attention in the Overseers of roads in general, and particularly the bad state of the following, viz.

The road leading from Sparta to Chambers's Mill as far as the Stoney Hill, the road leading from Sparta to the Piney woods house, the road from the Piney woods house to Greenesborough, the road leading from Chambers's mill to Powelton, the road leading from Chambers's mill to Montpelier, & the road leading from Thaddeus Holt's to Mapp's.

We, believing that the poor of every community are objects most worthy of Legislative contemplation, present as a grievance of a most serious nature that the provision made for their relief is not more simple.

We, believing that morality and true Religion constitute the firmest pillars in any Political system, but

Saturday the 31st August 1799 [347]

but particularly that of a Republican kind, do present as a grievance the loose and licentious conduct of those who keep dram shops or Tippling houses, whose scenes of the most flagicious nature are exhibited from day to day, the Sabbath not excepted, and as there is no existing Law so specific as to point out and denominate the various kinds of offences committed against the peace & dignity of Civil & Religious Society. We recommend that our next Legislature take it into mature deliberation to put a check to these growing evils, so far as they may have it in their power.

We congratulate his Honor the Judge on his arrival in our Western Circuit and return him our unfeigned thanks for his candid and assiduous attention to the business of our County, the steady & uniform displine introduced by him in the wholesome administration of Justice, believing it improbable that Justice can be administered without complete decorum.

We recommend that his judicious & well directed charge, together with these our presentments, be published in the Gazette of the State.

1. John Harbirt, Foreman	10. John Burch
2. Richard Rispes	11. William Hamilton
3. Thomas Mercer	12. James Greene
4. Francis Ross	13. James Bynum
5. John Henderson	14. William Chandler
6. William Yarborough	15. Ezekiel Smith
7. Stephen Horton	16. Joseph Bryan
8. Jerard Burch	17. John Ragan
9. William Horton	18. Reuben Jones

Saturday the 31st August 1799 [348]

The following persons having been drawn & summoned to attend as Grand Jurors at the present term, To wit.

Jonadab Reed, Josiah Beall, Benjamin Whitfield, & Robert Raines, having made default to appear, Ordered that they be fined in the sum of twenty dollars each, unless they shew sufficient cause of excuse agreeably to Law.

Ordered, that John Harvey, George Simpson, John Perkins, James Orrick, James Youngblood, & John Buckner be fined in the sum of ten dollars each for their nonattendance as Petit Jurors at the present term, unless they shall likewise make sufficient excuse agreeable to Law.

Ordered, that the charge, together with the presentments of the Grand Jury, be published agreeably to their request.

3 Exons iss^d 29th Octr 99.

Ex^d D. B. Mitchell

Court adjourned till Court in Course.

Attest. Mar Martin, Clk

Grand Jurors drawn for next Term [349]

1. James Alford
2. Woodlief Scott
3. Duke Hamilton
4. Robert Buchannan
5. William Alford, jun[r]
6. William Bullock
7. John Ragan
8. Francis Trawick
9. Solomon Phillips
10. James Harvey
11. Nath[l] Sledges
12. Miles Greene
13. Ephraim Moore
14. James Thweatt
15. Hugh M. Comer
16. Thomas Mitchell
17. Thomas Mathews
18. John C. Peak, Sen[r]
19. Lewis Graves
20. William Cureton
21. John Cook
22. John Kirk
23. Henry Moss, Sen[r]
24. John Rogers
25. John Mitchell, Esq[r]
26. Rev[d] John Brown
27. Francis Lawson
28. George Lee
29. John Humphries
30. Samuel Reid, jun[r]
31. John William Devereux
32. Rob[t] McGinty
33. Robert Tate
34. Joseph Kirk
35. Edmund Abercrombie
36. Loyd Kelley

Petit Jurors

1. John Whittington
2. Absalom Trailor
3. Sam[l] Betts, jun[r]
4. Singleton Holt
5. William Barksdale
6. Isaac Youngblood
7. Allen Brown
8. John Wilkinson
9. Nathan Youngblood
10. Thomas Goode
11. Jonathan Hearn
12. Levin Callaway
13. Joseph Barksdale
14. John Lee, Sen[r]
15. Thomas Fields
16. Minds Sledge

17. William Willis
18. John Callaway
19. Daniel Dyches
20. Isham Hogan
21. Benjamin Harper
22. Isham Brooks
23. Greene Williamson
24. James Jernigan
45. Benjamin Barnett [350]
46. Hamlin West
47. John Edwards
48. John Andrews
49. Stephen Stephens
50. Abner Wilkinson
51. Willie Burge
52. James Powell

25. James Felts
26. Wyatt Collier
27. Charles Allen
28. Greene Cato
29. John Freeman
30. Michael Maddux
31. John Wynne
32. James Pritchett
33. Swann Thompson
34. Isaac Moreland
35. Moses Powell
36. Robert Gilbert
37. William Ingram
38. Henry Rhodes
39. William Morgan
40. John C. Mason
41. William Brooks
42. David Strickland
43. Tilman Buckner
44. Sheldrake Brown

53. Archelous Ferrell
54. Clement Moore
55. Stephen Ellis
56. John Lee, jun^r
57. Daniel Melson
58. Jesse Allen
59. Henry Jernigan
60. Jonathan Black
61. James Simmons
62. William Williams
63. Henry Moss, jun^r
64. William Ferrill
65. James Lewis
66. Frederick Echols
67. Richard Pound
68. Laban Turk
69. Joseph Cooper, Senr
70. William Smith
71. John Roberts
72. John Carter

Georgia } At a Superior Court begun & holden in & for said [351] Hancock County } County on Monday the 24th February 1800. Present, His Honor Judge Walton.

John Brown, one of the original pannel of the Grand Jury, excused from any further services in this County as Grand Juror on account of his bodily infirmity.

Laban Turk excused during the present Term as a Petit Juror.

Absalom Trailor excused as a petit Juror during this term.

The following Grand Jurors attended, viz.

1. Myles Greene, Foreman
2. Woodlief Scott
3. Duke Hamilton
4. Robert Buchannan
5. William Alford, jun^r
6. William Bullock
7. John Ragan

16. John C. Peak
17. Lewis Graves
18. William Cureton
19. John Cook
20. John Kirk
21. Henry Moss, Senr
22. John Rogers

8. Francis Trawick
9. Solomon Phillips
10. James Harvey
11. Nathl Sledge
12. Ephraim Moore
13. Hugh M. Comer
14. Thomas Mitchell
15. Thomas Mathews

23. John Mitchell
24. Francis Lawson
25. John Humphries
26. Saml Reid, jun^r
27. John William Devereux
28. Robt McGinty
29. Edmund Abercrombie
30. Loyd Kelly

Whereupon, the first twenty three were empannelled & sworn as Grand Jurors & the rest dismissed until this Court will proceed on the trial of Appeals.

24th February 1800 [352]

William Hill }
  vs } Debt
Riverius H. Lee }

In this Case, the Defendant & Joseph Cooper, Senr came into Court and acknowledged themselves bound to the plaintiff in the sum of one hundred & twenty dollars, to be void only on condition that, if the said Riverius H. Lee shall be cast in this Suit, he will pay the condemnation money, or surrender himself in discharge thereof, or I (Joseph Cooper) will do it for him. Taken and acknowledged in Open Court this 24th February 1800.

Before Mar Martin, Clk   R. H. Lee
                 Jo^s Cooper

John Burch }
  vs } Sp^l Cases
Riverius H. Lee }

In this Case, the defendant came into Court with Joseph Cooper, his Security, who acknowledged themselves bound to the plaintiff in the sum of one hundred and sixty dollars, on this condition, that if said Riverius H. Lee shall be cast in this Action, he will pay the Condemnation money, or surrender himself in discharge thereof, or I (Joseph Cooper) will do it for him. Taken and acknowledged in Open Court this 24th Feby 1800.

Before Mar Martin, Clk   R. H. Lee
                 Jo^s Cooper

James Paul }
   vs   } Case
Rob{^{t}} Blakely }

Discontinued by plaintiff.

24th February 1800   [353]

Joseph Woodward }
   vs   } Slander
James Shorter   }

Plff{^{s}} Witness, Edm{^{d}} Corley 7 days prove, Ja{^{s}} Orricks

Defd{^{ts}} Witnesses, Hines Holt

Jury Sworn

1. Isham Hogan
2. Benjamin Harper
3. Daniel Dykes
4. Wyatt Collier
5. James Felps
6. Isham Brooks
7. Minds Sledge
8. William Barksdale
9. John Wilkinson
10. Sam{^{l}} Betts
11. Thomas Goode
12. Isaac Youngblood

Verdict. We, the Jury, find no cause of action.

Isham Hogan, foreman

William Stark &   }
Alex{^{r}} Cummins, exo{^{rs}} &c }
   vs   } Case
Charles McDonald   }

Discontinued.

William Stark   }
   vs   } Trover
Jeremiah Bonner }
Robert Bonner & }
Gabriel Hubert   }

Nonsuit.

Aaron Woodward & C⁰ }
      vs   } Attachment
James Shorter   }

Plff^s Witness, William Owsley, Jesse Connell

The above Jury Sworn. Verdict. We, the Jury, find for the plaintiffs two hundred thirty three dollars forty one & an half cents, with costs of Suit.

                                        Isham Hogan, Foreman

                      February 24th 1800   [354]

David Strickland, one of the original pannel of the petit Jury was excused from on account of his being over the age requiring services as a Juror.

John Little }
   vs   } Trespass
John Dent }

Bail discharged & bail bond delivered the def^t by order of Court.

Nicholas Long   }
      vs   } Attachment
Timothy Ricketson }

Abated by Defendant's death.

Ex^d Ge⁰ Walton

Court adjourned till tomorrow morning ½ past 9 o'Clock.

                        Tuesday 25th February 1800

Court met pursuant to adjournment. Present, his Honor Judge Walton.

John Whittington excused from service as a petit Juror during the present term on account of indisposition. James Lewis also excused on account of indisposition. George Simpson, a defaulting petit Juror at the last term, excused by the Court.

John Minor }
    vs   } Special Case
Henry Jones }

Settled at plaintiff's costs.

Tuesday 25th February 1800 [355]

Thomas Weeks }
    vs   } assault
Hugh Hall }

plff^s Witnesses, Gabriel Moss, Joseph Bryan

Jury Sworn

Greene Cato	William Brooks
Fred^k Echols	William Williams
Moses Powell	Hamlin West
Rob^{ts} Gilbert	Willie Burge
William Morgan	Archelaus Ferrell
John C. Mason	Clement Moore

Verdict. We, the Jury, do decidedly agree the plaintiff damaged to the amount of one hundred dollars, with cost of suit.

John C. Mason, Foreman

Appeal ent^d 3rd March 1800, Dixon Hall, Sec^y.

The adm^{rs} of Absalom Jackson }
    vs   } fi fa Shff^s report
William Low }

Stopped on aff^t of illegality. Affidavit withdrawn & Exon ordered to proceed.

The State }
    vs   } Indictm^t assault
Robert Flournoy }

A true Bill.   M. Greene, foreman

~~Richd Smith ex dem~~ }
~~of Wm Washington~~   }
    vs   } Ejectment
~~Wm Stiles, tenant in possession~~ }
~~James Wooten~~   }

~~The same jury as in the Case of Woodward vs Shorter~~. Cont^d till tomorrow.

The State }
    vs   } Indictm^t assault
Joshua Ellis }

We, the Jury, do find an assault, but no Battery.

                        M. Greene, foreman

          Tuesday the 25th February 1800   [356]

Robert Flournoy }
    vs   } Ejectment
Patience & Wm Gay }

On motion of Plaintiff's Attorney, it is Ordered That the County Surveyor, or one of his deputies, do make an accurate Survey of the premises in dispute, taking Care to designate the several lines & interferences, if any, and return the same to the Clerk's Office on or before the first day of the next term, both parties having liberty to take with them a Surveyor, if they think fit, the Plaintiff giving twenty days notice of the time of making such survey.

                        Flournoy, plff^s att^y

issued 5th June 1800.

Richard Smith, ex dem }
of Turner Hunt   }
    vs   } Ejectment
William Fenn, tenant in }
possession Stephen Evans }

Continued untill the decision of the Convention of the Judges at Louisville.

Elijah Lingo }
    vs   } Covers^t
John Kelley }

The same Jury as in the Case of Woodward vs Shorter. Verdict. We, the Jury, find for the plaintiff seventy six dollars fifty three and one third cents, with costs of of suit.

                          Isham Hogan, foreman

              Tuesday the 25th February 1800   [357]

John McCarty }
    vs   } Case
John Lamar }

plff^s Witnesses, Andrew Jeter, John Brewer

Jury Sworn. The same as in the case Thomas Weeks vs Hugh Hall. Verdict. We, the Jury, do find for the plaintiff forty four dollars & fifty eight cents and cost of suit.

                          John C. Mason, Foreman

26th August 1800 Received in full for the principal & interest in the above case.

                          Wm H. Crawford, plff^s

Hugh Hall }
    vs   } Spec^l Case
Joseph Bryan & }
Thomas Weeks }

plaintiff's Witnesses, Gab^l Moss

def^{ts} Witness, William Bishop 2 days proven, James Bishop

The same Jury as in the case of Woodward vs Shorter. Non Suit.

John Ogletree }
    vs   } Case
Isham Hogan }

The same Jury as in the Case of Weeks vs Hall. Verdict. We find for the Plaintiff fifty two dollars, with Interest from the tenth day December 1794.

        John C. Mason, Foreman

Exon iss^d 6th March 1800.

Zachariah Booth }
  vs   } Debt
John Cobbs   }

The same Jury as in the case of Woodward vs Shorter. Verdict, We, the Jury, find for the plaintiff seventy four dollars forty one and a quarter cents, with cost of suit.

        Isham Hogan, Foreman

Exon iss^d 6th March 1800.

     Tuesday 25th February 1800   [358]

John Macintosh to the }
use of James Hutchinson }
  vs   } Case
Charles McDonald   }

The defendant, by John Hamill his Attorney, came into Court and confessed Judgment for the sum of seventy nine dollars eighty cents.

        J. Hamill, Def^{ts} Att^y

Exon iss^d 4th May 1800.

At the request of the Grand Jury, Ordered That Francis Trawick, Esquire be henceforth discharged from services as a Juror.

William Morgan excused from furt^h services as a petit Juror during this term.

Francis Tennille }
& Arthur Fort }
  vs   } Case
James Wood }

I confess judgment to the plaintiff for the sum of three hundred ninety seven dollars eight cents, with cost of suit & stay of levy six months from this day 25th February 1800.

James Wood
Skrine, for the Defendant

Feby 1800. Exon iss^d 1st Novr 1800.

William Stark, Ass^{ee} }
      vs   } Case
Daniel Hunt   }
Isaac Daniel &   }
John Booth   }

I, one of the defendants in this suit, do hereby confess a judgment to the plaintiff for the sum of one hundred and forty eight dollars & ninety two cents, with costs of suit, with Stay of Execution Six months.

Daniel Hunt

Exon iss^d 15th Septr 1800.

Tuesday the 25th February 1800   [359]

Joshua Ellis, Att^y }
of Robert Knowles }
      vs   } Attachment
Littleton Carter   }

Settled.

Georgia   } To the Honorable George Walton, one of the Judges
Hancock County } of the Superior Courts for the State aforesaid

The petition of Jabez Bowen, jun^r Humbly Sheweth that he hath been a practitioner of Law in the State of South Carolina for a considerable length of time and is desirous of being admitted to practice in the Courts of this State; he therefore prays a committee of the bar may be appointed to examine the merits of his pretensions.

Jabez Bowen, Junr

By John E. Anderson }
    George Walker & } Esquires, a committee for the above purpose
    Thomas Flournoy }

The petitioner having produced to us satisfactory vouchers of his due admission in the Superior Courts of South Carolina of the year 1797, and also of his moral character, & finding him professionally qualified, We recommend that he be admitted and enrolled as a Solicitor & Attorney in the respective Courts within this State.

Ge° Walker
Th° Flournoy
John E. Anderson

Tuesday the 25th February 1800   [360]

Whereupon, the usual Oath of the profession was administered and the said Jabez Bowen was ordered to be admitted and enrolled accordingly.

Danl Parker for the }
use of Isham Hogan }
    vs   } Deceit
Abner Atkinson   }

Continued until decision of Convention by the Judges in similar cases.

Wayne & Anderson }
    vs   } Case
James Scarlett   }

I confess judgment for the sum of one hundred and seventy seven dollars & seventy five cents & cost of suit.

Ja^s Scarlett

Richard Wayne }
    vs   } Debt
James Scarlett }

Judgment confessed for the sum of seven hundred and ninety nine dollars ninetine & an half cents & costs of suit.

                                    Ja^s Scarlett

Ex^d Ge^o Walton

                    Tuesday the 25th February 1800   [361]

Sheldrake Brown }
    vs   } Assault & Battery
Edward Worsham }
& Reuben Slaughter }

Settled.

Riverius H. Lee }
    vs   } Case
Ransom Harwell }

Settled at plaintiff's cost.

Ex^d Ge^o Walton

Court adjourned till tomorrow morning 10 o'Clock.

                    Wednesday the 26th February 1800

Court met pursuant to adjournment. Present, his Honor Judge Walton.

Isham Hogan, Appellant }
    vs   } Case
Zachariah Glass, Respondent }

Resp^{ts} Witness, Jonathan Davis, Saml Barron

Special Jury Sworn

1. Myles Greene
2. Woodlief Scott
3. Duke Hamilton
4. Robert Buchannan
5. William Alford, junr
6. William Bullock
7. John Ragan
8. Solomon Phillips
9. James Harvey
10. Nathl Sledge
11. Ephraim Moore
12. John Rogers

Postponed by order of Court till tomorrow morning.

Wednesday the 26th February 1800 [362]

Ezekiel Smith, Appellant }
    vs } Case
John Shackelford, Resp{t} }

paid.

Robert Abercrombie, 15 days proven, Reuben Jones 12 days proven, William Chandler 9 days proven

Appeal withdrawn & original Verdict confirmed, with costs upon Appeal.

27th February 1800 Recd full satisfaction for this Judg{t}. John Shackelford, plff

Thomas McCall, Appel{t} }
    vs } Case
Robt Middleton, Resp{t} }

The same Special Jury as in the Case of Hogan, Ap{t} vs Glass, Respond{t}. Verdict. We, the Jury, find for the Appellant three hundred eighty five dollars twenty nine & a third cents.

                              M. Greene, foreman

Exon iss{d} 3rd Ap{l} 1800.

Benjamin Robertson, Ass^ee, Appel^t }
      vs   } Case
Dennis Trammell &   }
Josiah Dennis, Respondents }

Special Jury Sworn

1. Hugh M. Comer
2. Thomas Mitchell
3. Thomas Mathews
4. John C. Peak
5. Lewis Graves
6. William Cureton
7. John Cook
8. John Kirk
9. Henry Moss, Senr
10. John Mitchell
11. Robt McGinty
12. Edm^d Abercrombie

Verdict. We, the Jury, find for the Appellant seventy six dollars & sixty six Cents & cost of suit.

                John Mitchell, Foreman

Judg^t ent^d 1st March 1800. Exon iss^d 3rd Ap^l 1800.

Wednesday 26th February 1800   [363]

John E. Scott, Appellant }
      vs   } debt
Saml Hawkins, Resp^t   }

Resp^ts Witness, Saml Parsons

App^ts Witness, Fred^k Scott, Jacob Gore

Special Jury Sworn

1. Myles Greene
2. Duke Hamilton
3. Robt Buchannan
4. William Alford, j^r
5. William Bullock
6. John Ragan
7. Solomon Phillips
8. James Harvey
9. Nathl Sledge
10. Ephraim Moore
11. John Rogers
12. Loyd Kelley

Verdict. We, the Jury, do find for the plaintiff eighty seven dollars & cost of suit.

M. Greene, foreman

Exon iss^d 3rd May 1800.

John E. Scott &   }
Woodlief Scott, Appel^{ts} }
    vs   } debt
Saml Hawkins, Respond^t }

Appeal withdrawn by Consent of parties & original Verd^t confirmed.

John Pollard }
    vs   } Case
John Freeman }

Settled & cost paid.

Joseph Cooper, Appel^t }
    vs   } Case
James Smith & Co, Resp^t }

The same Special Jury as in the case Robertson vs Trammell & Dennis. Verdict. We, the Jury, find for plaintiff seven hundred & sixteen Dollars sixty six Cents & two thirds & costs.

John Mitchell, Foreman

Exon iss^d 6th March 1800.

Wednesday the 26th February 1800   [364]

The State   }
    vs   } Indictm^t assault
Thomas Raines }

A True bill.   M. Greene, Foreman

Dennis Mirarity, ex dem }
of John Hill }
    vs } Ejectment
Cornelius O'Triger, Ten^t in }
possession James Huckaby }

Ordered, that the County Surveyor, or his deputy, do make an accurate Survey of the land in dispute in this Case, and return a correct plat thereof to the next Superior Court of this County, giving the defendant ten days previous notice thereof.

iss^d 5th June 1800.

Saml W. Goode }
    vs } Case in the Inferior Court
Joseph Cooper }

Uriah Askey, the bail, surrendered the principal in the vacation of the Inferior Court, and the Sheriff having him in ~~his~~ custody in the present term of the Superior Court, it was moved by Mr Flournoy that this Court order the s^d principal to be liberated as not being liable to be so surrendered and received into custody.

Mr Walker opposed this and contended that the bail, being declared by the Act to be in the nature of Special bail, had such power. Whereupon

Wednesday the 26th February 1800   [365]

Whereupon, it is ordered that it be argued to morrow morning.

It was proceeded to draw the Jurors.

Grand Jurors

1. Jesse McKinne Pope
2. Michael Harvey, Senr
3. Ge^n Henry Mitchell
4. Robt Clark, jn^r
5. Jesse Vesey
6. Richard Ship
7. David Adams
8. Jo^s Turner
19. Seth Tatem
20. Theod^s Turke
21. Ja^s Thomas
22. Jonas Shivers
23. Jonth^n Adams
24. David Walker
25. Lazarus Battel
26. Henry Trip

9. James Lucas
10. Fred Tucker
11. Lewis Barnes
12. Thos Lamar
13. William Wyley
14. ~~Robt~~ Abner Atkinson
15. Richard Harwell
16. William Sanders
17. Robt Moreland
18. Saml Slaughter

27. Elijah Freeney
28. Johnth^n Miller
29. Jess Pope, jn^r
30. Jonth^n Anderson
31. William Hardwick
32. John Hamilton, Senr
33. John Hanby
34. Davis Mcgehee
35. Thomas Lancaster
36. Thomas Stevens

Petit Jurors

1. John Gualtney
2. Anselm Hudgins
3. Jo^s Candler
4. Shirly Sledge
5. Needham Journigan, Senr

6. Absalom Barnes
7. Vines Harwell
8. Peter F. Flournoy
9. Hardy Journigan
10. John Cooper

Wednesday the 26th February 1800 [366]

11. Ja^s Bonner
12. Thos Castlebury
13. Ja^s Emberson
14. Benjn Gilbert
15. Tunstil Roan
16. West Parker
17. William Gay
18. Robt Still
19. Ralph Lowe
20. Saml Hawkins
21. Jo^s Dennis
22. John Morris
23. John Dormond
24. John Patterson
25. John Murphy
26. Gray Andrews, Senr
27. Ja^s Lamar
28. Ja^s Crowder
29. John Herdman

31. John Harrison
32. Jno Smith
33. Robt Pollard
34. Jonth^n Milton
35. Saml Devereux
36. William Dennis
37. Joshua Turner
38. Robert Parham
40. George Gray
41. William Musgrove
42. Alex Hunter
43. Saml Pogue
44. Jacob Williams
45. Robt Kelly
46. Charles Waller
47. Joel Dickinson
48. Zeph^a Harvey
49. David Irvin
50. Thomas Morris

30. Ja^s Huckaby   51. John Thornton
                           52. Freeman Allen

           Wednesday the 26th February 1800   [367]

Mancil & Sherwood   }
Womack, Exo^{rs}, Appellants }
        vs   } Special Case
Philip Howell, Respond^t }

Settled by consent of parties.

Jesse Pope   }
      vs   } Deceit
John Holeford   }

Settled.

William Williams }
       vs   } Special Case
Abraham Smith   }

Settled at Def^{ts} costs.

The excuses of Jonadab Reid, Robt Raines, Benjamin Whitfield, & Josiah Beall, defaulting Grand Jurors at the last Term, were adjudged sufficient & their fines remitted, as also those of John Buckner and John Perkins, defaulting Petit Jurors.

The State   }
      vs   } fi fa for a fine as a default^g Juror
George Harvey }

Illegality sustained & excused for the fine.

The State   }
      vs   } fi fa for a fine as a default^g Juror
Joseph Cooper, Senr }

Illegality sustained & excused for the fine.

Wednesday the 26th February 1800 [368]

The State }
vs } fi fa for a fine as a defaulting Juror
James Orrick }

Illegality sustained and excused for the fine.

The State }
vs } fi fa for a fine as a default^g Juror
James Youngblood }

Illegality sustained & excused for the fine.

Ex^d Ge^o Walton

Court adjourned till tomorrow morning 10 o'Clock.

Thursday the 27th February 1800

Court met pursuant to adjournment. Present, his Honor Judge Walton.

Jesse McKinney Pope }
vs } Debt Award
John Harbirt, et al Adm^{rs} }
of John Cook, dec^d }

The above suit being submitted to us to settle & determine between the parties. We do award and determine that the said suit be discontinued on the

———

Thursday the 27th February 1800 [369]

the said Administrators paying all costs not exceeding seven dollars and fifty cents over and above the legal costs.

       John Humphries   Richard Fretwell
       Jonathan Hosea   Robt Buchannan
       Ab^r Womack   John Lamar
       Gale Lewis   B. Rogers &

Matthew Kinchen Chas McDonald
Hugh Horton 15th January 1800

The State }
    vs   } Indictm^t assault
Robt Flournoy }

Defend^t plead guilty. Fined twenty five Cents.

The State }
    vs   } Ind^t assault
Joshua Ellis }

Def^t plead guilty & Fined one dollar.

The State }
    vs   } Ind^t assault
Thomas Raines }

Def^t plead guilty & Fined twenty dollars.

Fine paid!

Martin Armstrong, Appel^t }
          vs   } Case
J^no Shaw, Ass^{ee} of Elihu Lyman, Resp^t }

In this case, it is agreed that a Verdict be entered for twenty one dollars & costs, with stay of Execution until the first day of January next.

                        P. L. V. Alen
                        Martin Armstrong

            Thursday the 27th February 1800   [370]

Upon the petition of Robert McGinty setting forth that the subscribing Witnesses to a Deed of conveyance made by Isaac Williams in his life time for a tract of land lying on Town Creek in the County of Hancock, containing one hundred and sixteen acres, cannot now be procured to prove the execution thereof so as to make it a matter of Record, it is Ordered that the Subscriptions, execution, & delivery of the said deed be established at the next term of this Court by the best evidence in the hands of the petitioner, if not gainsaid, and that this order be published three months in one of the Gazettes of the State.

Aaron Woodward & C⁰ }
  vs   } Attachm^t
James Shorter   }

In this case, Henry Shorter, Special bail for the def^t, came into Court & surrendered the body of the defendant. Whereupon, it is Ordered that the said Henry Shorter be exonerated & that said defendant do stand committed to the custody of the Sheriff.

      Thursday the 27th February 1800   [371]

John Andrew & C⁰}
  vs   } Case
Joseph Hambrick }

Judgment by defailt.

Starling Abernathy }
  vs   } Deceit
Thomas Cooper }

Nonsuit.

Richard Smith, ex dem   }
of William Washington   }
  vs   } Ejectment
William Stiles & James Wooten }

Verdict acknowledged for the plaintiff and Appeal entered by consent.

            Skrine for def^{ts}
            Walker for Plff

Appeal by Consent.

Thursday the 27th February 1800 [372]

Edward Brooks }
    vs   } Case
John Hudman }

Settled.

William Newsom }
    vs   } Debt
Ezekiel Stanley }

Settled.

John Cain   }
    vs   } Case
Job Tison &   }
William H. Hargrave }

This being the second case between the parties, the claim was united with the other & this case dismissed.

Benjamin Boyce }
    vs   } assumpsit
Isaac Jackson   }

Settled.

Presentments of the Grand Jury

We, the Grand Inquest for the County of Hancock, do present on oath the unlicensed practice of the Bar in general in said County & in particular Archibald Aaron, Esquire, in respect of his abuse of the unimpeached character of Jacob Gore & Saml Barnes, who gives them or afterwards their evidence in Court on the 26th Instant.

M. Greene, foreman, Woodlief Scott, Duke Hamilton, Robt Buchannan, W. Alford, j^r, Wm Bullock, Jno Ragan, Solomon Phillips, Ja^s Harvey, Nathl Sledge, Eph^m Moore, John Rogers, Hugh M. Comer, Fred^k Mitchell, Thomas Mathews, Jno C. Peak, Lewis Graves, William Cureton, John Cook, John Kirk, Thomas Moss, Senr, John Mitchell.

Thursday the 27th February 1800 [373]

Seth Kennedy, et al }
     vs   } In Equity
The Exo^{rs} of James Adams }

To the answer filed in this case, several exceptions were taken & upon argument, it is Ordered that the defendants answer over within four months.

Samuel W. Goode }
     vs   }
Joseph Cooper }

The point made in this case was this day argued and the Court was clearly & decidedly of opinion, that the Special bail, as declared by the existing Statutes, had full and complete power to surrender the principal, either in Term time or vacation, and to be thereby fully and completely exonerated.

Ex^d Ge^o Watson

Court adjourned till Court in Course.

Attest. Mar Martin, Clk

At a Superior Court begun & held in & for the County of Hancock on   [374]
Monday the 26th August 1800, present his Honor Judge Carnes.

The following persons attended & were sworn on the Grand Jury, viz.

1. David Adams, Foreman
2. Jesse McKinney Pope
3. Henry Mitchell
4. Robt Clarke
5. Richard Shipp
6. James Lucas
7. Frederick Tucker
8. Lewis Barnes
9. William Wiley
10. William Saunders
11. Robert Moreland
12. Seth Tatum
13. Theodosius Turk
14. James Thomas
15. Jonas Shivers
16. Jonathan Adams
17. Henry Trippe
18. Elijah Freeney
19. Jonathan Miller
20. Jesse Pope, Senr
21. William Hardwick
22. John Hamilton
23. Davis McGehee

Alexander Hunter, one of the original pannel of the Grand Jury, excused for the present Term.

William Wallace }
    vs   } Case
James Farley   }

Settled says plaintiff.

Trustees of the University }
    vs   } Case
Benjamin Cook   }

Jury Sworn

1. Ansel Hudgins
2. Joseph Candler
3. Absalom Barnes
4. Vines Harwell
5. Peter F. Flournoy
6. Hardy Jernigan
7. John Cooper
8. William Gay
9. Robt Still
10. Ralph Low
11. Saml Hawkins
12. Thomas Morris

Verdict. We, the Jury, find for the plaintiffs fifty six dollars twenty four & three fourth Cents, with Costs of Suit.

                Peter F. Flournoy, foreman

Exon iss^d 15th Septr 1800.

Monday 25th August 1800   [375]

The Exo^{rs} of Wm Minor }
    vs   } Case
John Freeman   }

John Freeman, Appellant   }
    vs   } Special Case
The Exo^{rs} of Wm Minor, Resp^{ts} }

The parties in the above two Suits refer all their differences in Said cases to the final award & arbitrament of Joseph Bonner & Jeremiah Bonner, mutually chosen.

The said arbitrators to meet at the house of John Freeman in Sparta on the 15th of next month & be set on their own adjournment. Their award to be returned on or before the first day of the ensuing term, then to become the Judgment of the Court.

> Jn° Minor
> John Freeman

John Brewer }
    vs   } Debt
George Rosser & }
Alexander Reid }

Plff^s Witnesses, Andrew Irby 4 days att^{ce} proven in Court

Def^{ts} Witnesses, John Coulter, Esqr, Turner Hunt

Jury Sworn

1. Gray Andrews
2. James Crowder
3. Robert Pollard
4. James Huckaby
5. Robt Kelley
6. Joel Dickinson
7. John Thornton
8. Nehemiah Harvey
9. Saml Devereux
10. John Morris
11. Micajah Cooper
12. Jonathan Day

Verdict. We, the Jury, find for the plaintiff one thousand dollars or Warrantee titles to two thirds of the said tract of land contended for, with cost of Suit.

> Gray Andrews, Foreman

Monday the 25th August 1800   [376]

The Sheriff having represented to the Court that he was under difficulty in procuring constables to attend the Court the present term, it is Ordered that Jesse Ellis, Richard Gay, & Noah Dodridge, three Constables now in Court, attend regularly during this Term & not absent themselves without permission.

The Court finding it impossible to transact the business of the Court with propriety on account of the noise & confusion produced by Sutlers with Carts & Waggons being so near the Court house, it is Ordered, that the Waggons & Carts & all other Carriages containing liquors, Cakes, and other things for sale be removed &

remain at least fifty yards distant from the Court house, and that the Sheriff & his Officers do cause the above order to be carried into full & immediate effect.

Richard Moon }
    vs   } False imprisonment
Isaac Newton }

Settled & cost paid.

John Howard & Wm Few }
adm^{rs} of Rhesa Howard }
    vs   } Assumpsit
Job Jackson }

Discontinued.

Ex^d Thos P. Carnes

Court adjourned till [smear]

Tuesday 26th August 1800

Court met according to adjournment. Present, his Honor Judge Carnes.

Samuel Devereux }
    vs   } Trover
John Massey }

Witness for Plff, Archi Devereux

Jury Sworn

1. Jonathan Day
2. Joseph Candler
3. Absolom Barnes
4. Vines Harwell
5. Peter F. Flournoy
6. Hardy Jernigan
7. John Cooper
8. William Gay
9. Robert Still
10. Ralph Low
11. James Bonner
12. Job Allen

Verdict. We, the Jury, find for the plaintiff Seventy five dollars, with cost of Suit.

                                             Peter F. Flournoy, Foreman

Judgment signed 30th Augt 1800. Appeal entered.

Jesse Cox }
    vs   } Case
Freeman Lewis }

Jury Sworn

1. Robt Hill
2. Gray Andrews
3. Jno Thornton
4. Ansel Hudgins
5. Thos Morris
6. John Morris
7. Robert Pollard
8. James Huckaby
9. Joel Dickinson
10. Saml Devereux
11. James Crowder
12. Nehemiah Harvey

Verdict. We, the Jurors, find for the plaintiff three hundred and seventy five dollars, with interest from the 10th of May one thousand seven hundred & ninety eight & the cost of suit.

                         Gray Andrews, foreman

          Tuesday the 26th August 1800   [378]

David Clements }
    vs   } case
Thomas Glynn]

The same Jury as in the Case of Jesse Cox vs. F. Lewis. Verdict. We, the Jury, find in favor of the plaintiff thirty five Dollars, with cost of suit.

                         Gray Andrews, Foreman

Judgmt signed 20th Septr 1800. Ca Sa issd 10th Decr 1800

Elijah Freeney }
    vs   } Debt
~~Robert Huddleton~~ }
William Owsley }
Joel McClendon }
& ~~Robert Owsley~~ }

The same Jury as in the Case Devereux vs Massey. Verdict. We, the Jury, find for the Plaintiff One hundred & Sixty seven dollars & forty Cents, with all lawful Interest and Costs of Suit.

       Jonathan Day, Foreman

[bound in margin] Augt 1800. Exon iss^d 15th Septr 1800.

Archibald Traylor }
  vs   } Covenant
Andrew Jeter }

Plf^s Witness, Zach Williamson 3 days, Pleasant Rose 2 days att^{ce} proven

       Jury Sworn

  1. Robt Kelley   7. Robt Pollard
  2. Gray Andrews   8. Jno Thweatt
  3. Jno Thornton   9. Joel Dickinson
  4. Wm Lewis   10. Saml Devereux
  5. Thos Morris   11. Ja^s Crowder
  6. Jno Morris   12. Nehemiah Harvey

Verdict. We of the Jury, find for the Plaintiff Forty Dollars, with Costs of Suit.

       Gray Andrews, Foreman

[bound in margin] 1800 rec^d fifty dollars. Mar Martin

26th Decr 1800 rec^d forty one dollars Seventy five cents in full of principal debt on this Judgm^t. Arch^d X Traylor, his mark

    Tuesday the 26th August 1800   [379]

The Grand Jury returned the following Bills, vis.

The State   }
  vs   } Indictm^t Trespass
Jeffery Barksdale }

No Bill.   David Adams, Foreman

The State }
    vs   } Indictm^t Assault
John Little }

True Bill.   David Adams, Foreman

The State   }
    vs   } Indictm^t Assault
William Sparks }
John Rogers & }
Kinchen Alford }

True Bill.   David Adams, foreman

The State   }
    vs   } Indictm^t Assault
William Thelford }

True Bill.   David Adams, Foreman

John Andrews & Co }
    vs   } Case
Joseph Hambrick }

The same Jury as in the Case of Devereux vs Massey. Verdict. We, the Jury, find for the Plaintiffs Thirty two Dollars and forty three & three fourths Cents, with lawfull Interest, with Costs of Suit.

                                            Jonathan Day, Foreman

Judg^t signed 28th Augt 1800. Ca Sa iss^d 6th Septr 1800.

James Scarlett }
    vs   } Case
Moses Marshall }

I do hereby appear in Court & confess judgment for the sum of sixty one Dollars, with stay of Execution until the twenty fifth day of December next & cost. August 26th 1800

                                             Moses Marshall

Exon iss^d 21st May 1801.

Tuesday the 26th August 1800   [380]

James Scarlett   }
    vs   } Case
Moses Marshall }

I do hereby appear in Court and confess Judgment for the Sum of Sixty Dollars, with stay of Execution until the twenty fifth day of December next, with Cost of Suit. Augt 26th 1800

Moses Marshall

Exon iss^d 21st May 1801.

The State   }
    vs   } Indictm^t Assault
Philip Spiller}

True Bill.   David Adams, foreman

The State   }
    vs   } Indictm^t Assault
Philip Spiller}

True Bill.   David Adams, foreman

The State   }
    vs   } Indictm^t Assault
John Brown }

No Bill.   David Adams, foreman

~~James Smith & Co~~ }
    vs   } fia fa
~~Joseph Cooper~~ }

~~Stopped on Aff^t of Illegality. Ordered, that the Execution proceed~~. Ent^d on another page.

Tuesday the 26th August 1800

The State }
    vs   } Indictm.t Assault
Philip Spiller }

The Same }
    vs   } D°
Same   }

The defendant, Philip Spiller, Came into Court with John Gray, his Security, who acknowledged themselves bound to his Excellency the Governor and his successors in Office in the sum of one hundred dollars each, to be levied of their respective goods, Chattels, lands, & Tenements, but to be void on condition that the said Philip Spiller shall make his make his personal appearance at the next Superior Court, abide the order and determination thereof, & not depart without leave. Taken and acknowledged in Open Court the 26th Aug.t 1800.

                                Philip Spiller
                                John Gray

The State }
    vs   } Indictm.t Assault
John Little }

The defendant, John Little, came into Court with Jonathan Day, his Security, who acknowledged themselves bound to his Excellency the Governor & his successors in Office in the sum of one hundred dollars each, to be levied of their respective goods, Chattels, lands, and Tenements, but to be void on condition that the said John Little shall make his personal appearance at the next Superior Court for the County of Hancock, abide the order & determination thereof, & not depart without leave. Taken and acknowledged in Open Court the 26th Aug.t 1800.

Attest. Mar Martin, Clk   John Little
                                        Jonathan Day

Tuesday 26th August 1800

Andrew Innes }
    vs   } Case
William Weeks }

Plea to the jurisdiction of the Court sustained And Suit dismissed.

Bartholomew J. Dowdles }
    vs   } Debt
John Waller, Senr   }

Dismissed.

William Hill   }
    vs   } Debt
Riverius H. Lee }

Death of Def^t Suggested.

John Burch }
   vs   } Special Case
The Same }

Death of Def^t Suggested.

Trustees of the University }
      vs   } Case
Josiah & Thaddeus Beall }

Settled says Mr Shackleford.

Andrew Baxter }
   vs   } Special Case
Nathan Barns }

Settled at the defendant's Costs.

Wimburn Dickenson }
    vs   } Special Case
Nathan Daniel   }

Settled says plaintiff.

~~B~~ Nathaniel Waller }
   vs   } fi fa
James Scarlet }

Stopᵗ by Affᵗ of illegality. This Affᵗ stating that a motion was made for a new trial after the verdict of a special jury and not the time by day return was given [illegible]

Tuesday 26ᵗʰ August 1800 [383]

James Smith & C⁰ }
    vs   } fi fa
Joseph Cooper   }

Stopᵗ by Affᵗ of illegality. Let the Execution proceed. [blot]

Anderson & Epperson}
    vs   } Case
Joseph Thomas   }

Settled.

Exᵈ   Thoˢ P. Carnes

Court adjourned till tomorrow Morning 9 o'Clock.

Index

Aaron, 110
Abram, 129
Esther, 42
John, 110
Philip, 110
Saml., 49
Thomas, 33
William, 129
Wm., 127
Aaron
  Archibald, 289
Abercrombie, 27
  Abner, 18, 81, 85, 134, 136, 139, 143, 151, 153, 159
  Chares, 34
  Charles, 17, 32, 36, 37, 39, 40, 44, 48, 66, 108, 111, 132, 141, 149, 157, 158, 165, 166, 177, 205, 206, 216
  Chas., 33, 110, 111, 169, 170, 171, 175, 177, 184, 187
  Edmd., 23, 29, 281
  Edmond, 192, 226
  Edmund, 209, 222, 243, 268, 270
  Edwd., 29
  Robert, 41, 201, 280
  Wiley, 23, 28, 157
  Willie, 157, 158, 162, 211, 216
Abernathy
  Starling, 288
Acee
  J. L., 88
  Joshua L., 65, 88, 129, 137, 188, 190, 194, 200, 215, 232, 233, 244, 246, 257

Adams, 229
  David, 32, 51, 53, 165, 178, 283, 290, 295, 296, 297
  James, 5, 6, 7, 42, 58, 135, 206, 228, 231, 246, 290
  Jas., 9, 10, 12, 33, 178, 264
  John, 201
  John, Jr., 93
  Jonathan, 17, 222, 226, 237, 243, 290
  Jonthn., 283
Alen
  P., 105, 119, 132, 149
  P. L. V., 173, 192, 287
Alexander
  Asa, 161
  Saml., 42
  Samuel, 196
Alford
  James, 5, 200, 222, 239, 268
  Jas., 51
  Kinchen, 296
  W., Jr., 289
  William, 83
  William, Jr., 268, 269, 280, 281
  William, Sr., 17
Allen
  Charles, 269
  Freeman, 285
  Jesse, 269
  Job, 82, 83, 110, 264, 265, 293
  Philip, 65, 204, 244, 247, 260
Anderson, 144, 156, 208, 253, 278, 300
  Ben, 23
  Benj., 29

Benjamin, 121
  Jno. E., 163
  John E., 8, 278
  Jonathan, 104
  Jonthn., 284
  Mary, 34
Andrew
  John, 288
  William, 38
  Wm., 40
Andrews
  Gray, 292, 294, 295
  Gray, Sr., 284
  John, 268, 296
  William, 79
Armstrong, 54
  John C., 189, 192, 195, 198
  Martin, 15, 93, 98, 143, 166, 168,
    177, 182, 187, 188, 190, 206,
    221, 287
Askey
  James, 188, 201, 204, 211
  Uriah, 235, 283
Atkinson
  Abner, 98, 103, 188, 190, 204,
    212, 221, 227, 228, 257, 262,
    278, 284
  Agrippa, 227
  Robt., 284
  Thomas, 186, 202, 248
Averet
  Benjamin, 11
Averett
  Benjamin, 10, 11, 22
  Benjn., 10
Bagby
  Geo., 134
  George, 5, 32, 78, 90, 100, 135
Bailey
  Jno., 33, 38, 108, 124

  John, 5, 6, 48, 66, 91, 146
  Lewis, 56, 104, 226
  Mary, 104, 226
  Robert, 56, 57
  Thomas, 56
Baits
  John, 200
Bandy
  Lewis, 5, 57, 69, 71
Bankston, 138
  Abner, 13, 36, 41, 50, 69, 70, 81,
    115, 147, 249
  Daniel, 13
  Danl., 83
  Henry, 14
  Jacob, 41
Barberae
  Isaac, 50
Barfield
  Richard, 56
Barksdale
  James, 245
  Jeffery, 136, 140, 145, 151, 159,
    295
  Jefry, 134
  Joseph, 268
  William, 85, 115, 176, 268, 271
  Wm., 115
Barnes, 74
  Absalom, 284, 291
  Absolom, 293
  Jno., 32
  Lewis, 16, 39, 43, 57, 58, 59, 65,
    73, 77, 78, 83, 85, 86, 88, 115,
    131, 284, 290
  Saml., 289
  William, 136, 139, 145, 151, 159,
    189, 191, 195, 198, 204, 206,
    211, 213
  Wm., 153

Barnet
  William, 93
Barnett
  Benjamin, 268
  John, 82
  Mary, 141
  Saml., 141
Barnhart
  George, 244
  Philip, 51, 222, 228
Barns
  Nathan, 299
  William, 124, 143
  Wm., 134
Barren
  Jno., 35, 43
  John, 17, 35
Barrington
  Nathan, 165
Barron
  John, 12, 20, 21, 28, 29, 37, 79, 265
  Saml., 20, 29, 165, 166, 177, 181, 226, 227, 279
  Saml., Jr., 166, 177, 182
  Samuel, 187, 233
  Samuel, Jr., 165, 187
Bates
  John, 239
Battaile
  Jessee, 133
Battel
  Lazarus, 283
Battle
  Dempsey, 244
  Jesse, 56, 57, 89, 90, 92, 135, 148, 164, 200, 239
  William, 53, 221, 226, 237, 243
  Wm., 51, 237
Baxter
  Andrew, 91, 133, 135, 148, 164, 299
  James, 93
Baynes
  Joseph, 251
Bayzer
  Caleb, 39, 43
Bazar
  Edward, 91
  John, 91
  William, 91
Bazer
  John, 189, 242
Bazor, 124
  Caleb, 234
  Edmond, 12
  Edward, 93, 97, 99, 105, 107, 123, 124
  Edwd., 102, 113, 115
  John, 123, 124
  William, 93, 124
  William, Sr., 123, 124
Beal
  Josiah, 51, 80
  Thadeus, 117
Beale
  Thaddeus, 5
Beall
  Jona., 244
  Josiah, 53, 242, 244, 267, 285, 299
  Thaddeus, 299
  Thadeus, 6
Beard
  Edward, 56
  Francis, 99, 124
  Henry, 99
  William, 104
Bearden
  Edmund, 223

William, 112, 119, 122
Beardin
  William, 93
Beardth
  William, 128
Beatty
  Hugh, 18
Beauchamp
  Littleton, 93
Benedix, 115, 116, 118
Benson
  Aaron, 228, 234
Betts
  Saml., 271
  Saml., Jr., 268
Bezar
  Edward, 90
  John, 90
  William, Sr., 90
Bird, 264, 265
  Peter, 222, 226, 234
Bishop
  James, 56, 57, 133, 135, 151, 164, 222, 226, 237, 243, 275
  Jas., 104
  Joshua, 5, 7, 9
  Stephen, 5, 6, 104, 165
  William, 275
  Wm., 51
Biven
  William, 249
Bivin
  William, 150, 222
Bivins
  John, 18
  William, 54, 93, 102, 107, 112, 119, 122, 148, 192, 194, 195, 197
  William, Jr., 57
  Wm., 51, 226

Black
  Jonathan, 32, 34, 35, 269
Blackney
  Robert, 134
Blair
  John, 93
Blakely
  Robt., 271
Blankinship
  Rubin, 74
Boice
  Benjamin, 17
  John, 134
Bolling
  Manning, 173, 174
Bond
  John, 76, 111, 138, 165, 166, 181, 187, 207, 257
Bonner, 239
  Henry, 40, 42, 54
  Hubbard, 250, 252
  James, 44, 69, 293
  Jas., 284
  Jereh., 54
  Jeremiah, 15, 30, 40, 42, 54, 81, 103, 136, 146, 148, 181, 250, 271, 291
  Jones, 40, 42, 69, 70, 71, 72, 74
  Jordan, 135, 171, 174, 178, 179
  Jorden, 230, 231
  Joseph, 148, 291
  Peter, 54
  Richard, 15, 42, 59, 90, 91, 131, 179, 210, 211, 238
  Richd., 21, 23, 39, 40, 42, 44, 45, 182, 237
  Robert, 15, 81, 148, 166, 169, 176, 271
  Robt., 30, 81, 82
  Thomas, 136

Thos., 136
Wyat, 40, 42
Zadoc, 134
Zadok, 136
Booker
  William F., 168, 191
Booth
  Jno., Sr., 99
  John, 49, 72, 186, 202, 248, 277
  John, Jr., 93
  John, Sr., 72, 103, 186, 260
  Zach, 237
  Zachariah, 222, 226, 243, 264, 276
Borland, 238
  A., 107
  Abm., 199
  Abraham, 44, 125
  Abram, 147
  Abrm., 52
  Andrew, 14, 56, 57, 73, 77, 86, 126, 136, 158, 221, 238
  Andw., 73, 110, 119, 250
Boron
  Aaron, 189
Bouldin
  Abraham, 45
  Andrew, 28
Bowen
  Jabez, 278
  Jabez, Jr., 277, 278
Boyce
  Benjamin, 289
Boyd
  John, 134
Boyle
  P., 54, 58, 108, 239
  Peter, 40, 42, 66, 91, 210, 213, 238, 247
  Pr., 57

Bradford
  Thomas, 18, 94, 190
  Ths., 189
Brantley
  Benjamin, 13
  Malachi, 165
Brantly
  Benj., 145
Braswell
  Benjamin, 165
  James, 94
  Joseph, 56
  Saml., 108
  Samuel, Sr., 244
  William, 84, 105
Braver
  Howel, 244
Breadlove
  Ben, 35
Breedlove
  Mary, 195, 246
  Nathan, 189
  Thomas, 162, 195, 246
Brewer
  George, 56, 165, 187
  Isaac, 134
  John, 165, 275, 292
  John, Jr., 56, 57
  John, Sr., 166
  Osborn, 242
Briggs
  Zebediah, 158
Britain
  James, 14, 23, 28
Briton
  James, 23
Brooks
  Edward, 134, 289
  Isham, 134, 268, 271
  William, 269, 273

Brown, 114
  Allen, 94, 268
  Burwell, 93
  Edward, 134
  Elisha, 222
  Eppes, 17, 18, 20, 55, 165, 166, 182, 187
  Epps, 20
  Eps, 45, 52
  Jno., 23
  John, 23, 56, 59, 65, 73, 77, 83, 85, 222, 268, 269, 297
  Moses, 244
  Sheldrake, 269, 279
  Sheldrick, 32
  Thomas, 49
  Walter, 93
  William, 6, 85, 93, 113, 115, 124, 125, 159, 170
  Wm., 6, 7, 36, 114, 115, 134, 191
Browne
  Epps, 57
  Jane, 167
  John, 57, 226
  William, 102, 107, 122, 128, 228
Bryan
  Joseph, 179, 222, 225, 228, 229, 235, 241, 243, 257, 259, 262, 263, 267, 273, 275
Bryant
  Benj., 133
Buchannan
  Robert, 268, 269, 280
  Robt., 188, 252, 281, 286, 289
Buckner
  Joel, 189, 191, 197, 198, 204, 206, 211, 213
  John, 166, 173, 175, 244, 267, 285
  Tilman, 269

  William, 165, 169, 173, 175
Bullock
  William, 268, 269, 280, 281
  Wm., 289
Bunkley
  Jesse, 200, 232
Burch
  Gerard, 244
  Jarard, 127, 129
  Jarerd, 204
  Jaret, 146
  Jarrard, 128, 131
  Jarratt, 5
  Jerald, 93
  Jerard, 96, 132, 188, 190, 246, 258, 260, 261, 267
  John, 243, 246, 254, 256, 258, 260, 261, 263, 267, 270, 299
Burge, 239
  Jno., 45
  John, 127, 210, 211, 238
  Willie, 89, 189, 197, 198, 206, 211, 213, 268, 273
Burges
  Joseph, 204
Burgess
  Joseph, 51
Burne
  Jane, 38, 40, 79
Burnley
  Henry, 56
Burns
  William, 105, 128, 144
  Willm., 111
Burton
  Allen, 89
  William A., 209
Butler
  Edmd., 22, 258
  Edmd., Jr., 244

Edmd., Sr., 17
Edmond, 164
Edmond, Sr., 133, 135, 148, 151
Edmund, 247, 260
Edmund, Sr., 175
Edward, 132
Edward, Sr., 19
Henry, 185
Jno., 99, 102, 105
John, 93, 97, 107, 112, 119, 140, 146
William, 189, 242
Butts
  Azariah, 5, 93, 108, 111
  Hazariah, 6
  James, 133, 138
  John, 189, 242
Buyas
  John, 251
Byas
  John, 244
Bynam
  James, 146
Bynum
  James, 92, 244, 246, 255, 256, 257, 258, 260, 261, 267
Cain
  James, 32
  John, 289
  William, 17, 129, 222
Cairy
  Thomas, 158, 162
Calbert
  Jonathan, 227
Caldwell
  Hy., 64
Callaway
  John, 268
  Levin, 268
  Thomas, 57

Cambell
  Dunkin, 234
Cammell
  Duncan, 228
Campbell
  Duncan, 229, 230, 231, 234, 235, 236
Candler
  Jno., 27
  John, 236
  John K., 166, 187
  Jos., 284
  Joseph, 291, 293
Carnelo
  Jno., 51
Carnes, 166, 172, 175, 180, 187, 225, 226, 233, 240, 290, 293
  P. J., 14, 27, 28, 97, 178
  Peter, 7, 8, 150
  T. P., 97, 114
  Thos. P., 167, 172, 175, 180, 189, 226, 233, 240, 245, 293, 300
  W., 87
Carr
  James, 244
Carrel
  Jesse, 144, 145
Cars
  Joseph, 104
Carson
  Joseph, 5, 31
  Wm., 124
Carter
  Hezekiah, 51, 245
  Isaac, 133, 140
  James, 222
  Jno., 32, 34, 43
  John, 37, 269
  Littleton, 277
Castleberry

Henry, 244
Jno., 37
Jno., Sr., 32
Richd., 41
Castlebery
  Asa, 139
  Richard, 139
Castlebury
  Henry, 93, 248
  Thos., 284
Cathel
  James, 146
Cathell
  James, 6, 14, 151, 152, 189, 242,
    249, 256
  Jas., 9
Cato
  Greene, 269, 273
  Starling, 151, 164
  Sterling, 133, 135
Chambers, 91, 266
  Robert, 199, 201
  Robt., 176, 202
Champen
  John, 167
Champion
  Hart, 51, 53, 64, 65, 98, 101
Chandler
  John, 23
  William, 166, 262, 263, 267, 280
Chapel
  Joseph, 16, 23
  Josh, 23
Chapman
  Henry, 252
Chappel
  Josh, 28
  Thomas, 191, 201, 206
Chappell
  Benjamin, 56

John, 210, 238
Thomas, 189, 197, 204, 211, 213
Thos., 17
Chapple
  Joseph, 18
Choice
  Tulley, 33
  Tully, 17, 32, 48, 132
Christopher
  James, 17, 44, 204
  Jas., 7, 52
Clark
  Cornelius, 84
  Henry, 36, 244
  Josh Robt., 32
  Robt., 84
  Robt., Jr., 283
  William, 5, 48, 120, 189, 191,
    195, 198, 206, 211, 213, 236
  Wm., 32, 33
Clarke
  Robt., 290
  William, 255
Clarr, 54
Clary
  Robert, 141
Clements
  David, 199, 294
  Jesse, 36, 180
  Philip, 36
Clemonds
  Jesse, 29
  Philip, 51
Clemons
  Jesse, 38
Clower
  George, 167, 231
  William, 234
  Wm., 232, 234
Coats

Lesley, 181, 207
Cobb
  John, 189
Cobbs
  John, 78, 264, 276
Coffee
  Peter, 51, 53, 133, 196, 197, 200, 235, 239, 244, 246, 256, 257, 263
Colbert
  Jonathan, 260
Coleman
  Harris, 195
  J., 118
  John, 165, 187, 242
  Josiah, 18
Colier
  William, 39
Collier
  Wyatt, 93, 96, 128, 129, 188, 190, 204, 206, 209, 212, 221, 269, 271
Colter
  Jno., 43
  Mary, 43
  Peter, 43
  William, 53
  Wm., 53
Comer
  Anderson, 39, 55, 137
  Hugh M., 268, 270, 281, 289
  James, 252
Connel
  Jesse, 214
Connell
  Jesse, 272
Conner
  Danl., 189
Cook
  Allen, 93, 103, 105, 260

  Benjamin, 291
  Drury, 5, 7, 8, 14
  John, 124, 160, 173, 238, 248, 252, 268, 269, 281, 286, 289
  John, Sr., 91
  Joseph, 232
  Philip, 160, 173, 248
  Zadok, 257
Cooper, 70, 125
  James, 93
  John, 284, 291, 293
  Jos., 205, 270
  Joseph, 17, 27, 69, 125, 130, 137, 165, 201, 204, 269, 270, 282, 283, 290, 297, 300
  Joseph, Jr., 132
  Joseph, Sr., 187, 270, 285
  Micajah, 292
  Thomas, 19, 87, 92, 96, 128, 175, 222, 228, 257, 258, 288
  Thos., 73, 87, 127, 129, 131, 258
Corley
  Edmd., 197, 271
  Edmond, 201
  Edmund, 197
Cormell
  Jesse, 21
Cotton
  George, 216
Coulter, 33
  Jno., 39
  John, 222, 292
  William, 33
  Wm., 43
Coventon
  John, 67
Cowden, 42
  James, 82, 83, 110, 166
Cowdon
  James, 187

Cox
  Jesse, 294
Craft
  Danl., 83
Crawford
  Wm. H., 275
Credenton
  Thomas, 110
Creswell
  Nancy, 150, 249
Crocker
  Arthur, 51
Crosby
  William, 151
Crouch
  John, 133
Crowder
  Edmd., 15, 17, 32, 33, 37, 38, 48, 232
  Edmond, 14
  Edmund, 41, 237
  James, 292, 294
  Jas., 284, 295
Culver
  Nathan, 106, 204
  Salathel, 94, 192
  Salathiel, 102, 107, 112, 119, 122, 125, 128, 188, 197, 201, 204, 206, 213
Cummins
  Alexr., 271
Cunningham
  Robert, 133, 135, 146, 147, 161, 164, 230
  Robt., 148, 149
  Robt. M., 253
  W., 120
Cureton
  Boling, 156, 161
  Bolling, 180, 214, 222
  William, 115, 116, 268, 269, 281, 289
  William, Jr., 57, 121
Currie
  John, 93
Curtis
  Blundel, 51
  Daniel, 74
  Isaac, 72, 127, 194, 277
  Levi, 145, 188, 195
  Nathan, 299
Daniell
  Levi, 191, 222
  Stephen, 175
  Ward, 14
Danielly
  Arthur, 145
  Aurther, 85
  Francis, 85
Darby
  James, 166
Daudle
  Prudence, 151
Davis
  Blanford, 8
  James, 200
  Jonathan, 279
  Vachel, 8
Day
  John, 130
  Jonathan, 98, 101, 103, 292, 293, 295, 296, 298
  Robert, 93, 98, 102, 125, 171, 178, 199, 213, 214
  Robt., 83, 101, 105, 107, 112, 119, 122, 128, 178
  Simon, 79
De Yambert
  John, 68, 69
de Yampert

John, 69
De Yampert
  John, 118, 183
Deal
  John, 168
  Thomas, 168
Denn
  John, 152, 162, 181, 182, 186, 195, 196, 200, 202, 208, 237, 239, 240, 246, 248, 250, 259
Dennis, 205, 282
  Isaac, 51, 134, 139, 143, 145, 151, 153, 159
  Jacob, 222, 226, 237, 243
  John, 165, 170, 172, 174, 175, 205
  Jos., 284
  Josiah, 129, 169, 223, 281
  Matthias, 207
  William, 284
Dent
  B. W., 222
  John, 247, 264, 272
  Peter, 133, 135, 148, 151, 164, 244
  Saml., 97, 99, 102, 108, 110, 112, 113, 114, 115, 116, 122, 133, 247, 253
  Samuel, 93, 108, 214, 258
  Thomas, 17, 253
  Thos., 43
  Walter, 29, 74
  William, 146, 179
  William, Jr., 165
Devereux, 114, 295, 296
  Archi., 293
  John W., 112, 113
  John William, 268, 270
  Saml., 284, 292, 294, 295
  Samuel, 293

Dickenson
  Wimburn, 299
Dickinson, 16
  Joel, 179, 188, 191, 195, 198, 204, 206, 211, 213, 284, 292, 294, 295
  John, 56
  Thomas, 6
  Wimburn, 93, 97, 99, 112, 115
  Wimbush, 108
Dickison
  Joseph, 45
  Josh, 45
Dickson
  David, 66, 108, 146, 184, 195
Diknson
  Thomas, 112
Dixon
  David, 57
  Henry, 157, 216
  J. L., 178, 225
  James, 242
  John L., 248
Dodridge
  Noah, 192, 197, 292
Dooly
  Geo., 31
Dormond
  John, 284
Dowdles
  Bartholomew, 299
Downs
  Isaac, 161
  Silas, 40
Duboise
  Lewis, 100
Dunn
  Alexander, 172
  John, 165
Durham

Mathew, 51
Matthew, 166, 170
Dyches
　Daniel, 268
Dykes
　Daniel, 271
Early, 156, 180, 190, 248
　Peter, 212
Earnest
　George, 5, 7, 14
　Jacob, 133
Echols
　Frederick, 269
　Fredk., 273
Edwards
　John, 268
　William, 32
Eiland
　Absalom, 223
　Absolem, 104
　Absolom, 228
Elholm, 156, 225
　A. C. G., 182
　Augustus C. George, 186
　Augustus Christian George, 181
Eliot
　Thomas, 73
Elliot
　Thomas, 226, 227
Ellis
　Jesse, 32, 34, 35, 37, 103, 114, 128, 158, 162, 204, 242, 292
　Joshua, 93, 274, 277, 287
　Levin, 56, 57, 162, 244, 247, 260
　Stephen, 56, 269
　Walter, 32
Emberson
　Jas., 284
Epperson, 300
Ernest
　Jacob, 135
Evans
　Benjn., 197
　David, 244, 247, 260
　George, 92, 189, 191, 195, 198, 202
　James, 146, 152, 163, 208
　Stephen, 133, 244, 251, 263, 265, 274
　William, 189, 191, 195, 198, 199, 201, 204, 206
Everet
　Benjamin, 24
Everett
　Archelus, 158
Ewin
　Samuel, 93
Ewing
　William, 77
Fail
　Jas., 176
　Thomas, 6
　Thos., 237
Farley
　James, 291
Farrell
　Archelous, 260
Feagan
　Aaron, 56
Felps
　David, 92, 96, 127, 128, 129, 131
　James, 271
　Samuel, 120
Felts
　James, 269
Fenn
　Richard, 152, 162, 181, 182, 195, 196, 200, 208, 237, 240, 246, 250, 259
　Richd., 239

William, 186, 202, 248, 274
Ferrell
  Archelaus, 273
  Archelous, 269
Ferrill
  Archelous, 156
  Bird, 156
  William, 269
Few
  W., 64
  William, 229
  Wm., 293
Fields
  Thomas, 56, 268
  Thos., 214, 255
Finch
  Charles, 49
  Robert, 187
  Robt., 165
Fitzgeareld
  William, 67
Fitzgerald
  William, 83, 87, 125
Fitzgerreld
  William, 75
Flornoy
  Robert, 11
Flournoy, 234, 254, 274, 283
  Peter F., 284, 291, 293
  R., 180, 245
  Robert, 19, 122, 132, 139, 140, 152, 159, 160, 168, 174, 180, 191, 208, 215, 245, 256, 273, 274
  Robt., 132, 163, 234, 241, 245, 254, 259, 287
  Tho., 160, 278
  Thomas, 19, 233, 278
  Thos., 160
Flowers
  Edwd., 244
Forsyth
  Fanny, 110
Fort
  Arthur, 276
Foster
  William, 244
Foxwell
  William, 94
Frazier
  Absalom, 39
  Benjamin, 94
  John, 93
Freeman
  Jno., 252
  John, 250, 269, 282, 291, 292
Freeneau
  Elijah, 188
  John, 189
Freeney
  Elijah, 190, 206, 209, 221, 284, 290, 294
French
  James, 56
Fretwell
  Richard, 166, 169, 173, 175, 252, 286
Fulsom
  John, 56
Fulwood
  Jane, 230
  Robert, 230
Fuquay
  Moses, 166
  Partha, 93
Gaither, 149, 183
  B., 152
  Brice, 133, 135, 152, 164, 215
  Henry, 136, 149, 181, 192, 203, 215, 242, 243

Gan
  Jno., 16
  John, 141
  Saml., 87
  Samuel, 87
Gander
  Mark, 139, 168
Gann
  Jane, 162
  Jno., 157
  John, 17, 147, 156, 157, 158, 176, 177, 204
  Mary, 158, 187, 204, 211
  Nathan, 98, 101
  Saml., 16, 17, 21, 23, 28
Garrett
  Henry, 185
  James, 137
Gay
  Allen, 232, 233
  Jno., 51
  John, 232, 233
  P., 189
  Patience, 227, 232, 233, 235, 259, 274
  Richard, 292
  William, 227, 232, 233, 235, 259, 284, 291, 293
  Wm., 274
George
  Elijah, 5, 6, 9, 14
Gibson
  John, 58, 98
Gilbert
  Benj., 65, 70, 86, 98
  Benjamin, 57, 58, 59, 65, 71, 88, 90, 101, 171, 249
  Benjn., 89, 284
  Felix, 27
  Martin, 21, 22, 51
  Michael, 12, 21, 22, 57, 79, 176, 192, 197, 204, 249
  Michl., 29, 39, 44, 52, 113, 115
  Robert, 269
  Robts., 273
  William, 22, 103
  Wm., 32
Giles
  Saml., 51
  Samuel, 80, 153
Gillaland
  Thomas, 93
Gilleland
  Wm., 176
Gilliland
  William, 93
  Wm., 27
Givens
  Saml., 240
Givins
  Samuel, 173
Glass, 280
  William, 8, 171
  Zachariah, 8, 18, 23, 45, 97, 279
Glynn
  Thomas, 294
Goar
  Jacob, 177
Golightly
  James, 146, 186, 202
Goode
  S. M., 197
  Saml., 17, 133
  Saml. W., 283
  Samuel W., 290
  Thomas, 268, 271
Goodright
  George, 173
Goodtitle
  James, 106, 254

Gorden
  Benjamin, 195
  Thomas, 195
  Thos., 23
Gordon
  Samuel, 49
  Thomas, 208
Gore
  Jacob, 96, 131, 157, 176, 204, 216, 281, 289
Grace
  Thomas, 5, 6, 7
Graham
  James, 103
Grammer
  John, 170, 172, 173
  Peter, 170, 172, 174
Grant
  Benjamin, 18
Grantham
  William, 19, 45, 89, 125
  Wm., 52, 53
Graves
  Lewis, 268, 269, 281, 289
  Wm., 134
Gray
  George, 56, 200, 284
  John, 298
  Joshua, 93
  Moreton, 262
  Robert, 244
  Robt., 189
  Thomas, 34
Graybill
  Hen., 6, 10, 18, 22, 25, 29, 38
  Henry, 10, 132, 175, 194, 200, 208, 232
Grear
  Jno., 38
Green
  James, 244, 246, 261
Greene, 141
  James, 188, 190, 204, 206, 209, 212, 221, 257, 258, 260, 263, 267
  James W., 206, 208, 209
  M., 273, 274, 280, 282, 289
  Miles, 268
  Myles, 210, 238, 269, 280, 281
Greer
  Betsey, 87
  Elizabeth, 158
  Elizabeth, Jr., 158
  Elizabeth, Sr., 187
  John, 58, 59, 65, 133, 135, 148, 151, 164
Grier
  Elizabeth, 204, 211
  John, 56
Griffen
  Jno., 22
Griffin, 190, 195, 202, 206, 258
  Jno., 138, 231
  John, 59, 212, 231
Grigg
  J., 96
  Jesse, 93, 97, 99, 100, 103, 114, 127, 128, 129, 130, 131, 146, 188, 190, 204, 206, 209, 210, 212, 221, 238, 239
Griggs
  John, 56, 57, 59, 65, 73, 77, 83, 86, 90
  William, 94
Grimmer
  William, 189, 191, 195, 198, 206, 211, 213
Gualtney
  John, 284
Guthrie

315

Alexander, 209
Haddock
  Richard, 145, 212
Hagan
  Isham, 98, 207
Hagerty
  Jonathan, 260
Halcom
  John, 96
Halcomb, 138
  John, 127, 128, 131
Hall, 276
  B., 118, 160, 185, 228, 235
  Benj., 97, 102, 115, 122, 128
  Benjamin, 93, 99, 105, 107
  Benjn., 113
  Bolling, 19, 89, 163, 208
  Bouldin, 21
  Bouldin, Sr., 27
  Dixon, 51, 53, 133, 135, 148, 164, 273
  Henry, 94, 103, 105
  Hugh, 140, 176, 273, 275
  Isaac, 165, 169, 173, 175
  James, 42
  Ject, 189
  M., 163
  Saml., 89
  Saml., Sr., 146
Hambleton
  Thos., 52
Hambrick
  Joseph, 288, 296
Hamil
  Jno., 38
Hamill, 156
  J., 241, 264, 276
  Jno., 256
  John, 9, 276
Hamilton, 18, 101, 105, 175

Duke, 89, 90, 184, 198, 268, 269, 280, 281, 289
John, 42, 54, 57, 88, 91, 113, 115, 132, 165, 166, 187, 290
John, Sr., 284
William, 93, 99, 102, 107, 112, 119, 122, 124, 128, 222, 234, 244, 246, 254, 256, 259, 260, 261, 263, 267
Wm., 97, 105
Hamlin, 31
  John, 26, 38, 81, 85, 134
  Richard, 30, 70, 81, 85, 130
  Richd., 29
Hammil, 79
Hanby
  John, 284
Hansel
  Jno. T., 83
  John, 166, 213
Harbirt
  Jno., 32, 33, 84
  John, 56, 57, 66, 67, 68, 75, 81, 84, 87, 91, 124, 250, 252, 254, 255, 256, 258, 259, 260, 261, 262, 263, 267, 286
Harden, 31
  Demsey, 133
Hardridge
  James, 222
Hardwick
  William, 284, 290
Hargrave
  William H., 289
Hargraves
  Geo., 133
  George, 135, 148, 164
Hargrove
  Eldridge, 247
Harney

John, 244
Harper
　Benjamin, 268, 271
　James, 8
　Robert, 17
　Robt., 42
　William, 170, 172, 173, 251
Harris, 130
　Absalom, 93, 222, 226
　Absolem, 96, 131
　Buckner, 45
　Edmund, 222
　Elisha, 244
　Harris, 153
　Micajah, 17, 69, 134
　Moses, 15, 70, 76, 84, 92, 118, 125, 129, 132, 140, 141, 152, 158, 192, 213
　Saml., 57, 59, 71
　Samuel, 56, 65, 77
　Thos., 244
Harrison
　John, 82, 222, 284
　Reuben, 210, 240
　Reubin, 153
　Thomas, 14
Harriss, 264, 265
　Buckner, 45
　Moses, 30
Hart
　Saml., 189
　Samuel, 200, 239
Harvey
　Evan, 70, 130
　George, 285
　James, 7, 51, 53, 120, 194, 268, 270, 280, 281
　Jas., 289
　Jno., 7
　John, 5, 14, 146, 267

　Michael, Sr., 283
　Nehemiah, 292, 294, 295
　Zepha., 284
　Zephaniah, 44, 52, 188, 190, 204, 205, 209, 212, 221
Harvie
　John, 134
　Wm., 134
Harwell
　Anderson, 165, 169, 173, 175, 194
　John, 241
　Ransom, 200, 232, 279
　Ransome, 232
　Richard, 284
　Richd., 189
　Vines, 284, 291, 293
Harwood
　Jesse, 57, 59, 65, 73, 85, 188
　Turner, 43, 94, 97, 99, 103, 105, 108, 112, 119, 122, 125, 128, 168, 253
Haverd
　John, 6
Hawkins, 149
　Matthew, 39, 44, 148
　Mattw., 52
　Saml., 281, 282, 284, 291
Hay
　Curtis, 56
Hayes
　Patric, 52
　Patrick, 50, 138
Haynes
　John, 121
Hays
　Patrick, 107, 147, 168, 191
Hearn
　Elisha, 56
　Jonathan, 268

Wm., 244
Hearndon
  George, 111, 138, 257
  Joseph, 77
Heath
  John, 50, 93, 107, 111, 112, 113
  Thomas, 6, 50, 113
  Thos., 107
Henderson
  John, 244, 246, 255, 260, 261, 263, 267
Henry
  Joseph, 121
Henson
  William, 203
Herbert
  John, 5, 243, 246, 247, 248, 256
Herdman
  John, 284
Hern
  Jno. P. Isaac, 32
Herndon
  George, 207
Herod
  Jesse, 56
Herring
  Alexander, 71
Heth, 109
Higgenbotham
  Joseph, 230
Higginbotham
  Joseph, 253
Hill
  James, 121
  John, 283
  Robert, 5, 56, 265
  Robt., 57, 294
  Thomas, 5, 6, 9
  William, 270, 299
Hilton
  Abrm., 189
Hinson
  William, 71, 88, 89
Hobby, 156
Hogan, 280
  Isham, 10, 68, 78, 101, 103, 106, 122, 125, 157, 159, 177, 180, 205, 210, 211, 214, 227, 228, 234, 235, 246, 262, 265, 268, 271, 272, 275, 276, 278, 279
Hogans
  Isham, 115, 228
Hogen
  Isham, 23, 35, 125
Hogg
  James, 127, 142, 216
  James, Jr., 137, 192, 197
  James, Sr., 186
Hogin
  Isham, 37, 41, 48
Hogins
  Isham, 35
Holcomb
  Jacob, 166
  Jno. C., 51
  John, 93
Holeford
  John, 285
Holley
  Saml., 140
  Samuel, 140
Holmes
  Richard, 231
  Richd., 229
Holsom
  John, 13
Holt
  Hines, 90, 162, 271
  Martha W., 34
  Singleton, 268

T., 191
Thaddeus, 16, 19, 21, 22, 23, 27,
   34, 41, 57, 74, 93, 96, 157, 161,
   191, 211, 216, 217, 222, 226,
   258, 266
Thadds., 17
Thadeus, 11
Thads., 191
Wm., 51
Holton
   James, 10
Hooring
   Alexr., 51
Horn
   Jonathan, 51
   Violet, 64, 65
   Wm., 51
Horton
   Hugh, 134, 199, 202, 252, 287
   James, 5, 32, 33, 48
   Stephen, 57, 89, 109, 112, 115,
      119, 179, 188, 190, 205, 221,
      243, 246, 252, 256, 257, 259,
      267
   William, 117, 118, 244, 246, 256,
      259, 260, 261, 263, 267
   Willm., 254
   Wm., 118
Hosea
   Jonathan, 252, 286
Hoskins
   Chas, 134
Howard
   John, 229, 293
   Josh, 43
   Resa, 114, 229
   Rhesa, 293
Howell
   Hezekiah, 230
   Joseph, 32, 230

Philip, 142, 192, 196, 215, 285
Hubbard
   Gabriel, 44
Hubert
   Gabl., 82, 86
   Gabriel, 81, 82, 86, 170, 271
   Mathew, 123
Huckaby
   James, 98, 125, 132, 182, 194,
      227, 244, 283, 292, 294
   Jas., 285
Huddleston
   James, 28
   Wm., 28
Huddlestone
   Wm., 133
Huddleton
   Robert, 294
Hudgens
   Ansel, 81
Hudgin
   Ansel, 39
Hudgins
   Ansel, 291, 294
   Anselm, 284
Hudleston
   William, 94
Hudman
   Jno., 226
   John, 289
Hudson
   Eli, 222
   Levin, 145, 244
Hughes
   Nicholas, 17, 139, 153
Hughs
   Nicholas, 134, 143, 145, 151
Humphries
   Isham, 244
   James, 230

John, 170, 252, 268, 270, 286
Hunt
  Daniel, 277
  Judkins, 51, 54, 136
  Turner, 194, 196, 222, 226, 237, 243, 263, 265, 274, 292
  W., 111
  William, 93, 97, 99, 105, 107, 112
  Wm., 102, 107, 109, 116, 119, 128, 129
Hunter
  Alex, 230, 284
  Alexander, 291
  Edward, 50, 141
  Edwd., 34, 44, 45, 52
  James, 230
  Sam, 184
  Saml., 184, 240
  Samuel, 175, 183, 184, 214, 265
Hurley
  David, 32
Hurt
  Joel, 18
  William, 172
Huster
  John, 134
Hutcherson
  James, 117
  Joseph, 8
  William, 147
Hutcheson, 30
Hutchinson
  James, 276
  Joseph, 7
Hutchison
  Wm., 52
Ingram
  William, 269
Innes

  Andrew, 298
Irby
  Andrew, 292
Irvin
  David, 284
Jack
  Jno., 70
  John, 69, 130, 185, 252
Jackson, 242
  Absalom, 77, 273
  Absolem, 122, 142
  D., 189
  David, 196
  Drury, 192, 195, 201, 204, 206, 211, 213
  Isaac, 133, 230, 253, 289
  James, 256
  Job, 39, 43, 49, 107, 113, 114, 229, 293
  John, 50
  Robert, 256
  Stephen, 39, 43, 49, 50, 107, 113
  Thos., 51
Jacobs
  Joshua, 134
  Mordecai, 136, 139, 143, 145, 151, 153, 159
  Mordicai, 134
Jarnigan
  Needham, 57
Jaxon
  Solomon, 206
Jenkins
  William, 72
Jernagan
  Needham, 27
Jernigan
  Hardy, 189, 191, 195, 198, 204, 291, 293

Henry, 107, 134, 146, 168, 191, 269
James, 268
Needham, 11, 56, 121
Needham, Sr., 132
Jeter
  Andrew, 275, 295
John
  William, 244, 251
  Zephaniah, 16, 146, 165, 166, 177
  Zepheniah, 69, 71
Johnson, 79, 109
  Abel, 45
  Hezekiah, 39, 143
  Hezh., 38, 39
  Israel, 167
  John, 222
  Martin, 93, 164, 223
  Samuel, 188, 190
  Thomas, 43, 72, 107, 204
  Thos., 39, 50, 57, 111
  William, 78
Johnston, 43
  Alexander, 56
  Charles, 56
  Hezekiah, 70, 130
  Thomas, 10, 56, 113
  Zephaniah, 113
Jones
  Benjamin, 11, 12, 165, 242
  Benjn., 187
  Hardy, 235
  Hartwell, 210, 238
  Henry, 244, 247, 260, 273
  Jno., 24
  John, 22, 199, 201, 202, 244
  Joseph, 228
  Nathan, 93

Reuben, 166, 177, 187, 201, 257, 259, 262, 263, 267, 280
Seaborn, 24, 31, 32
West, 125, 159, 210
William, 156
Jordan
  Solomon, 56, 57, 235
Journegan
  Henry, 138
Journigan
  Hardy, 284
  Needham, Sr., 284
Justice
  Dempsey, 244, 251, 253
  Jno., 108
  John, 93, 99, 112
Justices
  John, 97
Keaner
  Jacob, 165
Kelley
  Jesse, 94
  John, 6, 106, 179, 230, 231, 247, 275
  Lloyd, 139, 168
  Loyd, 268, 281
  Robt., 254, 292, 295
  Thomas, 93
Kelly, 110
  Andrew O., 124
  David, 188
  Jesse, 100, 101
  Jno., 9, 254
  John, 6, 73, 108, 158, 176, 180, 244, 260
  Loyd, 51, 106, 270
  Robt., 284
Kenley
  Loyd, 106
Kennedy

Caleb, 56
Seth, 264, 290
Kerr
  James, 188
Kilbee
  Tho., 188
Kilgore
  John, 74
Kinchen
  Mathew, 244
  Matthew, 246, 252, 254, 256, 257, 287
Kindrick
  Hezekiah, 195
King
  Andrew, 76, 116
  Thomas, 193, 207
Kinney
  Joshua, 177, 242, 251
Kinny
  Joel, 134
Kirk
  John, 145, 213, 268, 269, 281, 289
  Joseph, 268
  Stephen, 56, 73, 77, 91, 124
Knight
  Robt., 188
Knowles, 229, 231
  Edmond, 206
  Robert, 277
Lamar, 71
  James, 56
  Jas., 284
  Jno., 32, 33
  John, 17, 48, 50, 59, 101, 112, 113, 131, 252, 261, 275, 286
  Thomas, 80, 188, 190, 205, 212, 221, 230, 253
  Thos., 80, 284

Z., 80
Zachariah, 80
Lancaster
  Levi, 11, 31, 37, 39, 43, 126, 165, 166, 177, 182, 187
  Tho., 189
  Thomas, 201, 211, 213, 284
  William, 17, 102, 105, 107, 112, 119, 122, 124
  Wm., 111, 128, 235
Landcaster
  William, 93
Langford
  Moses, 252
Langham
  Thomas H., 197
Lanier
  Henry, 134, 135
Lary
  J., 189
Laurence, 21, 22, 24, 25, 26, 27, 29, 30, 31, 37, 38, 59, 72, 79, 109, 122, 126, 138
  Abraham, 263
  Alexander, 263
  James, 68, 75, 102
  Thomas, 84
Lawless
  Abraham, 144, 208, 255
  Abram, 179
  James, 146, 186, 202
Lawrence, 8, 10, 11, 13, 14, 31
  Abraham, 196, 197
  James, 68, 75, 117
  Jas., 98
Lawson
  ___, 39
  Francis, 44, 45, 55, 57, 67, 68, 75, 102, 117, 222, 226, 243, 254, 268, 270

Jane, 68, 75, 102
John, 117, 118
Thomas, 68, 75, 76, 102, 117
William, 22, 57, 87, 93, 108, 112, 115, 222, 234, 258
William, Jr., 56, 83, 175
William, Sr., 56, 67, 68, 75, 102, 117, 118
Wm., 28, 118, 226
Lea
  George, 222
  Temple, 222
Lee
  George, 92, 96, 127, 128, 129, 131, 268
  Green, 134
  Greene, 56
  John, Jr., 269
  John, Sr., 268
  R. H., 270
  Riverius H., 270, 279, 299
Leigh
  John, 94
Leneer
  William, 110
Leon, 115, 116, 118
Leonard
  Ben, 32, 34, 43
  Benjamin, 37
Lethro
  Robert, 13
Levar
  Philip, 93
Lewis, 138
  Daniel, 93
  F., 294
  Freeman, 294
  Gale, 252, 286
  H., 263
  James, 51, 269, 272

John, Jr., 90, 96
Wm., 295
Lidd
  David, 86, 87, 88, 89
Lightfoot
  Thomas, 223
Liles
  Ephraim, 228
Lincicomb
  Hezekiah, 36
Lindsay
  John, 152, 153
Lindsey
  John, 130
Lindsy
  John, 70
Lingo
  Elijah, 275
Linsacomb
  Hezekiah, 36, 44
Linsey
  Jno., 30
Lishman
  Edmund, 93
Lithgo
  Robert, 22
Little
  John, 247, 264, 272, 296, 298
Lloyd
  Moses, 185
Lockhart
  Abner, 249
  Richard, 188, 190, 204, 212, 221
  Richd., 51, 83, 174
Lofton
  Thos., 17
Long
  Arther, 72
  Davis, 88, 133, 135, 164
  Henry, 175

Nicholas, 272
Lord
  Wm., 133
Low
  Daniel, 55, 57, 245
  Henry, 134
  Jno., 32
  Ralph, 115, 133, 136, 139, 143, 145, 153, 159, 291, 293
  William, 6, 77, 122, 126, 142, 273
  Wm., 31
Lowe
  Ralph, 284
  Wm., 7
Loyd
  James, 18
Loyed
  John, 65
Lucas, 91
  James, 17, 188, 200, 232, 284, 290
  John, 247
  Moses, 14
  Sarah, 83
Lyas
  Lewis, 259
Lyman
  Elihu, 287
M___
  Edmd., 40
Macintosh
  John, 276
Madaus
  James, 222
Maddox
  Andrew, 99, 140, 226
  Ben, 26, 43
  Benjamin, 65
  Nany, 40

  William, 34, 37, 158, 244
  William, Sr., 32
  Wm., 21, 23, 29, 176
  Zachariah, 21
Maddux
  Andrew, 166, 177, 182, 187, 222
  Michael, 269
  William, 242, 247
Madox
  Andrew, 234
  Michael, 85
  Zack, 134
Magahee
  Wm., 244
Mahan
  Polly, 99, 103
Maher, 174
  Matthias, 173, 174, 179, 231
Mangham
  Wm., 213
Manor
  John, 134
Map
  Littleton, Sr., 91
Mapp, 110, 266
  Jno., 254
  John, 17, 106, 108, 158, 161
  William, 56
Marbert
  John, 198
Marcus
  John, 134
Marden
  William, 52
Maroney
  James, 215
Marony
  James, 147, 156, 161
Marshall
  Moses, 296, 297

Martin, 114, 258, 259
　Godfry, 42
　James, 119, 205, 223, 230
　M., 20
　Mar, 55, 57, 64, 69, 72, 73, 76, 82, 83, 86, 88, 89, 105, 106, 111, 133, 136, 141, 145, 150, 152, 167, 168, 174, 177, 178, 180, 183, 184, 185, 207, 223, 225, 226, 232, 233, 234, 240, 241, 245, 251, 254, 267, 270, 290, 295, 298
　Martin, 247
　William, 98
Mason
　John C., 140, 269, 273, 275, 276
　Thomas, 139, 170
Massey, 295, 296
　John, 293
　Russel, 145
Mathews
　Jno., 49, 112
　Thomas, 56, 91, 268, 270, 281, 289
　Thos., 124
Matthews, 19
　Thomas, 57
McAlister, 181
　David, 93, 181
McAlpin
　Robt., 141
McCall, 242
　Thomas, 280
McCarter
　Jeremiah, 134
McCarty
　John, 275
McClelland
　William, 51
McClendal
　Joel, 23
McClendon, 149, 183
　Jno., 192
　Job, 98
　Joel, 52, 80, 99, 124, 127, 142, 149, 166, 176, 181, 187, 199, 202, 215, 222, 294
McClure
　Tobias, 197
McCormick
　James, 222
McCoy
　Henry, 5, 6, 32, 33, 48
McCrary
　Jonathan, 104
McCreary
　Bartley, 82
McCue
　Dennis, 198
McCullers
　John, 242
McCullock
　Jno., 51
　John, 138
McDaniel
　Robert, 94
McDonald
　Charles, 79, 206, 252, 256, 271, 276
　Chas., 287
　Edwd., 244
　Thomas, 209
McDowell
　Daniel, 11, 158, 161, 180
　Danl., 249
McGaughey
　John, 265
　William, 18, 140
McGeehee
　Wm., 26

325

McGehee
  Davis, 115, 284, 290
  Saml., 51, 188, 209, 212
  Samuel, 190, 204, 205
  William, 79
  Wm., 122
McGinty
  Robert, 52, 133, 135, 143, 148, 164, 174, 176, 237, 287
  Robt., 80, 104, 174, 268, 270, 281
McInvail
  William, 18, 28
  Wm., 28
McInvaile, 27
  Wm., 23
McInvaill
  William, 236
McKay
  Chas., 188
  John, 244
McKenzie
  Aaron, 104, 196
  Jno., 32, 101, 174
  John, 15, 52, 101, 103, 105, 125, 129, 174, 196, 227, 231, 236, 237, 255
  William, 171
McKessack
  John, 93, 165
McKester
  David, 250
McKinney
  Jno., 33
McKinsey
  John, 139
McKinzey
  Jno., 52
  John, 42
McKinzie
  Aaron, 17

Jno., 48, 98
John, 80, 98
McLung
  William, 17
McVay
  John, 222
Medlock
  George, 165
Melson
  Daniel, 269
Mercer
  Thomas, 190, 209, 212, 221, 244, 246, 257, 260, 261, 263, 267
  Thos., 188
Merony, 161
  James, 148, 161, 180
Mgintee
  Robt., 28
Michael, 8, 10, 11, 13, 14, 21, 24, 25, 26, 27, 29, 30, 31, 37, 38, 79, 109, 122, 126, 138
Michl., 22, 24, 59, 72, 126
Middlebrook
  Thos., 51
Middlebrooks
  Micajah, 245
Middlebroox
  Micajah, 222
  Thomas, 222
Middleton
  Elizabeth, 151
  Robert, 144, 146, 150, 151, 186, 202, 236, 249
  Robt., 246, 248, 250, 256, 280
Miles
  A., 242
  Jno., 51
  Moses, 133
  William, 244, 247, 260
Milirons, 121

John, 99
Millar
  John, 21
Miller, 150, 257
  Alexander, 35, 144
  Andrew, 222
  Benj., 252
  George, 57
  Henry, 16, 18, 21, 23, 29
  James, 36, 40, 43, 125, 139, 145, 151, 159, 168, 170, 171, 210, 212, 256
  James, Jr., 44
  James, Sr., 44
  Jas., 212
  Jas., Jr., 212
  Johnthn., 284
  Jonathan, 197, 221, 252, 253, 290
  Joshua, 173
  Robt., 51
Millirons
  John, 104
Mills
  Richard, 106
Milstead
  Aaron, 244, 247, 260
  Zealous, 156, 176, 177, 204, 244
Milton
  Jonthn., 284
  Joseph, 74
Milum
  Dudley, 83
Minor
  J., 205
  Jno., 292
  John, 139, 192, 215, 273
  W., 252
  Will, 86
  William, 86, 136, 139, 171, 192, 203, 215, 227, 250, 252

Wm., 205, 253, 291
Minton
  Joseph, 9
Mirarity
  Dennis, 283
Mitchell, 91, 120, 189, 190, 195, 198, 203, 205, 210, 217, 221, 225, 245, 249, 254, 257, 258, 260, 262
  D. B., 64, 190, 194, 198, 203, 205, 210, 221, 223, 249, 254, 257, 258, 262, 267
  Daniel, 93, 96
  Danl., 127, 128, 129, 131
  Drury, 18, 244
  Fredk., 289
  Hen, 235
  Henry, 54, 93, 132, 134, 260, 283, 290
  John, 17, 33, 48, 104, 165, 268, 270, 281, 282, 289
  Joshua, 93
  Noel, 19, 45, 52, 264
  Thomas, 91, 93, 165, 166, 177, 181, 268, 270, 281
  Thos., 51, 53, 124, 187
  William, 21, 223
Mobley
  Reuben, 56, 148, 222
Moffat
  Henry, 190, 221
Moffatt
  Henry, 166, 176, 182, 187, 188, 201, 209
  Peggy, 83
Moffet
  Henry, 177
Monk
  Mial, 5, 7, 9, 135, 145
  Miel, 104, 133, 148, 164
Montgomery, 74

Hugh, 108, 115, 116, 118, 222
  James, 134, 136, 140, 146, 151, 222
  James M. C., 161
  John, 222, 226, 237, 243
  Robert, 56, 72, 101, 105, 167, 175, 194
  Robt., 18, 57, 127, 167
Moon
  Richard, 57, 71, 90, 293
  Susanna, 178
Moone
  Richard, 57, 69
  Richd., 77
Moor
  Susannah, 135
Moore
  Charles, 10, 17, 37, 51, 54, 157
  Chas., 83
  Clement, 269, 273
  Edward, 8, 14, 15
  Edward, Sr., 18
  Elijah, 223
  Ephm., 289
  Ephraim, 222, 268, 270, 280, 281
  Jachaniah, 44
  Jachariah, 52
  Jecamiah, 69, 86, 92, 96, 127, 128, 129, 131, 172, 192, 222, 226, 243
  Jno., 244
  Risdon, 132, 221, 225, 243
  Risdon, Jr., 216
  Thomas, 188, 192, 197, 198, 206, 211, 213
  Thos., 18
  William, 38
Moreland
  Francis, 18, 146, 165, 170, 172, 173, 181, 207
  Fras., 176
  Isaac, 269
  Robert, 136, 139, 143, 145, 151, 153, 290
  Robt., 133, 136, 139, 151, 153, 284
Morgan
  Asa, 94
  Isaac, 146
  Jeremiah, 6, 7
  William, 72, 99, 103, 109, 121, 269, 273, 276
  Wm., 133
Morris, 154
  Astin, 57, 69, 71, 77
  Austin, 56, 59, 83, 85, 90, 92, 115, 129, 152, 153
  Jno., 295
  John, 284, 292, 294
  Thomas, 284, 291
  Thos., 294, 295
Mosely
  William, 104
Moss
  Gabl., 275
  Gabriel, 273
  Henry, Jr., 269
  Henry, Sr., 268, 269, 281
  Thomas, Sr., 289
Mouland
  Francis, Jr., 93
Mowman
  Pleasant, 251
Mullings
  Thos., 29
Mullins
  Clement, 200
  Malone, 134, 139, 143, 145, 151, 153, 200
  Thomas, 74

Muppett
  Henry, 140
Murfey
  Wm., 251
Murphey
  William, 251
Murphy
  Daniel, 18
  James, 5
  John, 284
Muse
  Daniel, 56, 138, 207, 216, 257
  Danl., 111, 154
Musgrove
  William, 284
Myles
  Abm., 99
  Abraham, 103, 188
  Abrm., Jr., 189
  John, 101
Naylor
  George, 262
  James, 189
Nelson
  Jeremiah, 92, 165
Nesbit, 110
Newsom
  William, 289
Newsome
  Benjamin, 121
Newton
  Isaac, 293
Nichols
  Harris, 80
  Harriss, 51
Nicholson
  Harris, 18, 50, 80, 108, 153
Nisbet
  James, 119
  Jonathan, 168

Noble
  Saml., 189
Noles
  Edmd., 32
  Edmond, 135
  Zachariah, 32
Nolley
  Danl., 244
Nolly
  Danl., 251, 260
Noright
  Richard, 173
Nowles
  Edmond, Sr., 228
  Edmund, Sr., 178
  Mark, 165
  Zack, 134
Nuoman
  William, 183, 205
O'Triger
  Cornelius, 283
Oates
  Richard W., 5
  Richd. W., 9
Oats
  Richard W., 6, 23
  Richd., 28
  Richd. W., 22, 93
Ogletree
  John, 275
Oliver
  Benjamin, 55
  Benjn., 55
  James B., 116, 171
Onear
  John, 244
Orear
  Jno., 16
  John, 32
Orr

James, 51
Orrick
  James, 244, 267, 286
Orricks
  Jas., 271
Ousely
  William, 92
Ousley, 163
  John, 228
  Weldon, 85
  William, 13, 96, 144, 149, 163
  Wm., 6, 16, 21, 23, 28, 39
Owsley, 114
  John, 56
  Robert, 69, 294
  William, 5, 113, 129, 131, 145, 236, 272, 294
  Wm., 114, 127, 128, 162
Page
  James, 34
Palmer
  Joseph, 84
Paramour
  Thomas, 166, 169
  Thos., 173, 175
Pardue
  John, 189
Parham
  Jna., 45
  Robert, 284
  Stith, 144, 179, 208, 255
Parish
  Henry, 192
Parker
  Benj., 173, 175
  Benjamin, 166, 169
  Charles, 166
  Daniel, 262
  Danl., 278
  Jno., 9

  John, 5, 7, 14, 56, 57, 59, 69, 71, 77, 83, 86
  Richard, 222
  Richd., 92
  Saml., 244
  Samuel, 104
  West, 284
Parks
  Charles, 121
Parmeter
  Jason, 58
  Jesse, 43
Parmeton
  Jason, 36
Parmington
  Jason, 99
Parrish
  Henry, 76, 132
Parrist
  Edward, 18
Parsons
  Saml., 281
Paterson
  Joseph, 94
Patterson, 89
  Joel, 145
  John, 284
  Joseph, 89, 97, 99, 125, 173, 240, 261
Pattison
  John, 32
Paul
  James, 271
Peace
  John, 56
Peak
  Henry, 56, 222, 228, 234
  Jno. C., 289
  John, 251
  John C., 269, 281

John C., Sr., 268
John Comer, 211
Peavey
  Abraham, 59, 73, 83
Peavy
  Abraham, 56, 57, 65, 85
  Abram, 77
  Michael, 189
Pebbles
  Thomas, 56
Peckard
  Thomas, 51
Pennington
  Thos., 251
Pentecost
  William, 122, 140, 256
Penticost
  Will, 59
Perkins
  John, 118, 244, 267, 285
Permento
  Jesse, 32
Permetar
  Jesse, 34
Permeter
  Jesse, 37, 49
Philips
  Isham, 93
  James, 134
  Saml., 254
Phillips
  Hilry, 34, 40, 42
  Saml., 106, 158
  Samuel, 108, 222
  Solomon, 268, 270, 280, 281, 289
Pickard
  Frances, 99, 103
  Thomas, 66, 67, 84, 101, 102, 105, 106, 123
  Thos., 98

Pierce
  Abner, 66, 86
Pigg
  William, 165, 166, 177, 187, 243
Pinkston
  James, 45
  Jno., 45
  John, 179
Pogue
  Saml., 284
Polk
  Charles, 5
Pollard
  John, 282
  Robert, 292, 294
  Robt., 284, 295
Pollion
  John, 134
Pool
  Middleton, 197
Pope
  Allen, 32, 34, 37, 43
  Bamalea, 45
  Barnaby, 26, 27, 56, 72, 79, 122
  Henry, 6
  Isaac R., 72
  Jess, Jr., 284
  Jesse, 56, 57, 199, 202, 285
  Jesse McK., 169, 173, 175
  Jesse McKiney, 208
  Jesse McKinne, 175, 283
  Jesse McKinney, 144, 165, 169, 173, 199, 202, 238, 252, 255, 286, 290
  Jesse McKinny, 179
  Jesse Q., 197
  Jesse Quinae, 171
  Jesse, Sr., 290
  Richard, 5
  Saml., 24, 170

Samuel, 139
Porter
  Benjamin, 150
Potter
  Abram, 128
  Pleasant, 244
Pound
  Jno., 115
  John, 72, 209, 233
  Marryman, 99
  Merryman, 103
  Richard, 233, 269
  William, 40, 58
  Wm., 58
Pounds
  Jno., 30
  John, 35, 128
Powell
  James, 268
  Moses, 93, 96, 127, 128, 129, 269, 273
Price
  Jno., 52, 99
  John, 147, 199, 201
  M., 30
  Meredith, 199, 201
  Merideth, 23
Prichet
  James, 133
Pricket
  Philip, 134
Pritchett
  James, 140, 146, 153, 269
  Philip, 136, 139, 143, 145, 151, 153
Pruett
  Charles, 184, 185, 200, 203
  Jacob, 184, 185
  James, 184, 185, 200, 203
  John, 184, 185

John, Jr., 200, 203
Pruit
  Elisha, 55
Pruitt
  Charles, 169, 203
  Elisha, 55
  James, 169, 203
  John, 203
  John, Jr., 169
  Lucy, 176, 237
Pryor
  Aaron, 51
Rabun
  Matt, 33, 190, 193, 199, 200, 201, 204, 212, 213, 221
  Matthew, 176, 188
  Mattw., 177
  William, 53, 157, 216, 222, 226, 243
  Wm., 51, 211
Rachel
  Miles, 124
Rachels
  B., 189
  Miles, 93, 101, 103, 107, 113, 115, 122, 128
Ragan
  Jno., 248, 254, 289
  John, 198, 222, 260, 262, 267, 268, 269, 280, 281
Raglan
  John, 261
Raines
  Robert, 166, 181, 182, 237, 239, 244, 267
  Robt., 165, 182, 187, 285
  Thomas, 222, 226, 243, 282, 287
Rains
  Robert, 53
  Thomas, 5, 6

Thos., 33
Ralston, 110
Read
  Alexr., 48
  Jonadale, 51
  Saml., Jr., 51
Rease
  James, 255
Reddick, 114
  Abram, 9, 112
Reddock
  William, 26
Reed
  Alexander, 5, 17, 225
  Alexr., 6, 32, 33
  John, 222
  Jonadab, 244, 267
  Samuel, 18
Reedy
  Benjamin, 244
Rees
  Isham, 184, 226
  James, 204
  Littleton, 16, 23, 28, 187
  William, 21, 103
  Williamson C., 184
Reese
  Isham, 222, 237, 243
  James, 188, 190, 206, 209, 212, 221
  Joel, 188, 190
  Littleton, 88, 166
  William, 222, 226, 237, 243
Reid
  Alexander, 73, 92, 125, 132, 135, 148, 151, 164, 221, 292
  Alexr., 133
  Isham, 174
  Jno., 99
  John, 172

Jonadab, 285
Saml., 133, 136, 151, 153, 159
Saml., Jr., 270
Samuel, 139, 143, 145, 159
Samuel, Jr., 268
Reiley
  William, 11, 18
Reily, 114
  William, 113
  Wm., 9
Reins
  Robt., 51
  Thomas, 32, 48
Reives
  William, 93
Reynolds
  Harman, 17
  Harmon, 257
Rhodes
  Henry, 269
  William, 237
Richards
  Humphrey, 42
Richardson
  Danl., 26
  O., 195
  Obadiah, 51, 53, 146, 162, 192, 246
Ricketson
  Timothy, 272
Riely
  William, 97
Rigby
  William, 189
Right
  Constant, 144
Riley
  James, 93
Risby
  Richd., 39

Rispas
  John, 135
  Richard, 69
Rispes
  Richard, 256, 258, 260, 261, 263, 267
  Richd., 254, 257
Rispess
  John, 133, 148, 151, 164
  Richard, 246
  Richd., 243
Rivers
  Robert, 148, 150
  Robt., 242
Roach
  Samuel, 221, 225, 229, 260
Roan
  George, 93
  James, 134
  Tunstil, 284
Roberts
  John, 269
Robertson, 282
  Benjamin, 281
  John, 71, 127, 182, 194, 203, 227
  Moses, 189
Robison
  Frier, 5
  John, 88, 132
Rodgers
  Britton, 6
Rogers, 92, 132
  Allen, 189
  B., 286
  Britain, 5, 32, 33, 48, 170, 252
  Henry, 32, 148
  James, 93, 166
  John, 200, 239, 268, 269, 280, 281, 289, 296
  Joseph, 17

Michael, 92
Ullysses, 19
Ulysses, 132, 140
Ulyssis, 122
Rose
  Pleasant, 295
Ross
  Francis, 21, 23, 51, 53, 91, 188, 190, 244, 246, 255, 256, 257, 260, 261, 267
  Frederick, 36, 85
  George, 17, 32
  James, 69, 71, 264
  Littleton, 96
Rosser
  George, 292
Runnels
  Elijah, 166
  H., 58, 88
  Harman, 33, 138, 154
  Harmand, 40
  Harmon, 32, 48, 88, 90, 212
Rust
  Jacob, 36
Rutherford
  Robert, 222
Rutland
  Randolph, 69, 93, 96, 127, 128, 129, 131, 165, 166, 177, 182, 187
Rutledge
  J., 37
  James, 5, 19, 30
Rutlin
  Randolph, 69
Rutlind
  Randolph, 71
Ryan
  Michael, 100
  William, 32, 34, 37, 43

Ryly
  William, 45
Ryon
  Richard, 56
Sallard
  William, 17, 20, 21
  Wm., 20, 51
Salmons
  Ephraim A., 160
Salyers
  Elizabeth, 10, 11
Sanders
  Julius, 106, 113, 115, 264
  Mark, 17, 91
  Nathan, 198
  William, 284
Sanford
  Benjamin, 120
  Jesse, 120, 146, 188, 203
Sannard
  S., 38
Saterwhite
  Thomas, 139
  Thos., 168
Saunders
  Francis, 52
  Mark, 124, 174, 188, 204, 206, 209, 221
  Nathan, 189, 191, 195, 206, 211, 213
  William, 290
Scarlet
  James, 261, 299
  John, 134
Scarlett, 152
  James, 51, 54, 152, 198, 201, 206, 222, 278, 279, 296, 297
  Jas., 152, 278, 279
  John, 179
Scoggan
  Nehemiah, 165, 167
Scott
  Fredk., 281
  Jno., 174
  John E., 173, 231, 281, 282
  Mary, 174
  Mary S., 173, 231
  Thos., 174
  Woodlief, 268, 269, 280, 282, 289
Scurlock
  Geo., 39
  James, 145
  Joshua, 73, 226, 227
  Sarah, 226
  William, 56, 57, 59, 65, 73, 77, 86, 97, 99
Seale
  Enoch, 222
  Thomas, 251, 257
Selman
  William, 221, 226, 237, 243
Shackelford, 250
  Jno., 258
  John, 175, 201, 245, 248, 250, 280
  John, Sr., 135
Shackleford, 299
  John, 129, 201, 228, 234
  John, Sr., 133
Shakelford
  James, 138
Shakleford
  John, 17
Shaw
  Jno., 287
  Lena, 58
Shelby
  William, 230
Sherly

Jones, 124
Ship
  David, 222
  Richard, 14, 190, 221, 283
  Richard, Jr., 204
  Richd., 13
  Richd. B., 93
Shipp
  Richard, 82, 83, 165, 168, 244, 290
  Richd., 110, 188
  Thos., 51
Shippe
  Benjamin, 56
  Richard, 56
Shirly
  James, 103, 104
Shivers
  Jonas, 11, 133, 137, 166, 177, 182, 187, 199, 202, 215, 283, 290
Shivly
  Martin, 214
Shorter, 274, 275, 276
  Henry, 183, 185, 288
  James, 116, 117, 171, 183, 185, 193, 229, 235, 241, 252, 261, 262, 263, 271, 272, 288
Silman
  William, 74
Simmons
  Charles, 133
  Elijah, 85
  James, 269
  James M., 181, 250
  John, 93
Simms
  Robert, 22, 28, 32, 179, 247, 260
  Robt., 24, 129, 247, 250, 252, 261
Simpson

George, 124, 244, 267, 272
Sims
  Robert, 5, 6, 248
  Robt., 33, 48, 244
Skipwith
  Sir Peyton, 251
Skipworth, 252
Skrine, 190, 216, 277, 288
  Benj., 104, 212, 241
Slaughter
  Reuben, 279
  Reubin, 51
  Saml., 133, 181, 284
Slave
  Abram, 117
  Dorse, 120
  Frank, 9
  Harry, 117, 235
  Jane, 117
Sledge
  Minds, 268, 271
  Nathaniel, 84
  Nathl., 270, 280, 281, 289
  Shirly, 284
Sledges
  Nathl., 268
Smith, 92, 98
  Aaron, 201
  Abraham, 170, 285
  Archd., 237
  Archibald, 222, 226, 243
  David, 15
  Ezekel, 41
  Ezekiel, 76, 90, 91, 165, 201, 213, 249, 262, 267, 280
  Ezekiel, Jr., 83
  Ezekiel, Sr., 83
  George, 137
  Hardy, 184, 185, 222
  James, 282, 297, 300

Jesse, 245
Jno., 284
John C., 213
Joseph, 22, 98, 137, 140
Laurence, 78, 176, 227
Levin, 66, 107, 108, 157, 244
Nathan, 17
Nicholas, 18
Richard, 135, 179, 181, 182, 194, 206, 207, 228, 260, 274, 288
Richd., 59, 132, 178, 244, 255, 274
William, 103, 171, 269
Wm., 32
Sparks
 William, 222, 296
Spear
 Harris, 137, 215
 John, 57, 83, 165, 176, 188, 215
 Mose, 134
 William, 23
 Willis, 28
Spears
 John, 173
 William, 18
 Willis, 16
Spencer
 Jno. T., 30, 37
 John, 114, 165, 177
 John T., 167
 Thomas, 244, 250, 251
 William, 85
Spier
 John, 57, 71, 169
Spiers
 John, 69
Spiller
 Jeremiah, 134
 Philip, 143, 176, 237, 297, 298
Spillers

Jeremiah, 5
Spitters
 Philip, 28
Stallings
 Mary, 151
 Potter, 151
Stanbanks
 John, 189
Stanley
 Demsy, 32
 Ezekiel, 289
 Martin, 255
Stark
 William, 7, 81, 82, 148, 271, 277
 Willm., 30
Starks
 William, 15, 29, 35
Statam
 Charles, 133
Statham
 Charles, 55
Steele
 Alexander, 222
Stembridge
 John, 166, 169, 173, 175
Stephens, 134, 137, 142, 147, 150, 156, 164
 John, 244, 247, 260
 Stephen, 268
 Thomas, 110
 W., 64, 142, 147, 150, 156, 165, 166
Stevens
 Edward, 172
 Thomas, 284
Stewart
 Charles, 180
 Chas., 180
 William, 100, 104, 121, 124, 127
Stiles, 214

337

William, 59, 135, 178, 179, 181,
    182, 194, 206, 207, 228, 255,
    288
Wm., 106, 274
Still
    Robert, 293
    Robt., 284, 291
Stinson
    Zadok, 222
Stith, 6, 7, 13, 14, 15, 16, 18, 19, 20,
    21, 27, 32, 53, 120, 156
    ___, 132
    W., 66
    W., Jr., 6, 7, 13, 14, 15, 16, 18, 20,
        21, 27, 32, 34, 55, 163, 229
    W., Sr., 26
    William, Jr., 6
    Wm., 52
Strauther
    Francis, 151
    George, 207
    Henry, 151
Street
    William, 65, 88, 108, 129
Strickland
    David, 269, 272
    Jacob, 244
    Jephtha, 222, 234
    Jeptha, 226
Stringer
    James, 213, 257
Strother
    Geo., 9
    George, 6, 12, 34, 99, 103, 193,
        207
    Jno., Jr., 51
    John, 56
    Richard, 207
Stroud
    Isaac, 56

Mathew, 134
Matthew, 136, 139, 143, 145,
    151, 153, 159
Studdivant
    John, 125
Studivant
    John, 5, 6
Sturdivant
    Jno., 32
    John, 132, 133, 135, 151, 164
Sutton
    Garey, 16
    Garrett, 9, 14, 16
    Garry, 14, 15
    Gary, 9
    Solomon, 135
Swaringame
    Van, 222
Sweat
    John, 134, 146, 159
Swepson
    John, 196, 197, 263
Sykes
    Hubbard, 211
Taft
    George, 98
Talbert, 234
    Jesse, 151
    John, 234
Talbot
    John, 133
Taliaferro, 64, 70, 77, 80, 85, 87, 92,
    94, 96, 97, 101, 104, 106, 111,
    119, 121, 126, 131
    Ben, 59, 64, 70, 76, 80, 84, 87, 92,
        94, 96, 97, 101, 104, 106, 111,
        119, 126, 131, 133, 134
    Benjamin, 57
    John, 188
Tate

Charles, 244
Robert, 165, 268
Robt., 208, 213
Tatem
  Seth, 283
Tatum
  Nathaniel, 165
  Seth, 5, 6, 32, 290
Tayler
  Edmd., 49
Taylor
  Archibald, 85
  James, 244
  William, 223
Telmund
  John, 200
Temple
  Nancy, 88, 89
  Peter, 88, 89
Tennille
  Francis, 276
Terrel
  Archelous, 204
  Bird, 204
  Hubert, 124
Terrell
  Archelous, 177
  Byrd, 177
Terrill
  Archelous, 176
  Bird, 176
  Peter B., 172
Thelford
  William, 296
Thomas
  Frederick G., 242
  Fredk. G., 189
  J., 117
  James, 5, 6, 11, 19, 44, 45, 53, 115, 166, 167, 201, 290

Jas., 283
Jos., 9
Joseph, 244, 261, 300
Josiah, 118
Roberds, 5
Roberts, 6
William, 34, 37, 38, 44
Wm., 9, 38, 52
Thompson, 207
  Ben, 26, 29, 45, 208
  Benj., 131, 184, 200
  Benjamin, 137, 184, 205, 232
  E., 235
  Elizabeth, 234
  Geo., 43, 133
  George, 23, 29, 58, 116, 136, 140, 145
  Jesse, 5, 13, 43, 52, 53, 99, 103, 104, 106, 109, 147, 150, 162, 200, 201, 212, 232, 235
  Jessee, 161
  John, 134, 140, 145, 159
  Joseph, 137, 200, 213, 232, 235
  Swann, 269
  William, 108, 109, 212
Thomson
  Jesse, 80
Thornton
  Jno., 294, 295
  John, 285, 292
  Lindsey, 251
  William, 57, 65, 77, 85, 90, 201
  Wm., 73
Thweat
  James, 42, 51
Thweatt
  James, 40, 89, 91, 124, 146, 148, 184, 188, 210, 238, 239, 268
  Jno., 295
Tidd

David, 199, 213, 214, 246, 258
Tison
  Job, 289
Torrence
  John, 68, 118, 183
Tounsend
  Henry, 151
Townsen
  Henry, 22, 23
Townsend
  Eli, 223
  Henry, 151, 176, 201, 213
  Saml., 74
Townshend
  Samuel, 9
Trailer
  Absalom, 165, 167
Trailor
  Absalom, 268, 269
Trammel
  Dennis, 56, 65
  Jarard, 128
  Jared, 105
  Jarrard, 107, 124
Trammell, 282
  Dennis, 73, 83, 281
  Jared, 112
  Thomas, 99, 112, 166, 242
Trammil
  Dennis, 57
  Jarrard, 119, 122
  Jerrard, 93
  Jured, 102
  Thos., 93, 119
Trammill
  Thomas, 97, 187
  Thos., 108
Trawick
  Francis, 104, 151, 268, 270, 276
Traylor

Archd., 295
Archibald, 295
Traywick
  Francis, 133, 135, 164
Treutten
  Christian, 110
  John A., 110, 196
Trice
  Benj., 188
  John, 243, 246, 254, 256
Trip
  Henry, 283
Triplett
  William, 173, 248, 261
Trippe
  Henry, 290
  John, 179
Truman
  William, 93
Trutten
  Christian, 196
Tucker
  Fred, 284
  Frederick, 232, 237, 290
  Peyton, 55, 57
Tumons
  Abijah, 134
Tuplen
  William, 160
Turk
  Laban, 269
  Theodosius, 5, 33, 48, 290
  Theophilus, 32
Turke
  Theods., 283
Turner, 74, 130
  James, 16, 21, 23, 28, 32, 34, 37, 51, 108, 125, 128, 129, 141, 159, 204, 213
  Jas., 73, 141

Jos., 283
Joseph, 17, 19, 73, 77, 108, 115, 131
Joshua, 134, 284
Larkin, 66, 129, 244
Levin, 223, 227, 234
Lumpton, 51
Marshall, 115
Saml., 57, 59, 71, 77, 244, 247
Samuel, 56, 65, 90
William, 37, 66, 96, 107, 108, 125, 128, 129, 159, 213, 240
William, Jr., 259
William, Sr., 240, 259
Wm., 32, 34, 43
Tyus
Lewis, 222, 226, 237, 240, 243
Upright
Abraham, 146, 186, 202
James, 144, 179, 208, 255
Van Alen, 156, 163, 186, 223
P. L., 86, 109
Peter L., 28, 149, 163, 240
Van Allen, 27
Vaughan
Eliza, 82
Isaac, 98, 101, 103, 108, 109, 115, 216
Veasey
John, 190, 204
Veazey
Jesse, 5, 135, 164
John, 5, 6, 188, 206, 212, 221
Veazy
Jesse, 6, 133
Vesey
Jesse, 283
Vest
George, 31, 32, 85, 116
Vicars

Thomas, 134, 151
Vickars
Thomas, 136, 139, 143, 145, 159
Thos., 153
Vincent
Elisha, 158
Jane, 158
Vinson
John, 222
W___
James, 32
Wadsworth
James, 133
Walker, 24, 25, 26, 27, 31, 71, 101, 202, 240, 247, 248, 264, 283, 288
Alexr., 45
David, 184, 244, 283
E., 230
G., 29, 117, 132
Geo., 278
George, 6, 174, 278
J. H., 230
James, 29, 165
Jno. H., 24, 25, 29
John, 223
John H., 31, 93, 184
John Hunter, 74, 184
Martha, 230
Matt, 189
Sanders, 118
W., 138
William, 25, 65, 138, 216, 230, 236
Wm., 24, 25, 31
Wall
Francis, 222
Wallace, 111
John, 166, 169, 173
William, 138, 216, 236, 291
Waller, 79, 201

Benjamin, 121, 158, 258
  Charles, 284
  Daniel, 12
  Elisha, 157, 158
  Elizabeth, 211
  Handy, 170
  James, 23, 34, 242
  Jas., 21
  John, 111
  John, Sr., 299
  N., 91
  Nathaniel, 85, 90, 120, 123, 124, 152, 170, 198, 242, 251, 261, 299
  Nathl., 90, 124, 170, 172, 173, 174, 198, 241, 251, 260
  Nathl., Jr., 261
  William, 169, 181
Wallin
  P., 52
Wallis, 116
Walsh
  Edmd., 90
  Edmund, 86
  Walton, 32, 34, 43, 48, 50, 88, 89, 265, 269, 272, 279, 286
  Geo., 34, 37, 42, 50, 53, 130, 272, 279, 286
  George, 47, 277
  John C., 118
  William, 78
Wamack
  Abraham, 192
  Mancel, 192
  Sherwood, 192
Wambersie
  E., 114
  Emanuel, 177
Ward
  John, 134, 166, 167

Washington
  William, 160, 173, 214, 248, 255, 288
  Wm., 134, 274
Watkins
  Robert, 185, 229, 241
  Robt., 118
Watley
  Daniel, 28
  Michl., 34
  Richd., 23
Watson
  Geo., 290
  Wayne, 278
  Richard, 279
Weatherby
  George, 228
Wedington
  Robert, 227
Weekes
  Jno., 33
  John, 17
  William, 29, 35
Weeks, 116, 276
  John, 32, 48, 57
  Saml., 189
  Thomas, 273, 275
  William, 7, 111, 189, 228, 231, 242, 298
  William, Sr., 7
  Wm., 35, 229
Welch
  Edmund, 134
  Wm., 9
Welsh
  Benjamin, 24
  William, 5, 6, 14
West
  Hamlin, 268, 273
Weymore

John, 222
Whatley
  Allen, 12
  Daniel, 12, 25, 29, 34, 77, 171, 183, 205
  Danl., 126
  Elisha, 32, 34, 85, 115, 176
  John, 32, 35, 40, 58, 128, 209
  Michael, 10, 12
  Richd., 21
  Willis, 170, 172, 174, 198
Whatly
  Jno., 30
  Michl., 35
Wheloss
  Abner, 84
White
  John, 6, 7, 18, 244, 246, 255, 256, 257
  Joseph, 78, 122
Whitehead
  Joseph, 89
Whitehurst
  Jno., 204
Whitfield
  Benj., 200, 239
  Benja., 133
  Benjamin, 135, 148, 151, 164, 244, 267, 285
Whitney
  Jno., 104
  John, 124
Whittington
  John, 268, 272
Wigans
  William, 84
Wilcoxen
  Thomas, 190
Wilcoxon
  Thomas, 137, 172, 188, 209

Wiley
  Moses, 38, 164
  William, 290
  Wm., 30
Wilie
  Moses, 133
Wilkins
  James, 134
Wilkinson
  Abner, 268
  Jno., 226
  John, 222, 234, 268, 271
  Robt., 244
Willey
  Moses, 135, 151
William
  Jacob, 41
Williams, 150
  Jacob, 44, 98, 101, 139, 151, 168, 169, 170, 171, 172, 210, 256, 284
  John, 139
  John S., 56
  Josha., 30
  Joshua, 35, 209
  Paul, 44, 139, 145, 150, 159, 168, 170, 172
  William, 269, 273, 285
  Zorababel, 51
Williamson
  Greene, 268
  John, 255
  Micajah, 39, 41, 58, 246
  Mich., 42
  Peter, 50
  Saml., 32
  Samuel, 18
  Zach, 295
  Zachariah, 56
  Zorobabel, 170, 172, 173

Willis
  Francis, 54
  William, 268
Willson
  Andrew, 144
  James, 192, 194
  John, 138, 191
  Robert, 94
Wilson, 250
  Andrew, 246, 248
  James, 133, 197
  John, 189
  Robt., 51
  Saml., 32
  Samuel, 222
Womack
  Abr., 286
  Abraham, 93, 96, 142, 215, 252
  Abram, 244
  Mancel, 215
  Mancil, 285
  Shearwood, 215
  Sherwood, 285
Wood, 69, 141, 213
  Aaron, 6, 9, 59, 119, 134, 149, 159
  Aron, 109
  Ethd., 35, 82, 83, 178
  Etheld., 252
  Etheldd., 35
  Etheldred, 8, 14, 24, 25, 82, 83, 89, 121, 178, 249, 251, 265
  James, 5, 6, 15, 23, 24, 25, 26, 28, 29, 31, 38, 39, 41, 44, 52, 69, 73, 74, 78, 109, 118, 129, 132, 133, 141, 183, 197, 222, 227, 234, 276, 277
  Jas., 126
  Matthew, 247, 251, 252, 256
  Richard, 7, 8, 14
  Richd., 9, 24, 25
  Solomon, 71
Woodham
  Edwd., 44, 51, 52
Woodward, 274, 275, 276
  Aaron, 120, 183, 272, 288
  Abraham, 120
  Joseph, 31, 271
  William, 120
Wooten
  Hardy, 86, 104, 226
  James, 222, 274, 288
  Jno., 104
  John, 5, 53, 86, 153, 210, 240
Works
  James, 76, 116, 189, 191, 195, 201
  Jas., 196
Wormack
  Abraham, 98
Worsham
  Edward, 247, 254, 279
Wrangler
  Brazer, 144
Wright
  William, 18, 133, 135, 151, 164, 189
Wyche
  Bartholomew, 166
  Bartholw., 165
  Bat, 45, 187
  Batt, 182
Wyley
  William, 284
Wylie
  Wm., 37
Wynn
  Thomas, 165, 169, 231
  Thomas, Jr., 166
Wynne

John, 269
Robert, 167
Thomas, 167, 173, 175
Thos., 167
Yarborough
  James, 165, 175
  William, 13, 25, 186, 246, 259, 260, 261, 267
Willm., 263
Wm., 104, 176, 244, 254
Youngblood
  Isaac, 268, 271
  James, 189, 244, 267, 286
  Jno., 244
  Nathan, 268

www.ingramcontent.com/pod-product-compliance
Lightning Source LLC
Chambersburg PA
CBHW020639300426
44112CB00007B/167